Internet Future Strategies

How Pervasive Computing Services Will Change the World

Internet Future Strategies

*How Pervasive Computing Services Will
Change the World*

Daniel Amor

Upper Saddle River, New Jersey 07458

Library of Congress Cataloging-in Publication Data

CIP Data available

Editorial/production supervision: *Mary Sudul*
Composition: *Lori Hughes, Hughes Consulting*
Cover design: *Anthony Gemmellaro*
Cover design direction: *Jerry Votta*
Manufacturing manager: *Maura Zaldivar*
Acquisitions editor: *Jill Harry*
Marketing manager: *Dan DePasquale*
Editorial assistant: *Justin Somma*

Copyright © 2002 by Prentice Hall P T R
Prentice-Hall, Inc.
Upper Saddle River, New Jersey 07458

Prentice Hall books are widely used by corporations and government agencies for training, marketing, and resale.

The publisher offers discounts on this book in bulk quantities. For more information contact: Corporate Sales Department, Phone: 800-382-3419; Fax: 201-236-7141; E-mail: corpsales@prenhall.com; or write: Prentice Hall PTR, Corp. Sales Dept., One Lake Street, Upper Saddle River, NJ 07458.

Printed in the United States of America

10 9 8 7 6 5 4 3 2

ISBN 0-13-041803-X

Pearson Education LTD.
Pearson Education Australia PTY, Limited
Pearson Education Singapore, Pte. Ltd
Pearson Education North Asia Ltd
Pearson Education Canada, Ltd.
Pearson Educación de Mexico, S.A. de C.V.
Pearson Education — Japan
Pearson Education Malaysia, Pte. Ltd
Pearson Education, Upper Saddle River, New Jersey

To Sabine,

Your words are my food,
your breath my wine.
You are everything to me.

Sarah Bernhardt

Contents

Contents   **vii**

Foreword   **xiii**

Preface   **xix**

I Where the Future Begins   **1**

1 The Next Chapter on the Internet   **3**

    1.1   Introduction   3

          1.1.1   Human-Centered Development   5

          1.1.2   New Class of Computing   7

          1.1.3   The Tech Elite Duke it Out   9

          1.1.4   Business in a Brave New World   9

          1.1.5   Creation of a New Paradigm   10

    1.2   The Internet Today   11

          1.2.1   Internalized Outsourcing   11

          1.2.2   Subdivision   12

          1.2.3   Expensive and Complex Hardware   12

          1.2.4   Current Restrictions   16

    1.3   New Internet Technologies   17

          1.3.1   Application Service Providers   18

          1.3.2   Wireless Networks   20

          1.3.3   Framework for the Universal Network   21

          1.3.4   Metaservices   22

          1.3.5   Security Requirements   23

1.3.6   Operational Module   24
1.3.7   Virtualization of Applications and Information   24
1.3.8   A New Business Platform   26
1.3.9   New Interfaces   27
1.3.10 Context Awareness   28
1.4 New Internet Business Models   30
1.4.1   Device Manufacturers   32
1.4.2   Infrastructure Providers   33
1.4.3   Network Operators   34
1.4.4   Service Providers and Content Aggregators   35
1.4.5   Content Providers   35
1.4.6   "Regular" Businesses   36
1.5 Concerns   36
1.5.1   Strength of Traditional Links   37
1.5.2   Privacy and Security   37
1.5.3   Piracy   38
1.5.4   Disregard of Technology Standards   40
1.5.5   Capabilities of Hardware and Battery   41

2 **Mobile Commerce**   **43**
2.1 Mobile Architecture   45
2.2 Technologies   45
2.2.1   Global System for Mobile Communication   46
2.2.2   Short Message Service   48
2.2.3   General Packet Radio Service   53
2.2.4   Global Positioning System   55
2.2.5   Wireless Application Protocol   57
2.2.6   Mobile Internet Access System: imode   58
2.2.7   Differences Between imode and WAP   63
2.3 The Future of Mobile Technologies   64
2.3.1   Deployment   67
2.3.2   Applications   68
2.3.3   Infrastructure Providers   69
2.3.4   Time Scale   71
2.4 Mobile Applications   71
2.4.1   Mobile Internet   72
2.4.2   Mobile Commerce   73

2.4.3   Mobile Location Services   74

2.4.4   Mobile Entertainment   78

2.5   Mobile Business   79

2.5.1   Mobile Advertising   80

2.5.2   Mobile Banking   84

2.5.3   Mobile Devices   87

2.5.4   Mobile Payments   88

2.6   Portals   90

2.6.1   Device Portals   93

2.6.2   Personalized Portals   94

2.6.3   Situated Portal   96

3   **Home Automation Systems**   **99**

3.1   Introduction   99

3.1.1   Advantages of Home Automation   100

3.1.2   The First Generation   102

3.1.3   Existing Technologies   102

3.1.4   Basic Architecture   107

3.1.5   Home Automation Futures   110

3.2   Technologies   111

3.2.1   HomeRF   111

3.2.2   IEEE 802.11 Wireless LAN   112

3.2.3   X10   115

3.3   Business and Home Automation   116

3.3.1   Home Automation Applications   117

3.3.2   Techniques for Home Automation Profitability   117

4   **Technologies of the Future**   **119**

4.1   Internet Services   119

4.1.1   Enabling Technologies   119

4.1.2   Business Opportunities   121

4.1.3   Internet Services Standards   122

4.1.4   The Migration of Applications to the Web   123

4.1.5   Open Internet Services   124

4.2   Programming Models   124

4.2.1   Manufactured Component Objects   126

4.2.2   Design Advice for Developers   127

4.2.3   Basic Building Blocks   128

4.2.4   The Future   130

4.3   Device-to-Device Communication   131

4.3.1   ChaiServer   131

4.3.2   Inferno   133

4.3.3   Universal Plug and Play   134

4.3.4   Jini   135

4.3.5   Bluetooth   137

4.4   Information Exchange   139

4.4.1   JetSend   140

4.4.2   T Spaces   140

4.4.3   InfernoSpaces   141

4.4.4   Millennium   142

4.4.5   InfoBus   143

4.5   Service Broadcasting   144

4.5.1   E-Speak   144

4.5.2   Salutation   147

4.6   The Vision   148

4.6.1   E-Services from Hewlett-Packard   148

4.6.2   Microsoft .NET   151

4.6.3   Brazil from Sun Microsystems   155

4.7   Comparison of Pervasive Computing Technologies   157

4.8   The Future of Pervasive Computing   160

5   Applications in the Near Future   161

5.1   Wearable Computing   161

5.1.1   Augmented Memory   162

5.1.2   Augmented Reality   163

5.1.3   Intelligent Clothing   167

5.1.4   Standard Applications   168

5.2   Distributed Computing   169

5.2.1   Distributed Object Model Overview   170

5.2.2   One Computer   172

5.2.3   The Grid   174

II Future Strategies   177

6 Wedding Anniversary   179
6.1 The Solution Today   179
6.2 The Solution Tomorrow   182
6.3 Technology   185
6.4 Business Case   187
6.5 Similar Cases   189

7 The Thief   191
7.1 The Solution Today   191
7.2 The Solution Tomorrow   193
7.3 Technology   196
7.4 Business Case   197
7.5 Similar Cases   200

8 Party People   203
8.1 The Solution Today   203
8.2 The Solution Tomorrow   205
8.3 Technology   207
8.4 Business Case   209
8.5 Similar Cases   211

9 Toothaches   213
9.1 The Solution Today   213
9.2 The Solution Tomorrow   215
9.3 Technology   217
9.4 Business Case   219
9.5 Similar Cases   221

III Future Impact   223

10 The Future of the Internet   225
10.1 Social Impact   225
   10.1.1 Effect on Daily Life   225
   10.1.2 Effects of Automation and Mobility   227
10.2 Political Impact   229
   10.2.1 Managing New Technology   229

      10.2.2 Managing Global Technology   230

   10.3 Privacy Impact   231

      10.3.1 Effects from Marketing   231

      10.3.2 Effects on Security   232

   10.4 Financial Impact   232

   10.5 Technological Impact   234

A Future Strategies for Customers   **237**

B Internet Addresses   **245**

C Glossary   **255**

SUBJECT INDEX   **291**

Foreword

Trends in Information Technology

The combination of high-speed computers and intelligent devices is the exciting trend of information technology of the 21st century. The so-called pervasive computing will provide smaller, faster, and less expensive technology. Such devices, for example, are scientific instruments or online databases, all interconnected by wired or wireless networks and accessible anywhere in the world. This will have major impacts in education, manufacturing, and health care and other areas. These new trends are devoutly expected by modern industries, like biotechnology. On the other hand, there is a definitive need to focus on users and their tasks rather than only on computing devices and technology.

Business and the Idea of Services

Effective business is based on the challenging principle of facing relentless competition and still being better than all the business competitors together. Just exaggerating this notion slightly: each and every company which wants to be in the forefront—and remain there—must be able to offer and sell more products, with higher quality, in bigger numbers and in shorter time periods than its competitors.

And with better service. Especially with better service.

This is what pervasive computing has to be about: providing services. It is about making them common on a day-to-day basis, up to the point where they become ubiquitous and yet—mostly—unnoticed. We are already surrounded by all sorts of computing services in our daily life (e.g., flight reservation system, electronic car systems). Enabling these services to use existing and future network functionalities is the next logical step that only a few companies have begun to think about, let alone started to implement. The understanding of technologies and their social—therefore potentially economical impact is essential for the success of every business concept. Companies have to integrate new technologies seamlessly into their existing conceptual framework to be able to survive the fierce competition that inevitably arises when there is money to be made.

Services in the life-sciences and health care areas, for example, are of strategic importance for the years to come. Pharmaceutical companies and doctors likewise increasingly fall back on third parties to answer specific questions that are outside their usual knowledge base. Interestingly enough, a paradigmal shift is taking place at the same time: biology gradually moves away from a bench-based to a computer-based science, and biotechnology moves to a robot-based and computer-instructed technology. The common point of both these trends is the fact that specialized knowledge of a few experts is made available to a broad audience by interconnected knowledge management and the possibility to share and transfer vast amounts of pharmaceutical, genetic, medical, and other information. One outcome of this development is the emergence of industrial bioinformatics and the enhancement of the vitality of biotechnology companies.

Business meets Science

Companies have to handle business needs like managing customer relationships, electronic commerce, supply chain management, and enterprise resource planning. On the other hand, science requires effective ways to organize, store, manage, and retrieve the exponentially growing volumes of data that accumulate every day. Typically, advances in science lead to advances in technology, and these in turn enable business to create new products and services. However, customers tend to have a selective acceptance of new technologies as the life span of base technologies shortens with every innovation cycle. Not all technologies will therefore be able to generate profits and this is one of the major problems that solution engineers have to overcome. Companies can improve competitive positioning by use of enterprise-wide computational systems with strong organizational relationships.

The industrial bioinformation applications are a very good example of a pervasive technology. Industrial bioinformatics is not simply based on science, invention, or capital, but rather on the combination of these forces. Bioinformatics is an example for one of the emerging service industries that brings together resources, technologies, information, and highly skilled workers to form an integrated, high-throughput environment. The effort needed to analyze billions of molecular interactions demands researchers highly skilled in physics, chemistry, and computer science working together. Lone researchers are consequently replaced by interdisciplinary teams working in more or less tightly coupled environments. Industrial bioinformatics is an intellectual fusion of biomedicine, automation technology, and intensive computing, allowing us to scan biology in its entirety and to dig for answers in the mass of data. It involves partnerships between diverse disciplines: application scientists and engineers, biologists and doctors, applied mathematicians, computer scientists, and robot engineers. One advantage of using industrial bioinformatics is the potential for broad corporate viewing of both data and data models, encouraging interactions among individuals and improving discoveries. Therefore the biotechnology industry is very rapidly developing the infrastructure, modifying the infrastructure, the robotics, the network management, and so forth, to be able to handle these pervasive networks.

Service meets Customers

While the technological prerequisites have evolved and were improved continually, the most critical factor in business—the customers—still do not get the attention which they deserve. Many companies had to learn the hard way that rethinking the relationship with the customer is a complex process subjugated to continuous development. Only optimizing company processes is bound to fail whenever efficient customer relationship strategies are not applied consistently.

But generating services is not enough. The general bottleneck is teaching the customer to access those services, understand them, and use them on a regular basis. Have a look at today's first steps of integrated Internet services (which are mostly Web based at the moment). Regardless of how seemingly intuitive and easy to use they might seem, there is no prediction possible on how the human factor will react in certain circumstances. Take for example a company that invests heavily in its online order technology. Normally, the last page a customer sees is a summary of his order and a big button labeled "Order Now!" which commits the order when pressed. In a few obscure cases however, customers do not press this button but rather make a printout of that very same order page in their web browser and fax it to the company. Needless to say the company really should ask why customers do this, but such behavior will happen over and over again during the transitional phases of business/customer relationship over the Internet.

One of the most effective strategies to prevent such problems is called collaborative commerce. Collaborative commerce describes the interactions among and within organizations which surround a transaction and improves satisfaction by meeting the customers' needs on the first point of contact and creates a competitive advantage by providing a continuous stream of services to customers. It has to be viewed as a critical piece of business initiative.

Reacting to Customer Needs

The push to use pervasive computing is not coming from the IT-people in the company but rather the business process engineers or the business evolution teams thinking about it. What they are looking at is an opportunity to offer new services, to offer additional services, and get new customers. A good example is the life science industry. Genomic information provides many potential targets for drug discovery. One of the challenges is to convert this information into drugs that treat diseases. Diseases that affect people. Knowledge of the genetic factors will allow the development of drugs that deal with the roots of the disorders. The comprehensive knowledge of genetics available today is distributed worldwide on public and private databases and is accessible via the Internet. In the future, tight linking of these resources will allow biomedical research to find a molecular definition and diagnosis of diseases rather than the mainly clinical definition and diagnosis. The advantage will be a cost-effective medicine and the ability to prevent particular diseases.

The point of genes is to provide cells with instructions for molecular functions, e.g., making proteins to kill other infected or degenerated cells. Biomedical researchers now need the expertise to merge information technology with science in a productive way. These new pervasive methods should be complemented with deep support and collaboration from experts in allied fields. There is an ever increasing need for the development of new, more efficient, and more sensitive computational methods as our understanding of the complex biological interaction within living organisms grows.

The Everchanging World

Modern biotechnology brought costs down by a hundredfold in the last 10 years in biomedical studies. As a result, functional genomics primed automation and miniaturization. Data generated in the high-throughput areas of biological research has to be processed using automated modular components to ensure (1) high quality data, (2) low computation cost, and (3) quick exchange of applications/modules while reacting sensitively to changing market conditions or the availability of new methods, programs, and technologies. Flexibility of process support is a key requirement for current and future business applications of industrial bioinformatics.

Properly deployed mobile computing allows this flexibility to be streamlined. Pervasive computing brings the data from its source to the field truly ubiquitously through an enterprise data center, to those who need it most. Starting with the use of devices for managing corporate information like sales orders, the devices will be used for a variety of applications like inventory and medical computing, ending up in a data mobility model. In a production pipeline for instance, where capturing barcode data plays an integral role, the mobile devices can be used for location or tracking the customized product. Using an open wireless Ethernet the data can be synchronized with the corporate network.

Managing the Company Information Flow

For industrial computing and service applications, pervasive computing solutions are essential to extending the value of ERP systems. In a typical company, a number of technologies exist as islands of information with quasi inexistent interconnection. The transfer of data to, from, and within departments in a recognizable and secure format has challenged scientists and software developers. Custom interfaces are expensive to develop and maintain. Furthermore, the communication with corporate software solutions like manufacturing execution systems (MES), enterprise relationship management (ERM), supply chain management (SCM), sales force automation (SFA), computer aided selling (CAS), computer integrated manufacturing (CIM), management information systems (MIS), and e-commerce requires intimate knowledge of each software component.

One possible approach for linking two systems that both use a relational database, is simply to use SQL directly to read and write the data between the two systems. Two major problems arise when doing this: (1) complexity and integrity problems rise exponentially when more than two systems are to be linked, and (2) all security and business agreement rules that are contained within applications are circumvented. In the past few years however, the XML (extensible markup language) standard has emerged as a widely accepted method for transferring data in business applications.

There is a necessity for a minimum of communication between service provider and service customer. In some cases, this communication can be reduced to the point where fully automated processes can kick in (for example with XML formated messages), other cases can only be solved by intensive coaching, e.g., through contact centers. Even within a higher level of automation, advanced search engines, intelligent agents, and researcher profiler tools must exist. Although intelligent systems approach aspects of human beings, people are still the best adaptive general problem solver. By implementing pervasive computing capabilities, one can dramatically improve the access to ERP solutions by mobile staff giving the customers a significant competitive advantage.

MWG as a Dynamic Service Provider

MWG-BIOTECH is a leading provider of biotech products using e-business and CRM solutions for the research community. The company uses a comprehensive suite of business process management, applications integration and customer relationship management tools, training, and consulting to accelerate the drive toward e-business, enabling customers to reap the full benefits of MWG-BIOTECH's service.

The evolution of industrial bioinformatics to a customer care service seems to be a spectacular development now. Collaborative commerce has emerged to meet the growing demand for biomedical researcher interaction. Companies like MWG-BIOTECH are turning to collaborative commerce in order to boost biomedical researcher satisfaction. Drowning in a sea of irrelevant information about a gene or a gene function in which he or she is interested, the researcher has to find out all the possible information about this particular gene worldwide. In the field of DNA arrays, for instance, where the complexity of the product and services rises dramatically, a divergence exists between the information available and how much biomedical researchers can adsorb and interpret in the context of their particular needs. The result of the so-called complexity gap means that some biotech companies end up with orders for product configurations that cannot be produced.

Therefore, MWG-BIOTECH has invested both in computer technology and in the founding of a center of excellence to support collaborative commerce interaction with customers. The philosophy behind this idea is the effective transport of information from one specialist to another. It is one aim of MWG-BIOTECH to develop a framework of accepted, trusted, and easy-to-use tools supporting an enterprise-wide knowledge management system successfully integrated in the research process of modern life sciences.

Finding of Facts

It is the ability to easily upgrade services another notch that makes the Internet and pervasive computing services both powerful and attractive at the same time. Even if some services may sound simple, they may be bundled in an integrative way to form powerful packages meeting the needs of customers. The book provides insights in the fundamental working mechanisms of ubiquitous services as they are designed and created.

A person with facts does not need opinions, and facts are the principles that serve as the cornerstone of this book. The author presents them in a way that is useful for the expert reader as well as the beginner, providing a sound foundation and supplying details where needed. *Pervasive Computing* is the logical continuation of his previous bestselling textbook *The E-Business (R)Evolution* and I hope the reader will have as much enlightment and fun as I had while reading it.

Bernd Drescher
Life Science Information Director, MWG BIOTECH AG
Munich, Germany, 13 March, 2001

Preface

Pervasive Computing Is Persuasive

The idea for this book was born when Hewlett-Packard was looking for ideas for the so-called "CNN Vignettes," where a set of 60-second short stories was requested. I wrote four of them with the following ideas in mind. The short stories should present the next chapter on the Internet: the so-called e-services. They should explain the difference between Chapter One and Chapter Two. If we look at these differences we can show that in Chapter One, the current Internet, customers have to serve themselves on the Web. The cutting-edge concept/vision described in Chapter Two is how the Internet automatically services the customers and life therefore becomes easier.

In *The E-Business (R)Evolution*, which I wrote in 1999, I tried to open e-business and e-commerce to all readers. The book introduced the paradigms and concepts of the Internet as we see it today and how it is used in today's environment. The Internet as we know it today is based on computer-to-computer communication. Over the next few years, this PC-based communication will become part of a much larger network that will connect not only PCs, but also mobile phones, refrigerators, stoves, and television sets. In the last two chapters, I introduced the readers to a concept called "pervasive computing," which encompasses the technologies mentioned previously and introduces new business models.

One of these business models is mobile commerce (m-commerce), which allows people to use their mobile phones and personal digital assistants (PDAs) to buy goods and services over the new extended Internet. Key for the introduction of m-commerce are new technologies such as the Wireless Application Protocol (WAP) and Universal Mobile Telecommunications System (UMTS), which allow the transport of information to mobile phones (WAP) and high-speed links between mobile phone and servers. The UMTS standard allows transfer rates up to 2 Mbit/s, which is about 40 times faster than an ISDN connection today. WAP was introduced in early 2000, and UMTS will be rolled out in 2003.

But m-commerce does not mean that Amazon.com will now sell all books over the dishwasher instead of over the PC. Many companies think in this direction, and after reading the book, you should understand why this is not the right strategy. New business ideas are required. A mobile phone user will probably want location-based products and services. If the mobile phone user walks through New York City, information, products, and services that are near him are more interesting than a book available somewhere on the Internet.

One of the most advanced countries in the world, regarding m-commerce, is Finland where many location-based services have been introduced to the general public. The mobile phone can be used, for example, to buy a soft drink at the airport. Just walk up to the soft drink vending machine, call a certain phone number, and the soft drink will be released. Young people in Helsinki, Finland, can use a party finder service to locate a party nearby, based on some preferences, such as music, type, and size. When walking in downtown Helsinki, the user can have the mobile phone notify him about parties within the vicinity.

This book presents these and other examples in a broader context. It is not only about m-commerce, but also about all types of pervasive computing architectures and implementations, such as home networks and virtual enterprise networks. They all share the same infrastructure and the same basic technologies, such as Extensible Markup Language (XML). XML already plays an important role, but it will become even more important in the future as the devices connected to the Internet become even more heterogeneous.

Who Should Read This Book

Solution architects and implementers who need to know how to make the current e-business/e-commerce implementations future-proof will find here the key concepts and architectural designs required for expanding existing infrastructure and technologies. The book is not about programming, although it features some small excerpts to make the concepts easier to understand. E-Services and pervasive computing will change the way people work on and think about the Internet; solution architects will learn about the technologies and the new business models.

Individuals and companies can learn more about the new possibilities of the e-services revolution, which is about to take place. Technical and business managers in companies will also benefit from the book, since they are the people who prepare the long-term strategy for their companies. CEOs will recognize the new paradigm behind the stories.

Online startups will also profit from the book, as they will learn how they can create competitive e-services and how to integrate their existing solutions into an e-service. The book will give them an insight into the new business paradigm and the new economy, which are about to emerge.

The major question for all technologies in this book is: "Why should I use it?" There are enough books on how to use a technology; many people know how, but many forget to ask why. Sometimes it makes sense to avoid new technologies, because they only add extra overhead to the work that needs to be done. Whenever people explain a new technology to you, do not ask how it can be done, but why it should be done.

How This Book Is Organized

Part I opens the "next chapter" of Internet history as it explains the new technologies and business concepts: mobile commerce, home automation, and a variety of enabling technologies, some of which are already taking their first steps.

Part II presents four vignettes for the business-to-consumer world (B2C) or for the business-to-business (B2B) world. Each vignette illustrates a problem and its solution by the Internet of the future. Then, we look at real-world solutions possible today and envision future solutions. We examine a business plan for those solutions and extend that architecture to other business cases.

Part III speculates on how the Internet might look in 25 years and discusses the impact it will have on society, politics, finances, and technology.

The book contains many examples and links to web pages. As the Internet is changing every day, I cannot guarantee that every link will be available at the time you read the book. As a convenience to the readers, I have set up a web site that contains a list of all examples used in the book and will update the list at regular intervals. In addition, the web site will contain links to other e-business sites and more information on the topics in the book. The URL of the web site is http://www.futureinternetstrategies.com/ and will be available from the time of publishing.

Acknowledgements

First of all I would like to thank my wife Sabine for the continued support of my crazy ideas. Although it is sometimes difficult to maintain the work/life balance, I try as hard as I can to be there for her whenever she needs me. I wrote this book besides my real job as a consultant and solution architect for Hewlett-Packard in Europe. Sabine, I want to tell you that I love you.

I would also like to thank all readers of the *The E-Business (R)Evolution*[1] and *Dynamic Commerce*.[2] The feedback on these books was well received and I hope I haven't made the same mistakes again. If you want to get in touch with me, please go to my web site and use the feedback form. I usually get back to you within a day. If it takes longer, I may be traveling, so please be

---

[1]http://www.ebusinessrevolution.com/
[2]http://www.dynamiccommerce.org/

patient, because I travel a lot. A discussion forum is also provided to enable the discussion among readers. I have also set up a university area where students and lecturers can exchange information and download presentations for educational purposes.

I would also like to thank Jill Pisoni of Prentice Hall who supported the idea and helped me with all the details in getting this book published. My thanks also go to all other people involved at Prentice Hall to bring this book to the market. They were very responsive and helpful, and I want to thank them for the continued support during the writing of the book without which this book would not have been possible.

I owe Hewlett-Packard, my managers, Isabelle Roux-Buisson and Albert Frank, and my colleagues a big thank-you for their support and the many general discussions on business on the Internet that were conducted in the coffee breaks and during meetings that made me change some parts of the book while writing it.

Last, but not least, I would like to thank Thomas Kessler of Smart-SMS[3] and Uta Winter of MediaTechBooks[4] for reviewing the book at various stages and their input for changes during the writing. I would also like to thank them for their invaluable support, ideas, and suggestions.

---

[3] http://www.smart-sms.com/
[4] http://www.mediatechbooks.de/

Part I

Where the Future Begins

Chapter 1

The Next Chapter on the Internet

If you can imagine your doctor talking to your hearing aid or your refrigerator reordering milk, then you're ready to embrace the next Internet revolution called pervasive computing. The concept of pervasive computing, which describes the extension of the Internet beyond PCs and servers to form a truly universal network, has been around for several years, but only recently has it begun to find its way to the mainstream.

Although some pundits claim this development signals the death of the personal computer, that demise is unlikely, considering we haven't even moved past mainframes yet. What will start happening, however, is the expansion of the power of the Internet beyond traditional computing devices, enabling people to participate in a global network by using their mobile phones, TV sets, or refrigerators. And it will go a step further.

Pervasive computing will not only replicate the standard functionality of the Web in embedded devices, but it will also offer the services provided by such devices to other entities on the Internet. The idea is to reap the benefits of ever-broader networks without having to deal with obtuse, unwieldy technology. The first generation of embedded devices were passive, meaning that they relayed existing services to other devices, such as the TV. The second generation of embedded devices is more intelligent and can look for services on the Internet, collect them, and bundle them into "metaservices."

1.1 Introduction

Pervasive computing describes an environment where a wide variety of devices carry out information processing tasks on behalf of users by utilizing connectivity to wide variety of networks. In a 1996 speech, Rick Belluzo, executive VP and general manager of Hewlett-Packard,[1] compared pervasive computing to electricity, calling it "the stage when we take computing for granted. We

---

[1] http://www.hp.com/

only notice its absence, rather than its presence." While this may be true for Bill Gates's $53 million home, that level of pervasive technology hasn't trickled down to the mainstream—yet. Louis V. Gerstner, Jr., of IBM[2] once said, "Picture a day when a billion people will interact with a million e-businesses via a trillion interconnected, intelligent devices." Pervasive computing does not just mean "computers everywhere"; it means "computers, networks, applications, and services everywhere."

Pervasive computing has roots in many aspects of computing. In its current form, it was first articulated by Mark Weiser[3] in 1988 (even before the introduction of the World Wide Web) at the Computer Science Lab at Xerox PARC.[4] In his opinion, pervasive computing is roughly the opposite of virtual reality. Where virtual reality puts people inside a computer-generated world, pervasive computing forces the computer to live out here in the world with people. Virtual reality is primarily a horsepower problem; pervasive computing is a difficult integration of human factors, computer science, engineering, and social sciences. Weiser also calls this invisible, everywhere computing that does not live on a personal device of any sort but is in the woodwork everywhere. Its highest ideal is to make a computer so embedded, so fitting, so natural, that we use it without even thinking about it. By invisible, Weiser means that the tool does not intrude on your consciousness; you focus on the task, not the tool. Eyeglasses are a good tool: you look at the world, not the eyeglasses. Pervasive computing creates an augmented reality. It enriches objects in the real world and makes them "smart." This allows these devices to better assist people. With additional information about the environment and the context, these devices become better tools for the people using them.

The trick is to build devices to match people's activities that are related sets of tasks. Already you use 50 or more computers in your home. You don't care how many there are, as long as they provide value and don't get in your way. That's how it should be with the computers in our lives. Computers and motors are infrastructure; they should be invisible.

When computers merge with physical things, they disappear. This is also known as invisible computing and raises, of course, new issues with the user interface, since people do not know that they are using a computer. New, intuitive user interfaces are therefore required.

Realizing such a mass market revolution will involve new types of strategic planning that will connect individual organizations from different industries into an intricate network of alliances and interest groups. Additionally, this vision requires a simplified consumer-marketing strategy that focuses on customer solutions instead of technology products. But this will not be easy; very little of our current system infrastructure will survive.

---

[2]http://www.ibm.com
[3]http://www.ubiq.com/weiser/
[4]http://www.xerox.com/

Examples of Invisible Appliances

Here are some examples of information appliances. The list includes many things you wouldn't think of as computers, which is just the point: successful invisible computers won't be thought of as computers. So, you won't notice you are using lots of them.

- **ATM Machines** – Money delivery through a computer network

- **Cash Registers** – Calculators that are used in checkout counters

- **Navigation Systems** – Direction-giving devices and maps built into cars

- **Digital Cameras** – Images just like those from standard cameras

- **Electric Instruments** – Electronic simulation of guitars, keyboards, drums

- **Calculators** – A service to people who still use calculators even though they are sitting in front of a computer

---

1.1.1 Human-Centered Development

Personal computers are general-purpose devices, designed to do everything. As a result, they can't be optimized for any individual task. Another related problem is that in the design of the PC, many choices were made intentionally to make the PC as flexible and user friendly as possible. Users have complete control over their machines and can even modify the operating system at will, just by clicking on an e-mail attachment. This model makes any real security impossible. Furthermore, it makes it hard even for experienced computer experts to fix problems. Thus, long-range ease of use has been given up in favor of short-term convenience by enabling users to modify their machines on the spur of the moment. This approach is great for rapid diffusion of the next software application, but it leads to frustration when things go wrong, as they often do. Providing stability, security, or transparency requires limiting users' flexibility.

A tradeoff between flexibility and ease of use is unavoidable. However, there is no single tradeoff that is optimal for everyone. Donald Norman[5] argues that the PC was aimed at the "early adopters" and that its lack of success in penetrating about half of the households in the United States is a sign of its poor design. The success of Apple's iMac[6] is another sign that consumers do value simplicity. The iMac requires only a power cable and a telephone cable and within seconds it is on the Internet. No fuss about configuration, it just works. Norman argues that information appliances can and should be designed for the mass market. Proper design of simple interfaces, appropriate when a restricted set of tasks is to be enabled, does make this possible. This is one reason why more mobile phones than personal computers are sold in Europe. Mobile phones are easy to use.

Look at open source software. Linux is the major rival to Microsoft Windows today. Yet it seems that the main lesson to be drawn from the success of Linux and Apache is different. These systems are built by experts for experts. There are many people (although a tiny fraction of the whole population) who know what regular expressions are and can use text commands to execute programs much faster than a graphical user interface (GUI) would let them. They also tend to be in charge of important resources such as web servers, and they appreciate (and effectively use) the flexibility that access to source code provides. Apache and Linux are ideal for them. They are not satisfied with the black-box software from commercial vendors.

These expert users do not account for a large fraction of desktop computers but do control a large share of computing budgets. They form a substantial market for computers where flexibility is dominant, even at the cost of ease of use.

On the other hand, it is doubtful whether those among them who contribute to the code, as opposed to just using it, are interested in creating the easy-to-use but much less flexible interface that would appeal to a wider market. That is the province of Microsoft and Apple. Apple has always been strong on the user interface side, but now they are creating an even more powerful alternative to Windows, called Mac OS X. It uses a BSD kernel, which is similar to the core of Linux and has an easy-to-use interface, called Aqua. It is still a GUI, but built on more than 15 years of experience in this area.

To make computers invisible, designers must start a more human-centered product development, which studies the users for whom the device is intended. This could be in the field where they normally work, study, and play. Norman calls this method "rapid ethnography." Once this study has been conducted, rapid prototyping procedures, design, mock-ups, and tests, which take hours or days, try to find out how people respond to the product idea. This process needs to be repeated until an acceptable result is arrived at.

---

[5] Author of *Being Analog*, published by MIT Press
[6] http://www.apple.com/

The next step in the human-centered development is the manual, which needs be written in a short and simple manner. It should be as simple as possible. The manual and the prototypes are used as the design specs for the engineers.

The issue today is that a product usability test is done only after the product has been manufactured. It should be the other way around. The industry knows that you cannot get quality through testing. Quality must be built in at every step of the process. The result is faster production at higher quality. The same story holds for the total user experience. The total user experience is far more than usability. It is the entire relationship between the consumer and the product.

Human-centered product development is simple in concept but foreign to the minds of most technology companies. The youth of a technology is very exciting. Engineers are in charge. Customers demand more technology. There are high profits and high rates of growth. More technology is introduced, creating a collapsing market situation. After this, the technologies mature and become a commodity. They are taken for granted. Customers want value, quality, fun. Looking at the Internet, we have just left the collapse that happened in late 2000 and are now starting to see mature solutions. If you want human-centered development, you probably have to reorganize your company and create a mind-set to enable human-focused products.

1.1.2 New Class of Computing

Pervasive computing, sometimes called ubiquitous or nomadic computing, describes not only a class of computing device that doesn't fit the form factor of the traditional personal computer, but also a set of new business models supporting these devices. Where a desktop computer uses a familiar keyboard, monitor, and mouse interaction model, pervasive computing devices interact in a variety of different ways. They may use handwriting recognition, voice processing, or imagery. They're often portable and may or may not have a persistent network connection. A pervasive computing device is meant to integrate into your lifestyle and to extend your reach into a global network of computing, freeing you from desk-bound application interaction. With the ability to take corporate and personal processes and data with you, no matter your destination, opportunities abound for improving and enhancing your personal and professional life.

The first wave of computing, from the 1940s to the early 1980s, was dominated by many people serving one computer. In the early eighties the personal computer evolved and allowed the symbiosis between a single person and a computer. The third wave was introduced with the invention of the World Wide Web in the early nineties. Suddenly, the single person could connect to many other computers and users over the global network, the Internet. The fourth wave, which we are seeing on the horizon, extends the paradigm of the third

---

History of Computing

In the history of computing we are about to move to a fourth-generation of computing. Over time, cost and size of computers has reduced significantly to allow more people to participate in the world of computing.

- **Mainframe Computing** – Many people share one large computer

- **Personal Computing** – One person works with one little computer

- **Internet Computing** – One person uses many services on a worldwide network

- **Pervasive Computing** – Many devices serve many people in a personalized way on a global network

---

wave, allowing any device, not just computers, to connect to the global Internet and introduces the paradigm of automated services that serve the users, instead of users serving themselves on the Internet, everywhere in the world.

Picture the sales representative who undocks a portable device each morning before heading out on his route. As he travels his territory, he's able to transact with his customers either in real time or cached for his eventual return. Imagine finishing the last of the milk in the carton and casually swiping the bar code across a reader mounted on the refrigerator. The next time you enter the grocery store to shop, your PalmPC reminds you that you need milk or, better yet, if you don't find a trip to the market to be therapeutic, your household point-of-presence server simply forwards the milk request to the grocer and the required milk is delivered in the next shipment to your home!

While there's no doubt that pervasive computing will be a major part of the technological revolution in the 21st century, we have to ask ourselves whether or not it really benefits society. Many people believe that "pervasive" is just another word for invasive and that it comes at the price of our privacy. Ubiquitous computing affords us the ability to get information anytime, anywhere, but it also increases the risk that centralized personal information will be used without the owner's consent.

There are certainly advantages to having all of your personal data and the equivalent of hundreds of web search engines available on an embedded chip controlled by your voice and an invisible heads-up display. Sure, it sounds a little like the Jetsons, but so did an Internet appliance in the palm of your hand as recently as two or three years ago.

1.1.3   The Tech Elite Duke it Out

The race is on to create the standard for the next generation of the Internet, and as often happens with such efforts in their infancy, companies will compete to establish their own vision of the universal network. Sun Microsystems with its Jini technology is probably the best-known promoter of the universal network vision. But many other well-known companies have started to create similar technologies and incorporate the idea of pervasive computing into their corporate visions. Besides Sun, Hewlett-Packard, IBM, Lucent Technologies, and Microsoft are developing such technologies.

But lip service by the tech heavyweights isn't necessarily a precursor to widespread adoption. The tactical goal of championing these new technologies is often to make the companies developing the architecture appear innovative and to drive sales of more traditional products such as operating systems, servers, and printers. Though still in its formative stages, the concept of the universal network is now out of the bag, and strategically, the resulting technologies will open up a complete new world on the Internet for businesses of all sizes.

1.1.4   Business in a Brave New World

Pervasive computing is knocking on the door of today's economy. To sustain a profitable business in the future, you will need to change many business cases. Selling books to a fridge or sending information about software updates to a car will be easy through pervasive computing, but not successful. People using a fridge expect certain services from it, such as a list of food items inside, maybe a selection of shops in walking distance with good prices, and some recipes to make for dinner. But only a few people will go to the fridge to learn more about the latest thriller by Tom Clancy.

The same applies to all other devices that can now be connected to the Internet. People use them for a certain reason: to increase business and the value of the device; to offer services that support the device or the use of the device. Bringing "traditional" e-commerce and e-business applications to these devices will be easy, but commercially most probably a failure.

Pervasive computing will get at least 10 times more people onto the Internet than there are now, so it is tempting to offer the same services and products to these users through this new and alternative channel. Very few devices really offer the same type of functionality we are used to from today's personal computer. In Europe, WAP-technology has moved Internet functionality to mobile phones. But as you can imagine, doing business with your mobile is quite a challenge. Instead of viewing just a product category, a product detailed page, and a payment page, you will have to go through at least 25 pages on your mobile phone. Your mobile phone cannot display a large amount of information at one time, and slow download times make things worse.

1.1.5 Creation of a New Paradigm

A new paradigm is necessary if we are to create a business targeted to mobile phone users. Any company should first look at the current use of a device before starting with a business plan. In our case, our potential customers use the mobile phone for calling people, storing addresses and phone numbers, playing small games, and looking up calendar appointments, dates, and times. To make money, we could supply services and products to complement the existing services. The call functionality is already supported by the built-in address book, but we could offer an online address book of the whole world. People on business in another town often have difficulty locating an address, so we could have the mobile phone support them with directions. Since mobile phones contain small games, such as Tetris, Snake, and Memory, we could offer new games for download. And to keep a calendar up-to-date, we could synchronize it automatically with the user's existing calendar on his PC or server at work.

These are small services that can enhance the value of the phone, and people would be willing to pay a small amount of money for them. Although we can charge only a few cents per transaction, there is a good chance to become rich soon. The lower the transaction fee, the more likely people are to use the feature. Five cents for a phone and address lookup should not bother many people, and maybe 50 cents for directions to a certain address won't really bother a businessperson. Since the number of users is 10 times higher on mobile phones than on the Internet, we could offer a certain service at a much lower price.

We should now examine the functionality we have built for the mobile phone business to see how we can use it for other devices. All the functionality can, of course, be offered on the Web. People with older mobile phones would therefore be able to use the service. But let's not stop here. Other devices may also be in need of such services. For example, a driver could use the direction and location service, so the car should have access to it. Instead of receiving the information through a map, the driver needs the same information in spoken form. A voice should tell her to drive left at the next crossing and so forth. This means that the data should be stored in a device-independent format to obtain the maximum revenue from the service.

As you can see, every device is an aid for human beings; to make devices more valuable, it is necessary to offer additional services around them. Depending on the situation, the service, product, or information needs to be presented in a different manner in order to support people in the best possible way.

1.2 The Internet Today

(R)Evolutions are a way of life in the computer industry. Only 20 years ago, the computer world was dominated by mainframe systems. Only a few people had access to computers, and these computers were used for calculations in large corporations. Individuals did not possess computers. The personal computer in the early eighties and the GUI in the mid-eighties changed all that, thus giving computer access to millions of people. This turned the computer into a mass-market commodity. From there it was only a small step to the Internet.

Today, more than 350 million people worldwide use the Internet. According to International Data Corp., more than a quarter of a trillion dollars' worth of business will be transacted over the Internet this year. But today's Internet is very much restricted. Although many people believe that the Internet has opened up a whole new world, it has only created a single window into this new universe. In most cases, you need a personal computer to connect to a server, and you need a web browser to browse through the World Wide Web. Companies have set up web pages to allow customers to serve themselves, reducing the load and the cost to the company. For companies going online, the benefit is clear: less direct customer interaction, higher-quality orders, and fewer problems with orders because there is no media "middleman." These factors drive down the cost for every sale and increase the profit for the company.

This is not only true for B2C web sites, but also for B2B and business-to-employee (B2E) web sites. People accessing the services need to specify exactly what they want. They need to provide a set of information and type it into the browser window. Communication is reduced from a human-to-human interaction to a human-to-computer interaction without effectively reducing the workload. The only thing that has happened is a shift of work from the business to the partner, employee, or customer. There are other advantages for the web client, of course. The company, its services, and its products have become accessible 24 hours a day, the prices have been driven down due to the market transparency, and new competitors have created an even more dynamic market place.

1.2.1 Internalized Outsourcing

Most online companies today are forced to build their entire offering virtually from scratch. Even if they buy software solutions, they have to provide all the services themselves. Amazon.com, for example, provides the service of selling books to its customers. All services required to do that, such as inventory management, distribution, billing, and web store management have been implemented and operated by Amazon.com, making their web site proprietary, massive, and costly. Although it is not part of their core business, these services need to be implemented, maintained, and operated by the online retailer. Enter pervasive computing.

A universal network will allow the next generation of online retailers to outsource these services to inventory management, billing, distribution, and web store management solution providers, which will provide these services at a lower price and a higher quality. Right now companies can do this, but they lose control over vital business functions. Pervasive computing will tightly integrate these service providers and ensure centralized control.

1.2.2 Subdivision

For the outsourcing of Internet services to become feasible, every service needs to be able to communicate with the other. The concept of service then becomes more abstract, since it is made up of a series of smaller functions. The service of billing could be further subdivided into several simpler services. One service could be the bill handling. Bills are typically printed on the retailer's printer and then sent to the customer. To reduce costs, the bill could also be printed at a local billing office, or if the customer's printers are directly connected to the Web, the bill could also be printed at the customer site. Costs could be further reduced if the bill is entered directly into the Enterprise Resource Planning (ERP) system of the company and paid automatically. But it can't stop there.

For this new paradigm to work quickly and efficiently, all levels of service need to be integrated. A new layer must be added on top of the existing Internet layers to enable services to accept other services and to connect and create new metaservices, or simply broadcast their availability to the network. Next-generation Internet startups will concentrate even more on their core business and buy the use of building blocks whenever they need them. Instead of setting up a payment server, they will rent a payment service; instead of having to buy new hardware for peak usage, they will rent network and CPU capacity from a service provider.

1.2.3 Expensive and Complex Hardware

The Internet today has the problem that a rather complex computer needs to be used to access it. Although connecting a computer to the Internet has become easier, many people are still lost if a problem occurs, because they don't understand the underlying technology of computer and networking hardware.

To make the Internet more accessible to more people, we not only need devices that are much easier to use and configure than a computer, but we also need to change the whole paradigm of how the Internet works. We are already seeing the first postcomputer Internet generation that uses more mobile phones than computers to send e-mail, chat, and search for information. For example, once the plane has landed, the mobile phone will reconnect to send out the e-mails.

Television sets from Loewe[7] are Internet enabled. Mobile phones from Nokia[8] are WAP enabled. But even before the WAP era it was possible to surf the Web with a mobile phone. You could either connect a mobile phone to your laptop or use the Nokia Communicator to write e-mail and surf the Web. There is also no need to buy a new television to connect to the Web. For years you have been able to buy so-called set-top boxes to add the Internet functionality to your television set. This addition allows you to browse the Web without having to know how to install a browser or update the operating system.

Using a television or a mobile phone to access the Internet is not the same as using a web browser. Later, when we discuss WAP in more detail, both from a technological and a business point of view, you will understand better why this emerging technology has not lived up to its expectations. But even if WAP were the perfect technology, it would not remove some of the elementary problems of the Web, because WAP is only a technology to access the old Internet infrastructure.

These innovations over the past years did not change things a lot, because the existing functionality of a personal computer was introduced into new devices without respecting the limitations these devices had. The concept of pervasive computing does not stop with transferring standard Internet functionality to new devices, but also allows the creation of new applications and services. Turning on a washing machine, checking prices at a gas station, locating a plane en route could become possible through the Internet. Of course, this does not mean that everyone should be allowed to access all information and services through the Internet. It is important to realize that the pervasive computing ideal of any service to any device over any network is a statement of enablement; it does not mean that every service will be made available to every type of device over every type of network.

The owner of the washing machine should be the only one to switch it on or off. The prices of petrol should be visible to everyone, but only the owner of the petrol station should be allowed to reorder petrol or change the prices. The same applies to the services and information that are provided by an airplane. Everyone should be able to check whether a certain plane is late, but nobody except the pilot should be able to fly the plane. New security models and measures are therefore necessary to implement pervasive computing technologies.

There is still plenty of room for improvement. Despite bountiful bandwidth, information is still locked up in centralized databases, with "gatekeepers" controlling access. Users must rely on the web server to perform every operation, just like the old timesharing model. Web sites are isolated islands and cannot communicate with each other on a user's behalf in any meaningful way. Today's Web does little more than simply serve up individual pages to individual users—pages that mostly present HTML "pictures" of data, but not the data

---

[7]http://www.loewe.de/
[8]http://www.nokia.com/

itself (at present, making both available is too technically demanding for most web sites). And the browser is in many respects a glorified read-only dumb terminal; you can easily browse information, but it is difficult to edit, analyze, or manipulate (i.e., all the things knowledge workers actually need to do with it). Personalization consists of redundantly entering and giving up control of your personal information to every site you visit. You have to adapt to the technology, instead of the technology adapting to you.

Another major inhibitor to creating worldwide e-business web sites is the multitude of interfaces that are often incompatible, making it impossible to share information and services across a computer, mobile phone, and car, for example. Even if the interfaces seem to be compatible, the different devices provide varying levels of data access, meaning that there is a difference between the information you receive and visualize in the car and that at home. In some cases it does make sense to present the same data in different manners, but the amount and format of data should not vary from device to device. A car should be able to receive the same data as your computer at the same detail level. On your computer, you might be presented with a map and a textual description of how to get to a certain street. In the car, the information should be presented by voice, meaning that the car computer reads the textual information to make driving safer.

Things become even worse right now if you not only read data but also use different devices for data input. Many people already struggle because they have different calendars, one on their computer, one on their mobile phone, and a hard-copy one. They need to make sure that all meetings are recorded in all three calendars. In the future, all devices will be able to synchronize themselves without manual interaction. Okay, today you can synchronize your palmtop with your laptop, but you need to install additional software and connect them via a cable. In the future, no cables and additional software will be required.

Once the technology has been put in place, personalized "information spaces" on the Internet can be created. These repositories would contain all information about a certain person, a certain process, or a certain company. The information will be most likely organized in an object-oriented database whereby objects and attributes will have security settings allowing others to view them or not. This would mean that consumers don't have to reenter information on every e-business web page, but once they decide to buy something, the site will get access to the required data. And not only web sites will have access, but other devices will be able to retrieve data whenever they need it. These devices could be owned by that particular person, such as her mobile phone, his PDA, or any other mobile device. But it could also be other devices, such as a scanner at the airport that does an iris scan to check identity.

Most web sites today focus on fancy graphics and a strong marketing message, but very few can support business and commerce transactions, and those that do, often do so inadequately. The process is not often developed by a business unit, but by the IT department, which normally has no contact with customers and partners and therefore does not know their requirements very well. Developers of web sites face another problem: the interfaces to existing systems and to partner and customer online businesses. No system today lets developers write code for a particular system and deploy it to a variety of devices. Java technology comes very close, but it means that all software components need to be rewritten in the Java programming language to be supported; many companies are not willing to spend time, money, and effort for a software porting project if they have used a particular software solution for years.

Therefore, a new paradigm and vision are needed—ones that address all the issues raised here and that provide the foundation for the next generation of electronic businesses. Several technologies, paradigms, and visions have been developed. The book describes them so you can choose the right one for your business case. In the end, business is all that matters.

There are more reasons to create a pervasive computing vision of the future. Consider the following example. Today, people can use mobile devices and connect to a range of devices, but in most cases special knowledge is required. Physically connecting a PDA to a computer is usually simple. The cabling is standardized, and even unexperienced users will be able to plug in the cables. The problem arises as soon as they want to transfer data from one device to the other. If they use the proposed configuration of the PDA, the transfer will work, but most people configure their computer to their needs, with tools and programs that best fit their requirements without regard to the PDA. The PDA is not prepared to download data from any calendar, it is not able to communicate with every operating system, and it is not ready to use all existing services. Today, most standard applications, such as e-mail and calendar, work, but there is no *guarantee* that they will work. People with more in-depth technical knowledge are able to install additional drivers and configure them properly to work with the system, but the technical layman will not be able to use the network.

Therefore, the existing Internet technologies, communication protocols, and interface designs are unable to handle a heterogenous network properly. The existing paradigm does not scale with increasing numbers of services and computing devices. The knowledge and time required of users today will increase dramatically as more software services and computing resources become available, and do not scale with increasing user mobility. Manual configuration costs time. If a user remains in a computing environment for only 15 minutes, he does not want to spend the first 10 minutes restoring computing contexts manually. The existing infrastructure also does not tolerate change or failure of computing resources. The services available in an environment change in the presence of mobile devices such as laptops and I/O devices. Software services can be installed or removed without users' knowledge. Proximity-based networking (such as IrDA and Bluetooth) leads to dynamically changing net-

Today's Computing Model

Today's computing model is targeted toward the individual using a single device and can therefore be characterized by the following assumptions:

- **Desktop computing** – People typically sit in front of a desktop PC to do their work.

- **Stationary devices and software** – People tend to have total control over the few devices they use, including software and hardware configuration.

- **Monolithic applications** – Most applications are designed to interact with humans instead of with other applications.

- **Manual mapping** – Computing tasks are mapped manually to applications. Users need to know which application is capable of what.

- **Single device computing** – Users typically only use one device at a time.

- **Manual configuration** – Users are responsible for configuring applications themselves and keep a single configuration regardless of the environment.

works. Failures of services and networks can change the availability of computing resources. Manual configuration is simply too costly in this setting of transient services, networks, and devices.

1.2.4 Current Restrictions

Fundamental problems prevent current technology from becoming pervasive. Today, people typically sit in front of a desktop PC to do their work. This means that there is a one-to-one relationship between the device and the human. In the future, people are more likely to use a variety of different devices that need to be configured on-the-fly as the person using it wants it to be. Even if people use more than one device today, they typically use stationary devices such as desktop workstations and a couple of mobile devices (laptops, PDAs) and they do their computing primarily on those devices. People have complete control over those devices and how they are configured. People buy software and install it on their personal devices and compute primarily with that software. If they move with their laptops from one environment to another one, they need to reconfigure the laptop to work in the new environment. Network connection, printers, and online services need to be reconfigured manually.

Today's applications are designed to interact with humans only. This means that many companies invest a lot of money in the creation of GUIs that are designed to keep the human using the software happy, but most applications are unable to communicate with other applications in a heterogenous network. CORBA and E-Speak provide the ability to offer services and information across applications and modules, but only a few applications support these paradigms today—and if they do, they support only one of them, making them available to only very few other applications.

Another problem with today's computer environment is that the user needs to know which application performs which task. Users must keep track of how to use these applications and configure them to carry out each task that they want to do. The future needs to provide a single repository where users can locate all services available to them at a certain time, at a certain location, and with a certain device. Only then is the universal network really in place.

Computers and networks are isolated silos. Communication between systems is complex and inefficient. To extend an application or technology from one computer or network to another requires additional intervention, whether it is a file conversion or a complete systems integration.

Programs are tied directly to the operating system, which is tied to specific hardware. This prevents the user from accessing any given program from any hardware device—a prerequisite for pervasiveness.

Today's users are also not accustomed to using several devices to complete a task. Everything needs to be installed on one system to be accepted by the user. In the future, the user must understand that it may be more convenient to access a service that involves several devices at once. The user should not know which device does what in this setup. It should be a transparent service, and the underlying components should be managed by the service. Single-device computing should become a paradigm of the past. A new user interface is therefore necessary to control and use the new networking service environment. This interface will also obviate the need for manual configuration that drives users crazy. Today users are responsible for configuring applications; in the future, a service will configure the application to users' current needs.

1.3   New Internet Technologies

As new devices are connected to the Internet, the number of users will explode. As a result, the number of business opportunities will increase rapidly.

Pervasive computing technologies do more than connect these devices to the Internet. Not only can users view content through their WAP phone, but domestic devices, consumer electronics, and other devices, such as cars and planes, can access specialized services and provide services to other devices and users. Pervasive computing creates a universal network that will include business models such as m-commerce and home networks. It is the basis for the next generation of the Internet.

More and more devices contain computer chips and pervade every fabric of life. The concepts are not new; in the early nineties, many companies created visions of this future. The extension of the existing Internet is also often called the universal network.

A few years ago, Sun,[9] Oracle,[10] and a few others developed the network computer, which basically consists of a screen, a keyboard, and some memory. Applications and processing power were requested over the network as needed. Even files were saved on the Internet. By implementation of this paradigm, the existing hardware could be replaced by a newer generation that would be much cheaper and much easier to administer and configure. These technical tasks would be done by a system administrator who took care of hundreds of computers. If you look at the underlying paradigm, you can easily see it as a predecessor to the universal network.

1.3.1   Application Service Providers

The vision of the network computer was regarded as the end of the personal computer, but flaws in the concept prevented the network computer from really taking off. However, several ideas have been enhanced and introduced into the universal network. The basic idea of connecting less powerful devices to the Internet has been extended to noncomputer devices, such as mobile phones. More and more applications are now available through application service providers (ASP). One of the first applications, e-mail, has now become one of the most used applications on the Web, and it is now also possible to use Microsoft Word or SAP R/3 over the Web. By using a service instead of installing the software, the user does not have to pay a fee before using the software and does not need to buy the necessary infrastructure. In the ASP model, billing is done according to the pay-per-use model. The more often users connect to the ASP and use its applications, the more they have to pay.

The advantage is that the software and the infrastructure are controlled in a central environment; as soon as the software is updated, every user of the service can use it without having to install new versions of the software locally. As more and more nontechnical people use computers, this paradigm becomes more important. For complex software such as SAP R/3, the cost for the infrastructure can be very high, meaning that a company has to invest several

---

[9]http://www.sun.com/
[10]http://www.oracle.com/

million dollars or euros into the software, hardware, and network. Installation of a new version is also a major hassle. By outsourcing these applications, companies can focus on their core competencies. Today's ASPs are not yet compatible with the universal network, but they are the first step toward a truly networked business environment.

The major problem of ASPs today is to make the software network-friendly. Most software written today is not ready for the ASP model. Microsoft Word and SAP R/3, for example, need additional software wrappers to allow remote use of the software. The new technologies and programming paradigms will help to resolve this issue.

The vision of pervasive computing to interconnect all people by a globally integrated, ubiquitous network promises greater empowerment for the individual. Yet realizing such a vision requires the implementation of new technologies that, up until now, were merely visionary. Recent advancements in pervasive computing technologies promise the arrival of a new era in ubiquitous computing, marked by the emergence of high-speed, multilayer, in-home networks that will integrate traditional home automation and control technologies with real-time, media-rich applications like voice and video conferencing. Most importantly, these new technologies also involve new deployment strategies that will bring broadband internetworking applications to the domestic mass market.

Pervasive computing gives us tools to manage information easily. Information is the new currency of the global economy. We increasingly rely on the electronic creation, storage, and transmittal of personal, financial, and other confidential information, and we demand the highest security for all these transactions. We require complete access to time-sensitive data, regardless of physical location. We expect devices—PDAs, mobile phones, office PCs, and home entertainment systems—to access that information and work together in one seamless, integrated system. Pervasive computing can help us manage information quickly, efficiently, and effortlessly.

Pervasive computing aims to enable people to accomplish an increasing number of personal and professional transactions by using a new class of intelligent and portable devices. It gives people convenient access to relevant information stored on powerful networks, allowing them to easily take action anytime, anywhere.

These new intelligent appliances, or "smart devices," are embedded with microprocessors that allow users to plug in to intelligent networks and gain direct, simple, and secure access to both relevant information and services. These devices are as simple to use as calculators, telephones, or kitchen toasters.

Pervasive computing simplifies life by combining open-standards-based applications with everyday activities. It removes the complexity of new technologies, enables people to be more efficient in their work, and leaves more leisure time. Computing is no longer a discrete activity bound to a desktop; pervasive computing is fast becoming a part of everyday life.

Pervasive Computing Summary

Pervasive computing means many things to many people. Here is a short definition of all it encompasses.

- **Invisible devices** – Numerous, casually accessible, often invisible computing devices

- **Embedded microchips** – Microchip intelligence embedded into everyday devices and objects

- **Always on** – Access to information, entertainment, and communication with anyone, anytime, anywhere

- **Ubiquitous network** – Everyone and everything connected to an increasingly ubiquitous network structure

- **Life-enhancing applications** – Invisible penetration of technology into the mainstream mass market through a variety of life-enhancing applications

- **Consumer-centric solutions** – Device "gadgetry" for simple and practical consumer-centric solutions

- **Increasing productivity** – Mainstream market value propositions: Saving time, saving money, enhancing leisure and entertainment

- **Long-term vision** – Using technology in ways that empower people to work, live, and play more effectively

1.3.2 Wireless Networks

Simplicity can only be maintained if devices are connected in a wireless mode. That way you need not plug and unplug the devices as you move into a new location or introduce new components to a local area network (LAN). As long as only a few people use nomadic devices in a controlled environment, it is acceptable that they configure their devices themselves and plug/unplug them, but imagine hundreds of thousands of people in a city moving around using local services, switching context and using different services. If these multitudes needed to plug in every time, the time to set up the environment would take longer than using the service. With wireless technologies, it is easy to use an existing installed local infrastructure.

Two kinds of wireless networking are required. One kind provides long-range connections via cellular phones or satellite connections to connect to the Internet or special service providers that are not locally available. The other kind provides local, short-range connections to give access to local services; this can be achieved by Bluetooth or wireless LAN (WLAN) connections. An overview of the existing technologies is given in Chapter 4. A wireless network is, therefore, the basis for a pervasive computing architecture.

Although many people will carry around devices, they will not want to do so all the time. Many devices will be installed permanently in a certain location and can be accessed and used by many people for varying services. To allow access to these devices, a dynamic ownership needs to be implemented to allow the use of wired infrastructure and the seamless integration of the wireless and wired world.

Dynamic ownership means that the devices require a login for all people using it. Once a person logs in, the system will be configured to the needs of the user. This approach requires a centralized database with the profile of the user that can be accessed by all devices.

1.3.3 Framework for the Universal Network

To promote new services on the Internet, standards organizations must establish new standards that are as common and accepted as HTML for the Web. These standards include protocols and interfaces for the access of online services. The standards must allow the description and virtualization of services in order to allow access to services and information not yet available in digital form. Only if the framework supports this paradigm is it possible to create a large set of services in a short time.

A service should be viewed as an object on the Internet. At the moment, almost everyone agrees that objects should be described in XML, but different organizations have different approaches on how to describe these objects. Oasis,[11] RosettaNet,[12] and BizTalk[13] try to describe services, products, and information related to vertical and horizontal markets, to make them more easily comparable and usable. As long as the different organizations fail to create a single standard, it will be difficult to use all services on the Internet. XML allows the easy transformation of data from one format to the other, but if the granularity of the information is different, a manual process needs to be put in place to add missing details. For example, one standard could describe a personal computer as follows: 999 MHz processor, 128 MB RAM, 32 GB hard disk. The other standard would describe it as follows: About 1 GHz Pentium 4 processor, 128 MB DIMM RAMs, 32 GB IBM hard disk. Although both descriptions are structured, it is almost impossible to convert the first into the

[11]http://www.oasis-open.org/
[12]http://www.rosettanet.org/
[13]http://www.biztalk.com/

Components for the Universal Network

Four components are necessary to pervasive computing:

- **Universal cataloging system** – Users should be able to use any computer to find any program that suits their needs.

- **Universal application platform** – When users click on a file, a program should launch regardless of where it might be stored on the Internet and on what type of device.

- **Universal file management** – Users should be able to use any computer to not only access their own files but also to access any files which they have permission to view or access.

- **Universal payment system** – Users should have a set method for measuring what they use and specifying how they should pay for it.

---

second because essential information is missing. Fortunately, the organizations mentioned understand the problem and are cooperating to circumvent these problems.

1.3.4 Metaservices

By virtualizing applications and services, companies can build up new applications and services that are composed of several virtual applications and services, thus reducing the cost of development and implementation. New applications and services can be created on-the-fly and for a certain purpose only. Virtualizing the services and applications enables them to reconfigure themselves to work together seamlessly.

Support for these new metaservices on the universal network comes from support for the processes that create the metaservice. These processes are also being defined in new standards. One of these standards, called "Job Description Format," describes all processes in the print industry. Even the most complex processes will be described in this standard. Once all processes are documented in a simple way, everyone can review the stage a certain process is in, independently of the services and products used to implement the process.

Only if standardization can be achieved can metaservices on the Internet be controlled and guaranteed.

What I call metaservices is today known as a web site. Companies rely heavily on standard applications and interfaces between the different applications to create a complete business model on the Web. Using the concept of pervasive computing, companies can set up a virtual company with virtual organizations. Instead of implementing all components themselves, companies can tie in virtual processes, business models, and organizations. This allows companies to concentrate on their core competencies and think about innovative add-ons to their core business model. Companies like Amazon.com and Yahoo![14] have spent millions of dollars on components that are not part of their core competencies.

The business of Amazon.com is to sell products. To provide the basic business model, Amazon.com built up a complex infrastructure to support the business model. All services that are connected to the selling of books had to be implemented by Amazon.com. This undertaking built up a massive complexity in hardware, software, and services. Amazon.com has to implement and manage this complexity, making the whole site complex, proprietary, and expensive.

The web pages show only a small part of a complete company and its processes. To sell products, a company must set up a logistics service, an enterprise resource planning service, call center service, web-hosting service, and many other things a customer does not care about.

Many companies that enter the Internet world suffer because some components are missing. Manufacturers trying to target consumers, for example, often have problems supporting the needs of the consumers because the existing logistics services can handle the shipment of thousands of products, but not of single goods. Manufactures also often lack a call center for consumers and receive thousands of calls and e-mail instead of a few from dealers. Startup companies have even more trouble, since they have no departments at all. Through virtual departments, it is easier to set up a business without having to invest a lot into a business model that may fail after a short while. This gives new Internet businesses a better standing and also reassures the investors that their money is well spent.

1.3.5   Security Requirements

A new level of security will be required to support the universal network. Whereas access to the Web is easily secured through login and password, secured access to the universal network is more complex. Multiple access rights must be created for every object. Information and service objects must be set in context to provide different views of information and different aspects of services. Only then can the service be automated.

Simple login and password procedures will be inadequate in a universal network. Many devices won't have a keyboard—they will have an eye-scanner,

---

[14]http://www.yahoo.com/

a voice recognition system, or a smart card reader—but the universal network security method must be independent of how users or services are identified. Further, the security method must be able to identify the context in which a device is used. Context awareness becomes vital for every device, which we will see later in this chapter.

1.3.6 Operational Module

To support security needs, a central operational module is needed to provide the basic services for the pervasive computing platform. This operational module should be able to search for, broker, and execute services. To minimize delay, it should be relatively near to the person or device requesting a service. The person or device should be able to connect to another pervasive computing platform if the nearest one is not available.

Each of these platforms contains a directory of services available to the person or device in a certain situation. These services can be combined to form new metaservices, and the status of these services and their processes can be tracked. That way, the module can guarantee the quality of service of the network, and can predict when a certain result can be obtained and what needs to be done to optimize the result. The module should also be able to identify participants and restrict access to personal and other sensitive information to a certain group of people.

Virtualizing service objects makes it possible to use instances of a certain service in all sorts of different contexts without the need to recompile or reconfigure the service component. It also ensures that the service is implementation-independent and that a change in the service component will not affect the existing functionality that is broadcast to the Net world.

1.3.7 Virtualization of Applications and Information

The first steps toward pervasive computing have already been taken. The Web has virtualized processes and applications. Instead of using applications through their own user interface, the applications use the Web. Instead of using an e-mail client, many people use a web browser; instead of using a SAP GUI, many people use a web front to SAP. The advantage is that they are no longer restricted to a certain location or a certain installation. More and more applications use the Web to present and display processes and information.

When a service is moved to the Web, any device that contains a web browser can access the service. People can access their e-mail from anywhere in the world without having to carry around a local computer or a laptop. The application is not bound to a certain hardware installation or software configuration. A web browser is all users need.

Another problem will be solved in the near future: the distribution and access of files. Today, most data is on a local system, such as a portable or desktop

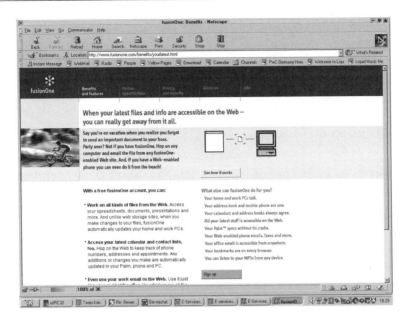

Figure 1.1. The Web Site of fusionOne

computer. This data is only accessible to a person or application service that is near this data. "Near" means that the data is on the same hard disk, in the same room, or on the same network segment. Putting data on the Internet today puts it at risk of being available to anyone. As more and more applications become pervasive and reside on the Internet, the next logical move is to put the data on the Internet as well, so users can access their applications and files from anywhere.

fusionOne[15] has developed a technology that allows users to manage their private data on the Internet. The technology allows users to collect information on a private network and provide it in a directory on the Internet to privileged persons. Business people who are traveling can access their data on their private network by connecting to the web site of fusionOne (see Figure 1.1) and entering a login and password. Private networks typically belong to companies or to families that are normally not accessible from the outside. With fusionOne's software, called Internet Sync, secure access to data on private networks is possible. Moreover, the risk of having several incompatible versions of the same document is reduced; with Internet Sync, users always have the most up-to-date version of a file, no matter where they are. The software is so far only a point solution, but it is easy to imagine a future version that allows controlled access to information relative to a certain person or situation.

---

[15]http://www.fusionone.com/

Many other applications—such as Gnutella[16] and Napster[17]—that deal with data distribution are already available. Both have been developed for MP3 files but the technology allows swapping of any type of file and could be used for business transactions if additional security were included.

Although file sharing on a network is a nice service, it does not handle transformation of the information contained in the files. It does not help to share a Word document across a heterogenous network if some of the devices are not capable of viewing the information. To use applications and files on any type of device, the programming paradigm must be changed to recognize the abilities of each device. These changes are described in Chapter 4 in detail. Only if these new standards are put in place can pervasive computing components without too much overhead be written. Only if you can virtualize information and services, can you use them on any device and participate in the universal network.

By virtualizing products, information, and services on the Internet, more companies can do business on the Internet. They don't even have to be completely online themselves. It is enough to have a virtual representation on the Internet that is managed by someone else. Although this approach is not optimum, it does allow all companies to take part in the new economy with little cost. Pervasive computing combines online services with offline services to create new, more powerful services for everyone in the online and offline world. Pervasive computing allows a new generation of Internet services, such as information, products, and service brokers that transparently handle both online and offline businesses.

Pervasive computing not only provides these services to the general public, but also allows only certain people to use a dedicated service. It is also possible to allow the automatic communication between certain devices. A car, for example, could check, on behalf of the driver, where the nearest and cheapest gas station can be found. The heater could participate in an energy auction to buy as much energy as possible for a certain amount of money.

To make pervasive computing successful, many small tasks must be done automatically so that users can concentrate on the real tasks. Achievement of this goal will mean an augmentation of life.

1.3.8   A New Business Platform

The introduction of pervasive computing technologies will create a new business-to-business platform that will bring a higher transparency to the market. Only with pervasive computing is it possible to compare all offers without missing one. It is also possible to combine service offerings from different companies and pick the best parts of each offer to create a new offer.

B2B exchanges are becoming more popular, where companies provide offers for products and services in response to requests from other companies.

---

[16]http://www.gnutella.org/

[17]http://www.napster.com/

Today this process is still manual because someone has to create a request for proposal and another person has to answer it. The first thing we will see in the future is automatic answers; later, we will see the on-demand creation of requests for proposals whenever a need for a certain good or service arises in production. Through pervasive computing, many processes that have been moved from the physical world to the Internet world will be automated in the future.

The technologies to support this automation are described in Chapter 4 in detail; which of them will succeed cannot be said at the moment, but it can only be a technology that can communicate with other pervasive computing technologies. No company in the world has such a market dominance that it can decide which technology will be the only one. E-Speak from Hewlett-Packard, for example, communicates with the Jini technology developed by Sun. Only if all technologies that are applied are able to communicate with each other will a truly universal network be born.

1.3.9   New Interfaces

Today, working across online and offline environments—even when using only a single laptop—can be a frustrating and inefficient experience. The world becomes more disintegrated. Applications that we use daily, such as web browsing, text editing, graphical design software, and communication technologies, require different software platforms with different functionalities. Although many services are already available through a web browser, each web service has its own user interface and its own formats. Most people would prefer a single, unified environment that adapts to whichever environment they are working in and that moves transparently between local and remote services and applications. Making an environment device-independent transmutes it to a sort of universal canvas for the Internet Age, as Microsoft calls it in its .NET vision.

A set of new interfaces makes the use of digital services much easier in the future. To make the interaction with the net-enabled devices as seamless as possible and to hide as much of their technology as possible, a set of natural interfaces will help a person use the devices as fast as possible without having to concentrate on the technology. Only this approach allows the vision of invisible computing. These interfaces will move away from "traditional" interfaces, such as keyboards and mouse devices, and move toward speech, vision, handwriting, and natural-language input technologies. More and more new devices will provide one of these interfaces, some of them in combination. The natural interface provides the right user experience for every device or environment.

Providing natural interfaces is not enough. All devices need to share a unified environment to enable users to interact with information in a unified way, no matter which device they are using. Therefore, it is necessary to create a compound information architecture that integrates all types of services into a single environment, making it easy to switch contexts, services, physical environments, and devices. Such an architecture creates a universal canvas from which users read and write information and use services from any device. This universality also allows a seamless view of information that may be distributed around the world.

Multiple ways of identification ensure the correct view of services and information. Once you have identified yourself, you need to provide your profile to the service you want to use. Therefore, a virtual representation of yourself is required to manage the personal interaction with digital services. These information agents can manage your identity and persona over the Internet and provide greater control of how Internet services interact with you. They should maintain your history, context, and preferences; basically, they should store your past, present, and future on the Internet in a secure way. With privacy support from agents, your personal information remains under your control and you decide which service can access it. This allows you to create your personal preferences just once, which you can then permit any digital service to use.

1.3.10   Context Awareness

As more and more devices with Internet access become available, their size is being reduced. Therefore, the interfaces to input and output information and use services become more irritating and boring to use. The user must enter a lot of information into each device to use the service. To reduce the amount of information is, therefore, one of the most pressing problems in making devices more user friendly. Part of the solution is known as context awareness. By means of hardware sensors and machine learning technologies, devices can detect the context of the user and adapt their behavior accordingly. The sensors detect what the environment is like. Mobile phones are already able to recognize whether they are used at home or outside. VIAG Interkom[18] provides its Genion mobile phone tariffs with a special service: if the mobile phone is used at the customer's home, the caller pays normal tariff; if used outside, the caller pays the higher mobile phone tariff. All mobile phone providers use the same system on a greater scale when crossing country borders, allowing the callers to use a roaming service by connecting them to the foreign mobile phone network.

Appliances that know more about their environment will be able to function better and will give their users a better, more personalized service. A device that knows about its own environment and that of its user could transparently adapt to the situation, leading to the realization of the invisible computer. To improve interaction with such a device, its context awareness must be augmented. The appliance will be able to give better defaults for the situation and could automatically make choices that the user normally would have to make, thus reducing the amount of time to access a service.

---

[18]http://www.viag.de/

Components of Context Awareness

To make devices aware of their context, the following components need to implemented. They need to answer the following questions:

- **Activity** – What does the user want to do?

- **Environment** – Where is the user currently?

- **Self** – Which status has the device?

The context-related information can be used to control incoming and outgoing information to and from the device and to set device controls. This could have consequences for the use of these devices. A washing machine could check the time of day and not start itself until the local power supplier reduces its prices for energy. A mobile phone may know whether to ring urgently or buzz subtly, depending on the environment—a meeting room or a beach—of the mobile phone owner. A PDA may know to immediately initiate a network connection or to wait until a connection is cheaper and more reliable, depending on whether the user needs to download information or send e-mail. A laptop can know to switch to low-power mode because its user is engaged in a phone conversation across the room or to check one more time for e-mail before a plane takes off so that the owner can read and respond to the e-mail while airborne.

Context awareness is not a new concept. Many appliances already use sensors to find out what is happening in their environment. Today, however, only a few sensors are used, and the recognition process is still very simple, based on very little input. Establishing a high-level notion of context, based on the output of a group of simple sensors, is not very common. The field of robotics started with this approach and has probably been responsible for most of the progress that has been made so far. The context awareness in robotics is still expensive and slow. In most cases, the robots are also fixed in a certain environment. In the future, devices need to adapt to a changing environment quickly and, even more importantly, cheaply. In the era of pervasive computing, context awareness is mandatory.

To make devices aware of their context, developers must implement the following components: activity, environment, and self. The activity component describes the task the user is performing at the moment, or, more generally, what his or her behavior is. This aspect of context is focused on the users of the device and their habits. This component creates the personalization

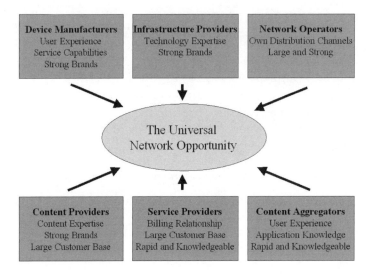

Figure 1.2. The Universal Network Opportunity

feature of the device. The environment component describes the status of the physical and social surroundings of the user. It takes into account the current location, the activities in the environment, and other external properties, like temperature or humidity. With the addition of this functionality, the device can set correct default values for its service and reduce the time for the user to use the service. Finally, the self component contains the status of the device itself. It indicates which capabilities are available for which person in a given environment. A device could give a set of services to person A in the house, but a different set of services while traveling. The same device could also provide a totally different set of services to person B regardless of its environment. When these components are onboard every device, they become personal and usable for anyone, anywhere.

1.4   New Internet Business Models

The universal network will provide a new chance for startups to play an important role. In Chapters 2 and 3 you will see some startups that already play a significant role in home automation networks and m-commerce. But the complexity and scope of the pervasive computing market means that it is difficult to single out any one type of player within any particular supply chain as having an advantage over any other. So, let us have a look at the different players in this new market segment (see Figure 1.2).

We will certainly see that six players in the market will make a lot of money. First, the device manufacturers: if they have a good story to tell, people will buy new devices. Infrastructure providers and network operators will be the next to quickly benefit from the new opportunities—even more than they did with the traditional Internet since the number of participants is much higher on the universal network. The large software infrastructure vendors that have the most expertise in providing the necessary solutions will realize the technological opportunities. They will have to bring their solutions to market through partnerships with brand owners. But technology alone will not enable pervasive computing.

Once the infrastructure, the devices, and the network are up and running and the new business ideas are accepted by the consumers, the following three players will be able to generate money in the market: Content providers, service providers, and content aggregators will offer information, products, and services through the universal network to the consumers and businesses. Service providers that can attain "critical mass" will have the potential to take up positions of strength by acting as brokers of service agreements and other commercial relationships and by specializing content, applications, and services for particular usage contexts (combinations of users' identities and preferences, user roles, and delivery channels). Branding strength lies in the hands of device manufacturers, service providers, and content aggregators because they are most likely known by the users and therefore able to drive the market forces.

Once the market is up and running, a new value chain (see Figure 1.3) will be in place. The device manufacturers will create handsets and other types of terminals for the users. Accessories manufacturers will provide new types of add-ons, such as headsets, car kits, PC cards, and much more to supplement the offerings of the device manufacturers.

The wholesaler manages the distribution of handsets and accessories and provides the intermediate service between manufacturer and distributor. The distributor then moves the devices to the end users via physical shops or electronic distribution channels.

On the other hand, software suppliers will write new software for the devices and the servers to support the business models of the companies in this emerging market. By making the software device independent, the whole concept of pervasiveness is established.

The network manufacturer will have to develop new network components to support the extended infrastructure of the universal network. Infrastructure operators will buy the network components to operate a network infrastructure on behalf of a licensee, which may also own and build infrastructure and sites. Existing network operators will enter the market and try to retain their leading role in the networking segment.

The third segment of the market, service (see Figure 1.4), will be dominated by the service providers that sell network services on behalf of the network

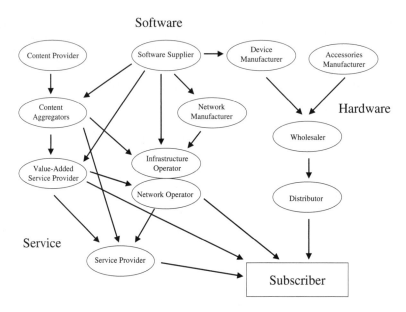

Figure 1.3. The New Value Chain

operators. They typically operate billing systems and customer services and collect a margin for doing so.

Content providers work in the background and collect, edit, and create information to serve content aggregators that provide menu services and protocol conversions to enable access to content. The content is packaged and passed on to a regular service provider or a value-added service provider.

The difference between regular service providers and value-added service providers is that the value-added service provider has a billing relationship with the subscriber that is independent of the network operator.

1.4.1 Device Manufacturers

The main opportunity for device manufacturers brought about by pervasive computing is for higher volume mass-market sales and the introduction of new devices and surrounding services. With the correct marketing and partnerships in place and the greater availability and accessibility of content, applications and services will make new and existing devices more appealing to purchase. By introducing next-generation devices, manufacturers can attract customers that refused to buy the old device for some reason.

Device manufacturers will no longer be able to sell hardware products in the future. If they want to remain an important player, they need to move away from promoting hardware and start to create value-added services for devices. The device manufacturers can easily use their established brands to move into

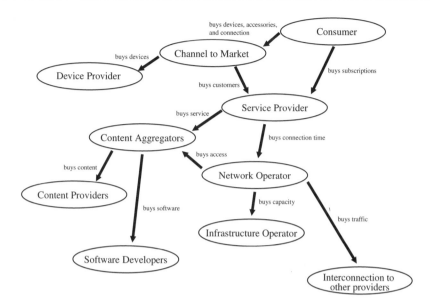

Figure 1.4. Revenue Streams in the Mobile World

this arena. Services could include a recipe database for the oven, a direct link to the next grocery store from the refrigerator, or an interactive TV information site from the television set.

Device manufacturers should not try to provide a single device as the solution for all problems. People like to have a device per problem, especially if the solutions provided are hardware dependent. People do not like to rely on a single piece of hardware, where if one of the functionalities is broken the whole device and all the other included functionalities need to be seen for repair. The devices should solve a simple question and should be even easier to use. Devices like VCRs that are difficult to program will not be salable in the future. Car stereos that have five buttons and 25 functions will also not be salable anymore. The devices of the future do not need any configuration; people buy them and are instantly able to use them, just like mobile phones, for example.

1.4.2   Infrastructure Providers

The universal network requires infrastructure. Infrastructure providers create the necessary devices and services to allow the connection of all devices that are enabled for pervasive computing services. The current Internet infrastructure based on routers, switches, and servers can be used for most of the universal networks needs, but new technologies are needed to support the increasing requirements of the new network. This means that the current network infrastructure must be replaced by new and more devices to support traditional Internet and universal network services.

The desire of content providers and content aggregators to offer their products and services to customers through multiple channels means that pervasive computing brings huge potential opportunities to infrastructure providers of all kinds. Infrastructure providers will have the opportunity to sell existing and new products into multiple industries that may have been closed to them in the past. For example, as the mobile telecommunications industry gears up to offer increasingly sophisticated digital content and services to subscribers, operators and service providers need sophisticated platforms that will enable them to make content available over wireless data network services.

The Internet infrastructure is already changing. It is, for example, moving from IPv4 to IPv6.[19] This means that every device on earth can have its own Internet Protocol (IP) address. With IPv4, the number of devices with their own IP address was limited. ATM backbones allow the creation of service level agreements (SLA) on quality of service (QoS) on the Internet. This means that video and audio streams can be viewed over the Internet in good and consistent quality. Today, the quality of video streaming over the Internet is variable.

New services will have other requirements from the architecture and infrastructure of the network. Infrastructure providers therefore need to create an open environment that allows users to plug in new functionality and services whenever required. In Chapter 4 we see several steps toward a unified infrastructure for a universal network.

1.4.3 Network Operators

Network operators provide data traffic to service and content providers and connect them to their customers. The most obvious benefit for network operators from pervasive computing will be the significant increase in demand for data traffic generated by two things. First, people will access content, applications, and services within a wider range of usage contexts. More people will access them through more diverse devices. Second, and even more important to network operators in the future, will be services and devices whose communication is initiated automatically by one of the participating services or devices. That one service or device handles context-switching and configures the other services and applications so that all devices can access crucial information without human interaction. More participating services will soon become available.

With pervasive computing technologies, network operators will be able to obtain more user-relevant information. They will know who uses what, when, and where. If permitted by the customer, they can leverage their customer information databases in order to cross- and up-sell new products and services. Selling targeted advertising space is also an option for the future. All mobile phone users in a certain area of the city could be informed about a price re-

---

[19]A detailed description of what this means can be found in Chapter 3 of *The E-Business (R)Evolution*, ISBN 013085123X, Prentice Hall.

duction in a nearby supermarket, for example, or all Madonna fans could be notified by their CD-player about a ticket auction for a concert in the area. Context-relevant information will become the new currency on the universal network.

1.4.4 Service Providers and Content Aggregators

Pervasive computing will erode current notions of subscriber segmentation. If people can access your service wherever, whenever, and however they like, it becomes very hard to tell whether a person is acting as a business user, for example, or as an individual consumer. On the one hand, you are able to offer your current service to more people around the world in more situations than ever before. On the other hand, your services need to be even more tailored than before to the needs of the individual user since the context of the usage can vary a lot.

Pervasive computing allows service providers and content aggregators to take advantage of this erosion and offer packages of content, applications, and services that can be tailored both to particular delivery channels and to content consumers, depending on the context in which they are consuming the content. Context-awareness services will become a major service that will provide the right flavor of service to a particular person. This key value-added service will greatly enhance content aggregators' value proposition. Content, therefore, must be provided in a device-independent way that allows users to maximize the potential service offering without being disturbed by conversion of content or unusual handling of a device. Pervasive computing technology only then becomes truly invisible.

Like network operators, service providers and content aggregators will also be able to leverage their customer databases to cross- and up-sell new products and services and to sell advertising space on their "portals." Forget today's portals with their personalization capabilities. Compared to the future, today's portals look like the good old printed Yellow Pages. Portals today require customers to come back to one place on the Internet to find a host of information and services. Next-generation portals will follow the customer around and offer a set of services based on the needs and the context of the user.

1.4.5 Content Providers

Content providers are highly interested in reusing their content as often as possible for as little incremental cost as possible. This inexpensive reuse can only be achieved if the content is created in a sophisticated and high-quality manner. Pervasiveness makes possible the reuse of a certain type of content in several contexts. Pervasive computing promises content providers multiple new routes to existing customers and the possibility of reaching entirely new customer bases.

Imagine the content type of an "account statement" from your bank. With the use of pervasive computing technologies, this content type can be provided through multiple channels. Content providers can not only reach larger audiences but can reach them more often. Today, many people view their account statements online with their computer. In the future, they will be able to review it through a large set of devices such as the mobile phone. This allows them to make decisions faster and more correctly because they can review all necessary information whenever they need it. If someone wanted to buy a car, she could verify the balance of an account and compare the price of the car to the current market value. Such audience expansion possibilities also offer content providers the opportunity to cross- and up-sell other products and services to customers. If more money than expected is available on that particular account, the purchaser might buy a better car.

1.4.6 "Regular" Businesses

Once the infrastructure has been set up, regular businesses will be able to profit from pervasive computing. Any company providing information and services will be able to participate in the universal network regardless of size, location, or business. The Internet today already provides a great enhancement, especially for small-to-medium enterprises. In the near future, through pervasive computing, all companies with a network connection will be able to provide services, target customers, and deliver value to new value chains.

For many companies, pervasive computing will mean that new competitors will show up, new business models will appear, and new products and services will become available. This sounds very much like what happened with the economy a few years ago when the Internet started to boom. The next boom will create another extraordinary situation to cope with. Don't forget what you learned during the first Internet revolution. Flexibility will remain a key. Businesses will have to adapt even more to their customers, because customers won't use a single standard interface called a browser. They will have an unlimited number of ways to communicate with your company.

Customer relationship management (CRM) therefore becomes even more important. While it is important to open new channels to your customer, at the same time you must centralize all efforts around CRM to make sure that all interaction with the customer is recorded. Only then are you able to provide the perfect trading environment because you can anticipate the needs of the clients even better. Customers become even more valuable than they are today. Knowledge about your customer will influence the value of your shares. The more you know, the better the company will be valued.

1.5 Concerns

Pervasive computing means change. And change means resistance. Many people are disturbed about change, concerned about its effects. Pervasive computing can only be successful if change is managed in a proper way. People need to understand the value of pervasive computing and how their concerns are treated. Change also means a loss of power to the currently powerful. Change redistributes power; this is something welcomed by the powerless and feared by the powerful.

Part of the change process therefore needs to deal with the concerns of the people involved. Technology can only be successful if people are willing to use it. So, in this section I present a set of concerns that may arise when pervasive computing technologies are introduced.

Treat concerns seriously. One of the biggest problems with e-business on the Internet was that concerns weren't addressed at all. The Internet hype made many believe that everything is possible and that the new technologies will make everything better. This is one of the biggest mistakes you can make. Technology does not do anything better. It just amplifies existing processes. If the process is bad, technology will make it worse.

1.5.1 Strength of Traditional Links

Existing supply chains will not necessarily embrace the idea of pervasive computing. Pervasive computing means that new intermediaries will be able to play a significant role. This means that a next round of disintermediation is about to happen. E-business already created a first round of disintermediation, but pervasive computing will be much more profound because content, for example, is channel independent. Content created for web browsers will be reused for television, radio, and newspapers. A web company can suddenly produce a newspaper or run a television station without too much trouble.

Many television and radio stations will therefore try to prevent others from entering the market. But as long as these current industry barriers are not torn down, these markets will remain closed stovepipe channels that other types of content and service provider will find expensive to access.

Solutions to this problem will break up many traditional industrial barriers. More and more companies will provide services and solutions in a cross-industrial manner while still addressing the personal needs of the single industry.

1.5.2 Privacy and Security

Through their pervasiveness, these new technologies can collect a lot of data about the users and their habits. Most people are concerned that this data will be misused by the companies collecting the information. To make the most out of pervasive computing technologies, information must be collected and shared among partners. Certain information about customers' online behavior, preferences, and so on will have to be shared between supply chains either explicitly or implicitly, to allow customers to navigate seamlessly around their information and services "universe." Without technology that can reassure customers about service providers' adherence to privacy policies, regulators may inhibit the sharing of such information. Many people will also be reluctant to share information with services they do not trust, so a trustworthy relationship must be built up. To ensure the privacy of the users, it may be useful to set up a trustworthy third party that collects all information on behalf of the services users want.

Pervasive computing will increase the number of service providers so significantly that the control of information flow between users and the service providers becomes impossible. A trusted third party could store personal information and provide the required information to preselected partners.

Security in general is also a sensitive area. On the Internet, people are afraid of giving away their credit card information. In a universal network, their houses and cars may be at risk if information is not properly secured. Application-level security in all networks must become at least as sophisticated as that available through the Internet to adequately address users' concerns. At the same time, these security barriers need to be easy to use. Today's firewall technologies are too complex for most people to configure. Future firewall technologies should be as easy to turn on as locking the front door of the house.

1.5.3   Piracy

Part of the reason that supply chains are currently so "closed" is that media owners are paranoid about unauthorized copying and distribution of their assets. Television channels, for example, buy broadcasting rights for a certain country. A universal network makes it difficult to restrict broadcasting rights to a certain country.

The Olympic games,[20] for example, cannot be broadcast live over the Internet at least until 2008. The International Olympic Committee (IOC) says that the Internet does not restrict the viewers to a certain region. And a major asset of the IOC is that it sells rights to certain countries and makes money selling the same content to different regions. An additional problem with advanced Internet technologies is that once you have converted the content, in this case the games, you can not redistribute the content via various channels, such as television sets, DVDs, radio, mobile phones, books, web sites, and so forth. Redistribution is not only cheap but, more importantly, very easy.

Another example is the MP3 hype, which makes record labels and some artists crazy, because suddenly they are no longer part of the supply chain and are unable to earn revenues. Well, at least not in the way they used to make money. Most record companies find it unthinkable to redesign their business models. But to survive, they need to.

---

[20]http://www.olympics.org/

Media owners, without significant advances in digital rights management technology and changes in their business models, will themselves inhibit their growth into multichannel media distribution.

Several companies work on solutions, but so far these are only point solutions. Some companies, such as DigiMarc,[21] work on solutions for adding digital watermarks to images. A digital watermark can be implemented in two ways. One way is to add invisible information to a picture: the images can retain their original format and can be viewed by appropriate viewing software. A JPEG image will be slightly modified but will remain a JPEG image. The advantage is that no additional software is required by the viewer. The major disadvantage is that the watermark can be removed rather easily in most cases; by resizing, for example. The other way is to create a format that can only be viewed with special software. This method ensures that nobody can remove the watermark, but makes it more difficult to use the content, since people need to have the right software installed on the right platform. In a universal network, this solution is not acceptable.

The Secure Digital Music Initiative (SDMI)[22] is a new format for music. It was created by the music and content industry to ensure that music distributed over the Internet can only be viewed by people who have paid for it. This is a nice idea, but as long as MP3 is out there, nobody will care about SDMI because it adds complexity—nobody will go for more complex solutions they have to pay for. This idea already failed once, when the banking industry tried to introduce the SET (Secure Electronic Transactions) standard. It failed because it created a lot of overhead and was more expensive. Here is the rule of thumb: The more people you want to reach, the easier and cheaper the solution has to be. Therefore, the music industry has to accept that MP3 is available and cannot be replaced simply by another format. To make money, the music industry needs to create value-added services.

Another company is working on creating links between users and their region. InfoSplit[23] (see Figure 1.5) is using a new technology to establish a relationship between a user and a geographic location. This technology would allow businesses to sell content to geographic regions. But of course, the technology is far from perfect. Right now it is fairly easy to fool this technology by faking IP addresses. But it can be expected that this technology will make advances and become more secure.

These are only point solutions and will not work perfectly in a universal network. A new standard to tag device-independent content needs to be created; instead of creating technology to identify the region of the user, industries need to rethink the whole concept of rights management. Just mapping the existing processes to the new realities is not enough. This is a lesson that many people did not learn from the e-business (r)evolution. Just replicating existing processes and ideas to a new technological platform is not enough. If the plat-

---

[21]http://www.digimarc.com/
[22]http://www.sdmi.org/
[23]http://www.infosplit.com/

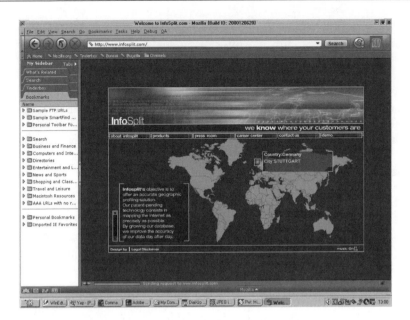

Figure 1.5. InfoSplit Can Find Out Where I Am

form creates new possibilities, the processes and ideas need to be extended or rethought.

1.5.4   Disregard of Technology Standards

Software standards have not always been a success. Especially in highly public areas, the best proposed standard does not always become the most pervasive. Some technologies have successfully been widely adopted across the corporate information technology (IT) world. IP is a good example of such a standard. However, IP is still far from being universally supported in the telecommunications industry. And there are only a handful of other nonhardware standards that are models of successful standardization. Even if a given standard has been adopted by most participants, a big problem can arise if some companies create their own "flavors" of the standard, making interconnection of different components difficult.

The problem is that when competitive differentiation can be obtained, vendors will always try to circumvent standardization processes. Vendors may pay lip service to standards by partially implementing them; but in many cases they will also implement features that are against the spirit of the standard or that offer "richer" or "advanced" alternatives. Particularly in the hype-fuelled software industry, vendors have historically been keen to do precisely that. Just look at the HTML standard and its very similar versions. Unfortunately they are not identical and therefore are sometimes problematic in implementation.

Unless one infrastructure vendor maneuvers itself into a position of colossal strength, wide adoption of standard technologies will be the only cost-effective route to pervasive computing. History would seem to indicate that such a situation would not be easy to engineer. True pervasive computing will be independent of certain standards. Pervasive computing would mean that different technologies and software standards will be able to connect to each other flawlessly. Bridging standards will play an even bigger role than they do today. And it seems that XML will play an important role, too.

1.5.5   Capabilities of Hardware and Battery

Mobile devices often are not connected all the time to a power plug; today we already experience this with laptops, mobile phones, and PDAs. My first mobile phone would last for a day (a Motorola[24] in 1995); my new Nokia[25] operates a week without recharging. My first laptop (a good old HP Omnibook 5700[26]) allowed me to work an hour without recharging; the new Apple iBook[27] allows me to work up to eight hours without recharging.

Personal mobile devices present the most complex technological challenges to vendors as potential platforms for accessing content, applications, and services. Mobile devices without connection to power or network outlets are becoming ever more important in an always faster-paced world. Therefore, their batteries must become smaller and more powerful.

However, the current state of battery technology is such that "advanced" features like sophisticated user interfaces and audio playback severely impact the mobility of compact devices. Perhaps more seriously, the other problem that hardware manufacturers currently face is that the hardware required to drive a 3G-capable wireless handset is currently too power hungry and inefficient to fit into a production device. Improvements will undoubtedly be made; some innovative technologies are in the pipeline, but the speed with which they come to market will have a profound effect on the suitability of mobile devices as pervasive computing access terminals.

Another big problem is the power-hungry Intel[28] computer chip. Compared to a few years ago Intel has made improvements, but for today's needs they may not be enough. Several companies are working on improvements. Probably the best-known company without a product was Transmeta[29] in 1999. It was famous because of one employee—Linus Torwalds, who headed the Linux

---

[24]http://www.motorola.com/

[25]http://www.nokia.com/

[26]http://www.hp.com/

[27]http://www.apple.com/ibook/

[28]http://www.intel.com/

[29]http://www.transmeta.com/

development. In 2000 it produced its first set of products, a new chip called Crusoe, which emulates all of the major chip designs in software and saves battery power by running very efficiently. Some companies, such as Sony,[30] are shipping laptops with the Crusoe chip; other companies have created stylish new devices for connecting to the Internet. Acer,[31] for example, has created a web pad that has a 50-meter wireless range and up to eight hours of battery life.

In the future we will see further enhancements in battery life and better, more powerful, yet less power-consuming CPUs. They will enable instant Internet access anytime and anywhere.

---

[30]http://www.sony.com/
[31]http://www.acer.com/

Chapter 2

Mobile Commerce

Mobile telephony is nothing that was invented in the last five years. In the 1980s, analog cellular technology was introduced; it allowed the efficient use of frequencies, enabling the connection of a large number of users. Among the well-known systems were the NMT900 and 450 (Nordic Mobile Telephone) and the AMPS (Advanced Mobile Phone Service). In the early 1990s digital cellular technology was introduced, and GSM (Global System for Mobile Communications) became the most widely accepted system around the world. Other such systems are the DCS1800 (Digital Communication System) and the PCS1900 (Personal Communication System), which are common in the United States.

GSM in Europe has become so popular that the number of mobile phones is larger than the base of installed fixed lines in most European countries. M-Commerce is one of the emerging trends based on the pervasive computing paradigm. M-Commerce uses wireless Internet technologies to reach its customers. Wireless Internet provides mobile and wireless access to the Internet or a company intranet; wireless Internet technologies provide interactive access to existing and new content and services. The wireless Internet is not a new or second Internet—it is the same content being accessed through other methods and devices. This means that content and services provided on the Internet are accessible by many more people through a mobile phone or PDA.

IDC defines m-commerce in the following way: It measures all purchases of products and services that occur across a mobile data platform as a result of some interaction with the subscriber. If stock is purchased, for example, the value of the stock is not included in the m-commerce calculation; only the fee to complete that stock transaction is included. This definition includes many types of transactions, such as bill payment, which includes the mobile telephony bill or prepay top-up. It also includes the purchase of products and services. A drink from a vending machine being charged to the mobile phone bill is one of the business models. You could also buy a movie ticket and pay on credit card, asking the phone to buy a movie ticket. Voice recognition could be used to initiate the transaction but the mobile data network would be used. You could pay airfare and be invoiced by the travel agent on your mobile phone bill; this would avoid the queue at the airport. Another thing you could do with

Why Does the Market Explode?

The mobile business market is about to explode for these reasons:

- **Mobile phone penetration** – Mobile phone use has increased dramatically as technology has advanced (bandwidth, billing systems, network capabilities, handset features).

- **Personalization** – People want to personalize their mobile phones (color covers, ring tones, logos, etc.).

- **Usability** – People are accustomed to mobile phones and new technologies and are willing and capable of using them.

- **Entertainment** – Because of its emotional aspect, entertainment is a powerful enabler.

- **Business models** – Mobile advertising and wireless music distribution will develop into multibillion dollar businesses after technological and commercial breakthrough in 2002.

your mobile device is to download music or videos to your multimedia device while you are travelling, to be ready to hear or see when returning home.

The definition does not include every business model. Online banking, that is, the transfer of money from one account to another, is not included because wireless Internet does not provide additional income for the bank or for the consumer. Also not included are voice-calling mobile-initiated purchases. For example, John receives a short message service (SMS) on his mobile phone stating that he can get 5 euros or dollars off a pair of jeans; he proceeds to the store and purchases the jeans with his credit or debit card. These business models can play a very important role in the future, of course, but they do not create additional business over the mobile device. They can be summarized as mobile marketing and accessibility models.

2.1   Mobile Architecture

A cellular network consists of mobile units linked to switching equipment, which interconnect the different parts of the network and allow access to the fixed Public Switched Telephone Network (PSTN). The technology is hidden from view; it is incorporated in a number of tranceivers called base stations (BSs). Every BS is located at a strategically selected place and covers a given area or cell—hence the name cellular communications. A number of adjacent cells grouped together form an area, and the corresponding BSs communicate through a so-called Mobile Switching Center (MSC). The MSC is the heart of a cellular radio system. It is responsible for routing, or switching, calls from the originator to the destinator. It can be thought of as managing the cell, being responsible for setup, routing control, and termination of the call, for management of inter-MSC handover and supplementary services, and for collecting charging and accounting information. The MSC can be connected to other MSCs on the same network or to the PSTN.

The frequencies used vary according to the cellular network technology implemented. For GSM, 890–915 MHz range is used for transmission and 935–960 MHz for reception. The DCS techology uses frequencies in the 1800 MHz range, and PCS in the 1900 MHz range.

Each cell has a number of channels associated with it. These channels are assigned to subscribers on demand. When a mobile station (MS) becomes "active," it registers with the nearest BS. The corresponding MSC stores information about that MS and its position. This information is used to direct incoming calls to the MS.

If during a call the MS moves to an adjacent cell, then a change of frequency will necessarily occur because adjacent cells never use the same channels. This procedure is called handover and is the key to mobile communications. As the MS approaches the edge of a cell, the BS monitors the decrease in signal power. The strength of the signal is compared with adjacent cells, and the call is handed over to the cell with the strongest signal.

During the switch, the line is lost for about 400 ms. When the MS is going from one area to another, it registers itself to the new MSC. Its location information is updated, thus allowing MSs to be used outside their "home" areas.

2.2   Technologies

This section describes in detail six technologies that implement the mobile architecture: GSM, SMS, General Packet Radio Service (GPRS), WAP, and imode, a mobile Internet access system.

2.2.1   Global System for Mobile Communication

GSM is a cellular network typically offering nationwide coverage, depending on the operator. With the possibility of international roaming, GSM users can use mobile services globally. National roaming is also supported by GSM.

GSM Coverage and Service

The GSM network is based on cell technology. The coverage area of each cell is different in different environments. Macrocells can be regarded as cells where the base station antenna is installed in a mast or a building above the average rooftop level. However, small cells or microcells are cells where the antenna height is under the average rooftop level. Thus, the cell radius can vary, depending on the antenna height, antenna gain, and propagation conditions, from a couple of hundred meters to several tens of kilometers. Officially, 35 km is the longest distance GSM specification supports, though the specifications define an extended cell, where the cell radius could be double. Indoor coverage is also supported by GSM. Indoor coverage can be built with power splitters that deliver a radio frequency (RF) signal from the outdoor antenna to a separate indoor antenna distribution system. When all the capacity of the cell is needed indoors, for example, in shopping centers or airports, the indoor coverage can be built inside the building with antennas only. In suburban areas, the indoor coverage usually originates from the in-building penetration of the radio signal, not by a separate indoor antenna system.

GSM was defined mainly for voice services, but operators also offer data services at speeds of 9.6 and 14.4 kbit/s [8]. Although a cellular network can never be regarded as completed, operators today are less able to compete in coverage area or quality of the network. However, in these days, data services start to play a big role in the operator business. A GSM service called High Speed Circuit Switched Data (HSCSD) offers data services at speeds up to 57.6 kbit/s, depending on the multislot usage. Some advanced operators launched a new data service named GPRS, which enables data communication in the first phase at speeds of 9.1–40.2 kbit/s, depending on the possible multislot usage and the coding scheme used. Also, SMS and a set of value-added services are specified in the GSM system.

In a cellular system like GSM, the network consists of cells. Each cell has its own serving area, and the user can move over the cell boundaries by handovers. This can mean a very high infrastructure cost, because several cells must exist before the user can move within the network. Moreover, complex mobility protocols and signalling are needed.

The operation frequency of GSM lies in the 900 MHz band. The reserved bandwidth can be divided into three areas. Each of these frequency areas is located in the 900 MHz band and uses separate frequencies for uplink and downlink directions. However, extra frequencies are also defined for GSM use in 1800 MHz band. The bandwidth specified for GSM use in 1800 MHz is three times wider than the bandwidth of primary GSM in the 900 MHz frequency band. The purpose of reserving frequencies in the 1800 MHz band was to fulfill the requirements of the increasing capacity needed in the future. Today, in most European countries there are several mobile operators that operate either on both bands or in the 1800 MHz band only. The specifications allow a handover between these two bands. Several dual-mode cellular phones are also available in the market which, in the last resort, enable the mobility in the dual-band network.

The physical layer of GSM defines the modulation scheme, which can be considered as a combination of frequency division multiple access (FDMA) and time division multiple access (TDMA). The spectrum available for GSM use is, according to FDMA technique, first divided into channels, each channel having 200 kHz of bandwidth. One or more frequencies are then assigned to each BS. Every 200 kHz channel is further divided into eight time slots. Each user is then assigned to a time slot or to a set of time slots. Transmission is possible only during this time slot; after that, the user has to wait until he receives another time slot.

Large-Scale Mobility

The purpose of the operator usually is to offer nationwide coverage; with international roaming, the user can also use mobile services globally. The mission for several operators and vendors is that the user can use his phone wherever and whenever. The need to move within the network is essential; otherwise, the concept of mobile services would not exist.

To ensure a large scale of mobility, several functions had to be designed. The mobility management of GSM is defined in the layer three specifications and is very complicated compared to that of a WLAN user. As stated earlier, the smallest unit of the radio network is a cell. Several cells build up a location area (LA). The concept of LA needed to be defined in order to handle large-scale mobility of the user. If a powered MS receives an incoming call, it is paged through the paging channel (PAGCH) of a cell. It would be a waste of bandwidth if the paging had to be done in every incoming call through every cell of the network. Thus, the network accurately knows the situation of each user in a location area [9]. The operator decides the size of the location areas in order to balance the signalling traffic of the network. Several cells are connected to base station controllers (BSC) and further BSCs are connected to MSCs. The number of BSCs and MSCs is a matter for the vendor but is also a matter of optimizing and maximizing the reliability of the network and is not discussed here. When the MS moves from cell to cell and from a location area to another area, two additional registers—HLR (home location register) and VLR (visitor location register)—are required.

Radio Resource Management, which controls the call setup, maintenance, and termination, also handles the signalling used in handovers. Different types of handovers are supported. One type is intracell handover, which can occur within a cell or within a frequency from a time slot to another time slot. This is normally done in case of interference. Another type is a handover between different cells. The cells can be situated in different BSCs or different MSCs. This, of course, affects the signalling need in handover. This type of a handover is the way to move within the network.

Handovers enable movement within the network, but they can also be used to control the traffic load of the cells. The MS measures the RX level of the surrounding BSs according to the neighboring list and reports the measurements to the BSC, where the handover decision is done. The suitable choices of handover and power control parameters make the BSC keep the connection alive by the help of power control. The handover attempt is not done until the user is really in the border of the cell.

2.2.2 Short Message Service

SMS is a globally accepted wireless service that enables the transmission of alphanumeric messages between mobile subscribers and external systems such as e-mail, paging, and voice-mail systems.

SMS appeared on the wireless scene in 1991 in Europe. The European standard for digital wireless, now known as GSM, included SMSs from the outset. Since then it has become the most popular service in the mobile world. In North America the service is slowly becoming available as digital mobile services become more popular. Pagers, which are popular in the United States, have never played a role in the European or Asian market. Therefore, there was no need to move from pagers to mobile phones with SMS.

Characteristics of SMS

SMS provides a mechanism for transmitting short messages to and from wireless devices. The service makes use of a local base station, which acts as a store-and-forward system for short messages. The wireless network provides the mechanisms required to find the destination station(s) and transports short messages between the base station and wireless stations. In contrast to other existing text-message transmission services such as alphanumeric paging, the service elements guarantee delivery of text messages to the destination.

Additionally, SMS supports several input mechanisms that allow interconnection with different message sources and destinations. A mobile phone that is switched on can receive and submit SMS whether or not a person is talking on the phone. Senders of SMS can receive a receipt that an SMS has been transmitted and a receipt that the SMS has arrived. Temporary failures due to unavailable receiving stations are identified, and the short message is stored in the base station until the destination device becomes available.

SMS can be characterized by the following features: out-of-band packet delivery and low-bandwidth message transfer. This results in a highly efficient means for transmitting short bursts of data. The maximum length for text is 160 characters for Latin text or 70 characters for Chinese and other complex alphabets. Initial applications of SMS focused on eliminating alphanumeric pagers by permitting two-way general-purpose messaging and notification services, primarily for voice mail.

SMS Applications

As technology and networks evolved, a variety of services have been introduced, including e-mail, fax, paging integration, interactive banking, information services such as stock quotes, and integration with Internet-based applications. Every mobile phone user, in Europe at least, can get the latest weather forecast, political news, and results from sporting events on the display of the mobile phone. It is even possible to check the balance of the owner's bank account.

Wireless data applications include downloading of subscriber identity module (SIM) cards for activation, debit, profile editing, wireless points of sale (POSs), and other field-service applications such as automatic meter reading, remote sensing, and location-based services. Integration with the Internet spurred the development of web-based messaging and other interactive applications such as instant messaging, gaming, and chatting.

Today it becomes more difficult to differentiate from other service providers. Standard voice telephony over mobile networks is the same from every provider, and prices are almost the same. SMS provides a powerful vehicle for service differentiation. SMS represents an additional source of revenue for the service provider by delivering information and services.

SMS Benefits to Subscribers

The benefits of SMS to subscribers center around convenience, flexibility, and seamless integration of messaging services and data access. From this perspective, the primary benefit is the use of the handset as an extension of the computer. SMS also eliminates the need for separate devices for messaging because services can be integrated into a single wireless device—the mobile terminal. These benefits normally depend on the applications that the service provider offers.

Besides these basic benefits, provided by any mobile service providers offering SMS, is more sophisticated functionality offered by the telecom service providers. They have started to offer the delivery of messages to multiple subscribers at a time, reducing the load on the network and the typing burden for users. This feature is especially useful at Christmas and New Year's Eve, when everyone is trying to send out SMSs at the same time. In Europe, mobile networks regularly break down at this time of year. Sending a single SMS to multiple addresses will alleviate these problems.

Benefits of Short Message Service

At a minimum, SMS benefits include:

- **Notifications** – Delivery of notifications and alerts

- **Warranty** – Guaranteed message delivery as opposed to pager services

- **Reliability** – A reliable, low-cost communication mechanism for concise information

- **Selectivity** – Screening of messages and returning calls in a selective way

- **Productivity** – Increased subscriber productivity

Users can receive diverse information, as described earlier. These information services depend on the telecom provider and can vary from providing a few basic facts about the service to supporting complete news sites.

Another important feature is standard Internet e-mail connectivity. Through this gateway, SMS and e-mail can be exchanged transparently. For example, to send e-mail to my mobile phone, you can use +49171xxxxxxxx@td1-sms.de, where +49 is the prefix for Germany and 171 is the prefix for the mobile communications provider T-Mobile (D1), a subsidiary of Deutsche Telekom.[1] When SMS is sent to an e-mail address, the e-mail address is used as the reply-address. Using any standard e-mail program, e-mail recepients can reply to that address with one limitation: The maximum length of the e-mail is 160 characters in ASCII code and 70 Japanese or Chinese characters. Longer e-mail will be truncated or, in some instances, divided into several SMS transmissions.

Some mobile service providers let users create closed user groups, enabling work group information exchange and application sharing. This feature is popular with teenagers who want to share MP3 files or chat with their friends online. It is also popular with project teams in companies that work in a distributed environment. It allows them to share project information and applications to make their work more efficient. To make the mobile phone even more useful, some service providers offer a tight integration with other data and Internet-based applications. This opens up the whole world of the Inter-

---

[1]http://www.telekom.de/

net to the mobile phone through SMS. Although not very user-friendly at the moment, it offers a cheap way to access a large information pool.

Benefits to Service Providers

SMS not only benefits users, but it also benefits service providers. Thanks to the increased number of calls on wireless and wireline networks by leveraging the notification capabilities, SMS provides a good chance to increment the average revenue per user. For the United States, it provides a way to integrate paging services with the mobile phone system. It will replace or complement an existing paging offer. Through SMS, corporate users can access wireless data. New revenue streams result from the addition of value-added services such as e-mail, voice mail, fax, and web-based application integration, reminder services, stock and currency quotes, and airline schedules. The more services offered to the customers, the more revenues generated.

SMS also provides key administrative services such as information about charges, over-the-air downloading, and over-the-air service provisioning, reducing the cost for the service provider.

SMS can control traffic channels and protect important network resources, such as voice channels, from overload. SMS provides a notification mechanism for newer services such as those utilizing WAP. All of these benefits are quickly attainable, with modest incremental cost and short payback periods, which make SMS an attractive investment for service providers.

Future Applications

Although SMS was originally designed to support limited-size messages—mostly notifications and numeric or alphanumeric pages—it has since created an infrastructure for many more services. These applications are and will continue to be widely used, but SMS can exploit other, newly identified niches.

Short bursts of data are at the heart of many applications and have been used in the past on the Internet to provide alerts and notifications. By adding the data communication capabilities to the mobility of the station, the station can be used in new situations. A waiter, for example, can charge a customer's credit card right at the table, offering customers faster, more convenient service and saving time.

Any application that needs only a small amount of information can profit from SMS. Location tracking, for example, just needs to interchange small amounts of information, such as the longitude and latitude at a current time of the day, and perhaps other parameters like temperature or humidity. This allows the tracking of the location of a moving asset such as a truck or its load, a valuable service for both providers and clients.

Banking is another important niche application for SMS. The built-in data transport mechanism can reduce the cost for a transaction. Enabling wireless subscribers to check their balances, transfer funds between accounts, and pay their bills and credit cards is valuable both for subscribers and financial institutions. SMS has some security issues, so it is used for presenting balances only, but other services will be available in the near future.

Besides business applications, entertainment plays an important role in the mobile world. SMS also plays an important role. Examples are simple, short message exchanges between two parties, the so-called texting, or between multiple participants, the so-called chatting. Typing information on a mobile phone is a bit tedious, as you can imagine, so some companies have tried to make it more convenient. Some offer additional keyboards that can be attached to the mobile phone, and others offer software that simplifies message generation. This software uses predictive text input algorithms, such as T9 from Tegic,[2] that anticipates which word the user is trying to generate and thus significantly reduces the number of key strokes needed to input a message. Widespread incorporation of such algorithms into the installed base of mobile phones will typically lead to an average 25 percent increase in SMS traffic for each enabled user. These predictive text algorithms support multiple languages.

Another emerging SMS-based application is downloading ringtones. Ringtones are the tunes that the phone plays when someone calls it. Because the same phone is often sold with the same default tune, phone users want to be able to change their ringtone to distinguish it from others. Phones often come with a range of different ringtones built in to the phone's memory from which users can choose. However, it has become popular to download new ringtones from an Internet site to the phone. These ringtones tend to be popular television or film theme tunes. One company offering such a service is Smart-SMS.[3] Although it is easy to set up a site, it is important to consider copyright issues when offering ringtone services, since such commercial tunes need to be licensed before they can legally be distributed. Ringtone composers are also popular because they allow mobile phone users to compose their own unique ringtones and download them to their phones.

As mobile phone penetration increases and everyone has a mobile phone, unique ringtones to help determine just whose phone is ringing will become increasingly popular. Expect to see this application grow in availability and popularity over time. In Germany alone, more than 100 web sites offer ringtones. A whole ringtone industry is being built up. Although some startups have made a lot of money in the past, I don't believe that it will be possible to become rich from this area in the future, but ringtone customization will be a required service for any portal in the mobile area.

Delivery of information that subscribers can tailor to their lifestyle represents an attractive proposition for wireless users. More and more applications will continue to be developed for SMS until newer technologies replace SMS. Although WAP has been around for a while, it does not have the same status

---

[2] http://www.tegic.com/
[3] http://www.smart-sms.com/

as SMS, since it is not built into every mobile phone and is not service provider independent.

2.2.3 General Packet Radio Service

GPRS is a new, nonvoice, value-added service that allows information to be sent and received across a mobile telephone network. It is an addition to today's existing mobile phone network and supplements Circuit-Switched Data and SMS. GPRS is a module that can be attached to GSM and TDMA mobile phone networks. GSM is popular in Europe and Asia, whereas TDMA is predominant in the Americas. By introducing GPRS in both systems, the industry associations that support these two network types want to create a single evolutionary path toward the 3G mobile phone networks based on UMTS.

The theoretical maximum speed of GPRS is currently set at 171.2 kbit/s, which can be achieved by use of all eight time slots at the same time. This is approximately 10 times faster than current data transfer over standard GSM networks, but it is also much more expensive. Many telecom providers won't allow their customers to use all eight time slots at a time.

The GPRS technology enables instant connectivity whereby information can be sent or received immediately without requiring a user to dial-up first. This technology is referred to as "always on." Immediacy is an important feature for time-critical applications such as remote credit card authorization where it is unacceptable to keep the customer waiting for even 30 extra seconds.

With GPRS, users can create applications that would not have been possible on GSM networks because of the limited bandwidth (9.6 kbit/s) and limited message length (up to 160 characters via SMS). Through GPRS web browsing, file transfer, home automation, and newly designed mobility service become reality.

Mode of Operation

GPRS involves overlaying a packet-based air interface on the existing circuit-switched GSM network. With GPRS, the information is split into separate but related packets before being transmitted and reassembled at the receiving end. Packet switching can be likened to a jigsaw puzzle. The puzzle is divided into pieces at the factory and put into a plastic bag. During transportation of the now boxed jigsaw from the factory to the end user, the pieces get jumbled up. After the recipient empties the bag with all the pieces, he reassembles them to form the original image. All the pieces are all related and fit together, but the way they are transported and assembled varies. The Internet itself is another example of a packet data network, the most famous of many such network types.

Packet switching means that GPRS is only used when data is actually sent or received. This behavior makes it possible to share a single channel with several other people. This principle is similar to the one used on the Internet. Over a single line, thousands of users communicate with each other without having to worry that their communication is disrupted by other data flows on the same line. This efficient use of scarce radio resources means that large numbers of GPRS users can potentially share the same bandwidth and be served from a single cell.

To use GPRS, users specifically need a mobile phone or terminal that supports GPRS (most of the existing GSM phones do not support GPRS) and a mobile phone provider that supports GPRS. Typically, GPRS is an additional service customers have to pay for. On top of this, they need new software and a new hardware configuration to support data transfer between the mobile phone and a laptop, for example. If used for WAP or imode, no additional hardware is necessary.

GPRS Advantages

For mobile network providers, GPRS has several advantages. It allocates scarce radio resources more efficiently by supporting virtual connectivity by using packets instead of circuits. Therefore, it reduces the load on the circuit-switched part of the network. It also reduces the number of SMS that are sent over the circuit-switched part since all messages can be easily rerouted using the GPRS/SMS interconnect that is supported by the GPRS standard.

GPRS fully enables mobile Internet functionality by allowing interworking between the existing Internet and the new GPRS network. This means that any service that can be used on the Internet can also be used on the mobile

---

Advantages of GPRS

The GPRS is the next step in the mobile (r)evolution. It provides a set of features and functionalities that make the mobile business become reality. Some of the most important features are the following:

- **Always online** – Enhanced e-mail, info, and telematics

- **Simultaneous voice/data** – First multimedia services

- **Pay per use** – Increased market acceptance

- **High bit rate** – Enhanced QoS

- **Spectral efficiency** – High density of subscribers

connection. Web, chat, FTP, and all other services are instantly available on the mobile network. This makes it possible to share information with colleagues by accessing a virtual private network (VPN), to check bank account details using a secure connection, or to chat with friends while traveling. It also supports central information storage and remotely accessing files.

GPRS Limitations

It should already be clear that GPRS is an important new enabling mobile data service that offers a major improvement in spectrum efficiency, capability, and functionality compared with today's nonvoice mobile services. GPRS has some limits, though.

First, GPRS does impact a network's existing cell capacity. Only limited radio resources can be deployed for different uses. The use for one purpose precludes simultaneous use for another. For example, voice and GPRS calls both use the same network resources. The extent of the impact depends upon the number of time slots, if any, that are reserved for exclusive use of GPRS. However, GPRS does dynamically manage channel allocation and allow a reduction in peak time signalling channel loading by sending short messages over GPRS channels instead.

Second, the speed of the Internet connection is much lower in reality than predicted. Achieving the theoretical maximum GPRS data transmission speed of 172.2 kbps would require a single user taking over all eight time slots without any error protection. Clearly, it is unlikely that a network operator will allow all time slots to be used by a single GPRS user. Additionally, the initial GPRS terminals are expected be severely limited and will support only one, two, or three time slots. The bandwidth available to a GPRS user will therefore be limited. As such, the theoretical maximum GPRS speeds should be checked against the reality of constraints in the networks and terminals. The reality is that mobile networks are always likely to have lower data transmission speeds than fixed networks.

But even with these two issues, GPRS is a huge step ahead.

2.2.4   Global Positioning System

The Global Positioning System (GPS) is a U.S. military space system operated by the U.S. Air Force. The space segment of GPS consists of a constellation of 24 satellites that broadcast precise time signals. When the satellites are in view of a suitable GPS receiver, these signals aid position-location, navigation, and precision timing. GPS was developed by the U.S. Department of Defense and deployed over two decades at a cost of over $10 billion. The U.S. armed forces increasingly rely on GPS signals for a variety of purposes, from navigation to munitions guidance.

Over the past 10 years, GPS has evolved far beyond its military origins. It is now a worldwide information resource supporting a wide range of civil, scientific, and commercial functions, from air traffic control to the Internet. GPS has also spawned a substantial commercial industry in the United States and abroad with rapidly growing markets for related products and services.

Mode of Operation

GPS consists of three segments: a space segment of 24 orbiting satellites, a control segment that includes a control center and access to overseas command stations, and a user segment consisting of GPS receivers and associated equipment.

GPS satellites transmit two different signals: the Precision or P-code and the Coarse Acquisition or C/A-code. The P-code is designed for authorized military users and provides what is called the Precise Positioning Service (PPS). To ensure that unauthorized users do not acquire the P-code, the United States can implement an encryption segment on the P-code called antispoofing (AS). The C/A-code is designed for use by nonmilitary users and provides what is called the Standard Positioning Service (SPS). The C/A-code is less accurate and easier to jam than the P-code. It is also easier to acquire, so military receivers first track the C/A-code and then transfer to the P-code. The U.S. military can degrade the accuracy of the C/A-code by implementing a technique called selective availability (SA). SA thus controls the level of accuracy available to all users of the SPS.

GPS Applications

GPS has many applications, such as land navigation, which is used in cars, planes, and ships. It enables pilots or drivers or ships' captains to find their exact location and can guide them to a target. In combination with wireless technologies, a center could track the movement of these vehicles. This is, for example, used by taxi centers to find the next taxi for a request. Ship owners can track their ships worldwide and airlines know exactly how late their planes are.

GPS is widely used in farming and agricultural applications. Through the exact location of fields, growers can navigate efficiently through their fields, for example. GPS is used for mapping and as a geographical information system to verify the correctness of a map, for example. The military uses GPS to make it easier for soldiers to find their target, and missiles use it to avoid mountains and cities while flying toward a target. Intelligent highways and vehicles use GPS to find routes without traffic jams, and automatic vehicle location (AVL) is used by insurance companies to detect stolen cars. Although not yet built into all cars, it is likely that all new cars will have a built-in AVL to make theft unprofitable, if not impossible.

2.2.5 Wireless Application Protocol

WAP defines a global wireless protocol specification to work across heterogeneous wireless network technologies and is a communications standard for digital mobile phones, supported by over 1,200 companies. WAP makes it possible for mobile phones to access the Internet and retrieve information on simplified display screens or through a voice interface. WAP phones can receive text and data, including pages downloaded from the World Wide Web, as well as voice using an implementation of WAP. The first mobile phones to make use of WAP were introduced by Nokia and Ericsson in 1999.

The WAP Forum and the World Wide Web Consortium (W3C) have announced a formal liaison relationship to define next-generation web specifications that support the full participation of wireless devices on the World Wide Web. The WAP Forum and W3C are working together to develop a common process of producing next-generation, XML-based web specifications, define testing and implementation processes, and promote these specifications to the industry at large. Part of the work will concentrate on enabling wireless devices to "participate as full peers in the universal information space of the Web," largely through the incorporation of WAP's Wireless Markup Language (WML) features into the W3C's XHTML, the next-generation markup language for the Web. At the same time, WMLScript is being incorporated into standard JavaScript called ECMAScript.

The WAP/W3C coordination committee works jointly on XHTML, which is compatible with Synchronized Multimedia Integration Language (SMIL). The committee is trying to ensure user control over privacy information and to develop CC/PP, a universal device profiling system based on W3C's RDF metadata technology.

WML is used to create WAP pages on mobile phone systems. WML is similar to HTML and provides basic functionality to display text and graphics on the mobile phone. WMLScript is a lightweight procedural scripting language similar to JavaScript that allows you to create dynamic pages and respond to input from the user. WML is based on XML, which means that if you provide content in XML, it is easy to display it in web browsers and WAP phones without having to worry too much about conversion.

IDG expects that in 2004 nearly all mobile phones will have WAP access. See Figure 2.1 for graphical information. There are multiple assumptions for this model. The main two are that all digital handset shipments from 2001 are WAP capable (on the assumption that it is cheaper to include than exclude) and that the carriers follow through and implement some services.

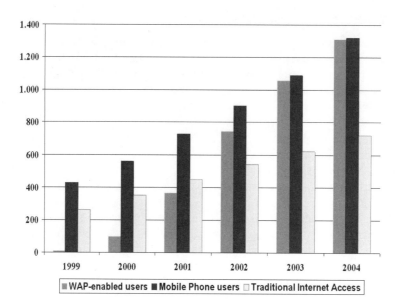

Figure 2.1. Importance of WAP

2.2.6   Mobile Internet Access System: imode

imode is NTT DoCoMo's mobile Internet access system. NTT DoCoMo[4] is a
subsidiary of Japan's incumbent telephone operator NTT. The majority of NTT-
DoCoMo's shares are owned by NTT, and the majority of NTT's shares are
owned by the Japanese government. At the beginning of 2001, there were over
10 million users, and the number of users increases by about 50,000 per day.
Since there are 60 million mobile users in Japan, imode may potentially have
around 60 million users in Japan. At the moment 99.999 percent of imode
users are Japanese. imode users are a cross-section of Japan's society—young,
middle-aged, and old people.

Mode of Operation

Technically imode is an overlay over NTT DoCoMo's ordinary mobile voice system. Whereas the voice system is circuit-switched, (i.e., you need to dial up),
imode is packet-switched. This means that imode is in principle always on,
provided you are in an area where the imode signal can reach you. When you
select an imode item on the handset menu, the data is usually immediately
downloaded. There is no delay for dialling to set up the connection. However,
the data is delayed in reaching you. This delay is similar to the delay on your
PC-based Internet connection after you click a link or after you type in a URL

---

[4]http://www.nttdocomo.com/

Features of WAP

The following features show the advantages of WAP:

- Flexible delivery of personalized content

- Interworking with existing and future networks, such as GSM, CDMA, GPRS, UMTS

- WAP applications that target the whole market: handsets and smartphones subscribers (critical mass effect)

- WAP server that allows Internet subscribers management

- Full e-customer care and one-to-one marketing facilities

- Dedicated billing facilities

---

and press Return or Enter. Of course there are further delays if the information you download is too big or if the network is overloaded.

Users send e-mail, look at the weather forecast, look at sports results, load ringing melodies into their handsets, play games, do online banking, trade stock online, purchase air tickets, download cartoons and images, look for restaurants, and look for new friends.

The maximum speed for download is 9.6 kbit/s. This is approximately six times slower than a 64 kbit/s ISDN connection, but it is sufficient for simple imode data. Of course, this speed makes it impossible to download live movies through imode.

Use of imode

To start imode, you press a special imode button on your mobile phone, and the imode menu appears. On the imode menu, you can chose one of several options: you can look at your private "my menu" page, where imode sites are listed to which you are subscribing, you can look at the menu of approximately 600 imode partner sites, or type in a URL to look at any Internet site, bookmark web sites, send e-mail, or change your settings.

To use imode, you must have a basic mobile phone subscription with NTT DoCoMo. In addition, you pay 300 yen (approximately three dollars or euros) a month for imode use. This is all you pay if you never actually use imode. However, when you start using imode, you incur additional charges. There is a basic data charge per packet, 0.3 yen (approximately 3 U.S. cents) per 128 byte data packet transmitted. As an example, looking at the basic imode menu, the standard DoCoMo welcome screen or user interface will set you back about 2.7 yen (i.e., approximately 2.7 U.S. cents). There are no connection charges for imode, but there are other charges for using e-mail and for premium subscription services.

In principle, you can look at Internet sites, which are not specifically formatted for imode. However, in many cases you will only see a small portion of the page, and the information you see may not be meaningful. Also, it is likely that the information will overflow the cache of your handset; in this case, the displayed information will be truncated, and there will be an error message as well.

Many (if not most) of DoCoMo's partner sites are pay sites. These sites have a public free area for basic information, but most of the content requires that you register and pay a monthly charge to the site. imode services include e-mail; however, if you wish, you can disable e-mail service on imode.

imode displays gif images and animated gif images, but no movies right now. Some handsets have color screens and can display color images. imode uses cHTML (compact HTML), which is in part a subset of ordinary HTML. However, in addition to HTML tags, there are special imode-only tags (for example, a tag to set up a link, which when pressed dials a telephone number, or another imode-only tag, informing search machines that a particular web page is an imode page). In addition, there are also special DoCoMo characters, which are symbols for joy, kisses, love, sadness, hot spring baths, telephone, Shinkansen train, encircled numbers, and so forth. There are quite a large number of these special nonstandardized characters.

Since cHTML is an extended subset of HTML, you can use your Netscape or IE browser to look at imode pages. Some imode web pages can be found at the web site of EuroTechnology[5] or on Eu-Japan.com's web site.[6] However, there are some restrictions. At the moment, 99.999 percent of imode users are Japanese and therefore almost all imode content is in the Japanese language. Therefore, you will need a Japanese-enabled browser. At the moment, you will not be able to see imode-only tags (such as the links that dial a telephone connection directly from the imode handset in Japan). And, of course, you will not be able to see the many special DoCoMo imode symbols; they will usually be replaced by a question mark. So, looking at an imode page with an ordinary PC-based browser will give you an idea, but will not exactly reproduce what imode users see on their handsets.

---

[5]http://www.eurotechnology.com/i/
[6]http://www.eu-japan.com/i/

imode Advantages

There is no one single reason for the huge success of imode in Japan (see the related sidebar). One reason is the relatively low street price to consumers for imode-enabled handsets. Instead of buying an expensive computer and paying for local Internet access, which is also very expensive in Japan, consumers can buy a cheap device and bypass this large expense. Consumers in Japan don't pay the true cost of imode-enabled phones. Typical total costs (including DoCoMo's charges) when switching to imode are on the order of U.S. $70, but this can be lower (even down to zero in extreme cases) or higher, depending on the popularity of the model or the geographic area in Japan.

Another reason for success is that Japanese spend a lot of time commuting and have time on their hands. Using a mobile device, they can chat with friends, download information, and exchange e-mail. The Japanese are used to using mobile phones; more than 60 million mobile subscribers have set the stage for further growth in this area. The Japanese are also very interested in new technological gadgets. They are more likely to buy new technology than are residents of more conservative countries, such as the United States.

Another advantage of imode is that it uses a packet-switched system. It is basically always on, but the customer is charged not for the time usage, but for information and service usage. NTT DoCoMo introduced an efficient micro-billing system that all participants of imode can use. The portal-like menu of partner sites gives users access to a list of selected content on partner sites, which are included in the microbilling system and can sell content and services. Therefore, all expenses can be charged to the mobile phone bill. Subscribers can pay for value-added, premium sites. This feature is attractive to site owners who sell information to users. In Japan, imode already reached "cult status," meaning that young people want to be part of the network and spend a lot of money. This state was reached through efficient marketing in all media, including traditional newspapers and television.

E-mail and chat are the killer applications for imode users, just like they are on the Internet; the difference is that imode devices are ready to accept Japanese characters. All information, products, and services are in Japanese, making it easier for people with lower education to participate, as they could not do on the early Internet, where a knowledge of English was essential. The programming language cHTML is easy to use, making it possible for companies and users to quickly implement web sites. This has led to explosive growth of Japanese content.

M-Commerce on imode

Real m-commerce, including mobile banking and online trading, is conducted on imode; therefore, security has to be treated seriously. Several areas are vulnerable to security breaches. The connection between the imode device and the cellular base station needs to be secured and encrypted. This link uses

Reasons for the Success of imode

There is no one reason for the huge success of imode in Japan. It has a lot to do with the Japanese market and culture.

- **Low price** – Relatively low street price to consumers for imode-enabled handsets

- **High penetration** – High mobile phone penetration (more than 60 million mobile subscribers)

- **Japanese culture** – Gadget-loving population

- **Low PC penetration** – Relatively low PC penetration at home; high local loop access charges

- **Always on** – Uses packet-switched system, meaning imode is always on

- **Microbilling** – Efficient microbilling system through the mobile phone bill

- **Efficient marketing** – High-profile marketing campaigns in Japan

- **E-mail** – A killer application

- **Uses cHTML** – Developers and ordinary consumers can esily develop content

- **One portal** – Portal-type menu list of partner sites that share infrastructure such as access and microbilling

proprietary protocols and encoding controlled by NTT DoCoMo. From there on the connection needs to be secured to link up to the public Internet and the imode sites on the cHTML layer. Also important is the secure transmission of passwords and information. NTT DoCoMo says that the system is secure, but because it uses proprietary protocols, it is difficult to check whether this is really the case.

As you can see, imode has a lot of potential, but are you able to do business over imode? The easiest way of doing business is to sell content. You can also sell services via imode, and you can have a VPN on imode; there are many other business applications for imode.

What Is Compact HTML?

Compact HTML (cHTML) is a well-defined subset of HTML 2.0, HTML 3.2, and HTML 4.0 recommendations, designed for small information appliances. HTML defines a flexible, portable, and practical document format for the documents on the Internet. One direction of HTML is to grow toward richer multimedia document format. On the other hand, there must be another direction for small information appliances. Small information appliances have hardware restrictions such as small memory, low-power CPU, small or no secondary storage, small display, monocolor, single-character font, and restricted input method (no keyboard and mouse). The browser for cHTML can be implemented in such a restricted environment. Once such a subset of HTML is defined, content providers and information appliance manufacturers can rely on this common standard.

More than 10 million users are connected to imode, and the number of users increases by about 50,000 per day. This corresponds to about 10 percent of Japan's population. This number will increase dramatically in the future. Since almost every user of imode speaks Japanese, it is helpful to have your content and services ready in Japanese. You could try to attract niche markets in Japanese, expatriates to whom you provide information and services in English, but that market is very small. For the G8 meeting in Okinawa in summer 2000, some English pages were prepared, but the content and the services did not reflect the richness of the Japanese version.

imode can be used not only to target end consumers but also to share information and services within a company. By setting up a VPN, you avoid the public Internet to exchange information and services.

To learn more about doing business in Japan, consult one of the many resources on the Web, such as EuroTechnology's web site.[7]

2.2.7 Differences Between imode and WAP

Comparing imode and WAP is not straightforward. WAP services today are used in Europe, Japan, Korea, and other areas in the world. In some sense, imode and WAP-based services compete in Japan and will possibly compete

---

[7]http://www.eurotechnology.com/doing-business-in-japan/

worldwide in the future. Both imode and WAP are complex systems, and it is really only possible to compare present implementations of imode and WAP, as well as their business models, pricing, marketing, and so forth. There are several important differences in the way imode and WAP-based services are presently implemented, marketed, and priced. For example, imode uses cHTML, which is relatively easier for web site developers to learn than WML, which is used in WAP devices.

Another difference is that at present in Japan, imode is implemented with a packet-switched system, which is in principle always on whereas WAP systems in Europe are at present circuit-switched, that is, dial-up. WAP users are charged for the connection time; for example, if a user looks at a newspaper headline or a football result for 10 minutes, that user is charged for 10 minutes of connection time. In Japan, imode users are charged per packet of downloaded information. So, if an imode user looks at a news item or at a football result for 2 seconds or 3 hours on a mobile handset, the charge is the same for 2 seconds or 3 hours, as long as the user does not download additional information. Packet-switching or circuit-switching is a technical difference of the telecommunication system on which the services are based; it has nothing to do in principle with the imode and WAP standards. In principle, imode and WAP encoded web pages can be delivered over packet- and circuit-switched systems.

Another major difference is who can operate portals. In the case of WAP as implemented in Europe, in theory anybody with an Internet connection can operate a WAP portal—there can be multiple WAP portals. In Japan's imode, NTT DoCoMo operates the official menu and the imode center. Anybody can operate an imode site but must enter into a partnership with DoCoMo in order to have the site to appear on the official imode menu. Only NTT DoCoMo operates the imode center.

Future development depends on user/consumer choices, operators' choices and commercial decisions, technical limitations, and even health issues that continue to be raised. Therefore, unexpected developments are not to be excluded. Who would have predicted imode's success a few years ago? Of course this does not prevent intelligent guesses about the future—but they may well turn out to be wrong.

2.3 The Future of Mobile Technologies

Yet another revolution is emerging in the wireless technology industry. The telecommunications world is changing as the trends of media convergence, industry consolidation, Internet and IP technologies, and mobile communications collide. As subscriber growth continues to increase in the United States, Europe, and the rest of the world, carriers and infrastructure providers face a huge challenge in addressing bandwidth problems associated with this exploding capacity. Significant change will be brought about by this rapid evolution in technology, with third-generation (3G) mobile Internet technology radically departing from the technology of the first and even the second generations of mobile technology.

The next-generation wireless standard is expected to address the capacity issue as well as the disparate wireless standards. The 3G technology has GSM roots from Europe and is expected to bring together diverse wireless standards like CDMA, TDMA, and PDC. All these standards have prevented a global roaming of mobile phones. In the United States, it is impossible to roam from one state to another and use the same mobile phone, whereas Europeans can travel to any place in Europe and use their phones. Roaming is a feature that allows users to connect to a foreign carrier and use their network to make phone calls. The billing is handled by the home carrier. The foreign carrier adds a percentage on top for the use of its own network. This makes it possible to have unique phone numbers in the GSM network. No matter where I am, my number is always the same.

In the future people will look at their mobile phone as much as they listen to it, so the display becomes more important. As such, 3G will be less safe than previous generations because television and other multimedia services tend to distract users. It could well be that law enforcement agencies will require car drivers to have not only hands-free kits but also eyes-free kits, to make sure the driver is not distracted by images on the 3G mobile phone. 3G enables the use of complex applications, but the challenging part will be to present these applications in an intuitive way. Screens are small, and it will take some time before we see screens that can be folded or that are based on holographic technologies.

The amount of data or nonvoice transmissions of 3G will be as important as and very different from the traditional voice business. Data communication is expected to grow much faster than voice communication on the mobile network. Mobile communication will be similar in its capability to fixed communications, so many people will have only a mobile phone. The mobile phone will be an integral part of most people's lives; it will not be an added accessory but a core part of how people conduct their daily lives. In Europe, it is sometimes difficult to find people without a mobile phone. The mobile phone will become akin to a remote control that lets people do what they want when they want. It will be more than just calling people; the mobile phone will become a center for communications.

IMT-2000[8] is the global body to coordinate the global standard and spectrum allocation for 3G services through the World Radio Congress (WRC)[9]. The major challenge ahead for the carriers (telecom providers) to advance to 3G service is to establish an evolutionary path from the current 2G services to 2.5G and then to 3G. Most of the European players are already in the process of

---

[8]http://www.imt-2000.net/
[9]http://www.wrc.net/

moving the current infrastructure from 2G to 2.5G. 2.5G basically means moving to the GPRS technology. Some carriers like British Telecom,[10] Deutsche Telekom,[11] and Vodafone[12] have the services complete and operational in Europe. The carriers around the world will transition from 2.5 to 3G services in two ways. In Europe and Asia, carriers will take the GPRS or Enhanced Data for GSM Evolution (EDGE) route, which will provide high-speed connectivity to customers. GPRS promises to provide always-on connection with a practical speed of 19.2 Kbps. GPRS uses packet technology and allows operators to maximize network efficiently by allowing multiple data subscribers to share channels on the network. Just as SMSs take advantage of spare network capacity to deliver brief text messages, packet-based technologies extend the same concept. The carriers are expected to move to 3G technology (UMTS) by late 2001. Japan has already started building up its UMTS networks. The good thing is that Europe and America can watch in peace and quiet how things develop in Japan and then import the most promising business models and technologies. The disadvantage is that the Japanese are far ahead, meaning that they will probably dominate the global market. NTT DoCoMo, for example, has bought 20 percent of KPN,[13] the Dutch telecom, and founded a company together with KPN and Telecom Italia[14] to promote imode in Europe.

In the United States and the countries that support CDMA, the carriers will have to take an alternative path. To move toward 3G they will adopt the CDMA2000-1x standard, known as IS-2000, which is CDMA's 2.5G technology. Two of the carriers in the United States, Verizon[15] wireless and Sprint PCS,[16] are already deploying these services with the help of technologies provided by Qualcomm[17] and Lucent Technologies.[18] The CDMA2000-1x provides a data rate of 153 kbps transmission, which is already suitable for a streaming video application. The CDMA2000 is a spread spectrum technology developed by Qualcomm.

The first phase of CDMA2000-1x will provide the capability of a 144 kbps data rate, and the second phase will offer more than a 1.5 Mb data rate. The major issue of the United States is that this technology will be available soon in the urban areas on the East and the West coasts, but it will take quite some time before it will be available in the Midwest. In Europe, regulations state that rural areas have to be supported within the first two years after the start of the service. Because of the nature of rural areas, few people will require the service, so the cost will be increased and revenues will be reduced. But everyone should have the same opportunities no matter where they live.

---

[10] http://www.bt.com/

[11] http://www.telekom.de/

[12] http://www.vodafone.com/

[13] http://www.kpn.com/

[14] http://www.telecom.it/

[15] http://www.verizon.com/

[16] http://www.sprint.com/

[17] http://www.qualcomm.com/

[18] http://www.lucent.com/

Japan is a step ahead with 2.5G fully in place and accepted by the public. The successful imode service uses packet data network (PDC-P). Carriers like NTT DoCoMo[19] have already started working on the 3G technologies. First trials have been conducted and with the move to the W-CDMA standard, 3G should be available in 2001 throughout Japan.

The two prime candidates for the 3G standard will be wideband-CDMA and broadband-CDMA, otherwise known as CDMA-2000. Whatever the winning standard, they will both offer global, seamless communication. The 3G service will also support the newly upgraded IPv6 scheme, since many device and infrastructure vendors have raised concerns about the number of IP addresses the current Internet protocol can support. IPv6 extends the existing IPv4 technology used on the Internet, with some interesting features. A much larger IP address range, for example, gives every device on earth its own IP address, and QoS features make it possible to guarantee bandwidth. A detailed discussion of this topic can be found in my book, *The E-Business (R)Evolution*.[20]

2.3.1 Deployment

Asia, especially Japan, and Western Europe, are leading the way to the next generation of wireless technology with the United States lagging behind. Finland, Japan, and the United Kingdom will be the first to market in deploying 3G, according to the Strategis Group.[21] While the United States was auctioning the 2G mobile phones in late 2000, Japan and Germany, were already deploying so-called 2.5G services, which are considered interim steps to 3G. 2.5G, based on the GPRS standard, is also now available in some parts of Canada. 3G service will support wireless access speeds as high as 384 Kbps; access with 2.5G service is half that speed or slower. The fastest commonly available wireless access speed is currently 19.2 Kbps.

As early as 1992, the International Telecommunication Union (ITU)[22] identified specific frequency bands for IMT-2000. Similarly, it is expected to identify additional spectrum to cater to the anticipated growth in broadband 3G services that will be in common use by the middle of the next decade. The GSM Association, the largest interest group in 3G, believes that in addition to the existing GSM and IMT-2000 bands, extension bands totaling about 190 MHz will be required for 3G applications. Such additional frequency bands would ensure a global spectrum for everyone's mobile future. 3G offers the unique possibility to move toward a truly global standard. GSM has done a good job internationalizing a mobile phone standard; unfortunately, some countries, such as the United States, did not participate.

---

[19]http://www.nttdocomo.com/
[20]http://www.ebusinessrevolution.com/
[21]http://www.strategis.com/
[22]http://www.itu.org/

It is questionable whether the device capabilities in terms of memory and screen size support 3G features like video and audio. There are already announcements from wireless manufacturers like Nokia, Ericsson, Sony,[23] and Samsung[24] about their new devices that support 3G. Most of them talk about video and audio services, but realistically they will only upgrade mobile phones to small music receivers. It will take at least a year to see the proliferation of such devices that take advantage of 3G services. These new devices should be designed to transmit and receive bandwidth-intensive applications. After that, it will take another year until really useful applications become visible.

Three types of mobile devices dominate the mobile devices market. The largest share is mobile phones that contain mostly proprietary OS and browsers. These phones are sometimes called *smart phones*. U.S.Robotics has produced 5 million Palm computers so far. Nokia alone produces about 2 million phones a week. Although many people in the United States buy a Palm computer, its market share is neglibile in the rest of the world, where mobile phones are the most important device for mobile communication. Besides mobile phones, PDAs play a (small) role, having extended their functionality by incorporating a mobile phone. Moving from a mobile phone to m-commerce is easy; moving from PDAs to the Internet is more difficult, because PDAs were not designed for communications—they were designed to provide mobile access to nonmobile data.

2.3.2 Applications

The next generation of mobile communication will support more than basic features like voice, e-mail, text, notifications, and SMS. They will support a wide range of applications from streaming video, multimedia, and m-commerce to file transfer.

A number of music distribution companies have expressed interest in marketing music by providing downloadable channels that use UMTS services. The quality of the music transmission needs to be good, and the combination of higher bit rate and compression techniques should ensure high-quality reception. This type of service is not tolerant of delays, unlike SMS-based e-mail or messaging service. It is not clear how the distribution companies price this service at this time. But many different models are discussed. Some companies such as Napster[25] and Bertelsmann[26] want to provide music for a flat fee of 15 dollars/euros. Others want to charge one dollar/euro per song that is downloaded. At the time of this writing, many different companies are planning to set up music portals that can be accessed through a web browser or mobile phone in the first generation; later, home automation systems will be able to access the services and the music.

---

[23]http://www.sony.com/
[24]http://www.samsung.com
[25]http://www.napster.com/
[26]http://www.bertelsmann.com/

Video streaming service will be similar to audio streaming and is an another marketing channel for retailers and content distribution companies. UMTS will offer the standard desktop streaming speed and compression rate. Along with audio streaming, industry observers don't expect to see this service in GPRS-based system, because it is too bandwidth intensive. But new technologies are about to remove the bandwidth issues. While the infrastructure is about to expand its possibilities, new technologies reduce the file size of videos. DivX ;-) is already the most popular format for videos and has features similar to MP3 for music. DivX films are widely available on the Internet, and the file size is comparable to MP3 music, which means that everyone, even those with slow connections, can download it and view it in reasonably good quality. The film industry is just about to realize the potential of DivX.

File transfer is a general category of service that covers general information browsing. This application is delay tolerant and will most probably be priced by the megabytes used in the transfer. These qualities enable file sharing among many different devices and users if required. Instead of having copies on every device, a single copy of every document will be available on the Internet.

M-Commerce will also become more interesting as images, sounds, and other multimedia plug-ins become available; devices will have better displays, and higher download rates will enable users to create more interesting offers.

2.3.3   Infrastructure Providers

Infrastructure providers face a huge challenge in addressing the needs for 3G technologies. Two of the major providers, Ericsson[27] and Nokia,[28] are competing to sell the 3G hardware/infrastructure products and solutions both in Europe and the rest of the world to telecom providers like British Telecomm[29] and Vodafone.[30] Ericsson claims that the 3G technology will grow faster than expected and, by 2004, 100 million people will use it for voice and data service. Ericsson launched its first macro BS using 3G WCDMA technology.

While in Europe and Japan auctions have been held for 3G licenses, both Nokia and Ericsson have been actively involved in selling high-end 3G products, network solutions, and operational support. They have already signed up with a number of telecom players in Europe and the rest of the world. 3G cannot be called cheap in any sense. In Germany, for example, a license for Deutsche Telekom[31] cost more than 8 billion dollars/euros. With this license, Deutsche Telekom is allowed to operate a 3G service. To build up the necessary infrastructure, another 4 to 5 billion dollars/euros would be needed to make sure that the whole of Germany is covered.

---

[27] http://www.ericsson.com/
[28] http://www.nokia.com/
[29] http://www.bt.com/
[30] http://www.vodafone
[31] http://www.telekom.de/

Race for 3G Licenses

The race toward 3G has started, and licenses have already been sold in many countries. Germany and the United Kingdom have been the most expensive countries for licenses so far.

- **France** – France tried to hold an auction in early 2001 but delayed it because only two companies turned up for four licenses.

- **Italy** – Five 3G licenses were awarded in 2000. The telecommunication regulator in Italy received more than $4 billion for the five UMTS licenses.

- **Japan** – There are three contenders in Japan: NTT Do-CoMo, DDI, and J-Phone, which are vying for the allocated three licenses from the government.

- **Germany** – The total amount being bid for 3G licenses was over 50 billion dollars/euros. There were seven bidders for the six licenses being auctioned.

- **United Kingdom** – The total amount being bid for 3G licenses was over 30 billion dollars/euros. There were seven bidders for the five licenses being auctioned.

- **United States** – Qualcomm and Sprint PCS have started trial service of 3G broadband wireless network services in the U.S. market. No auctions have been set up so far.

Another issue for infrastructure providers is that people will have to move from their existing mobile phones to the next generation to use the features of 3G. Depending on the business model, this move will happen sooner or later. In Italy phones are rather expensive, but costs per call are very low. This means that many people buy a phone and use it for all calls. Because of the low cost of calling fees, almost everyone has a mobile phone. But the high costs of the phone itself prevent the Italians from moving on to a new mobile phone. In Germany mobile phones are sold for a dollar/euro, but people have to pay higher calling fees. This constellation makes it easier to change to the next generation. When somone renews a contract or moves on to another one, a mobile phone comes with the deal. So, once the carriers offer 3G, the new mobile phones will push people to the next generation. Let us hope the carriers learned the WAP lesson: When you introduce a new technology, you had better have the devices available. (At its beginning, WAP was called "Where Are the Phones?" Everyone talked about WAP, but nobody had access to it.)

2.3.4   Time Scale

The introduction of 3G started in 1999, when the 3G radio interface was standardized and initial 3G live technical demonstrations of infrastructure and concept terminals were shown. At that time, very few people knew about the technology and the concepts behind it; people were starting to get second generation mobile phones.

Early in 2000 the standardization effort was continued with network architectures, terminal requirements, and detailed standards descriptions on how to implement such a network. In May 2000, formal approval of the IMT-2000 recommendations was given at the ITU Radio Communication Assembly. Later that year, 3G licenses for Phase 1 spectrum were awarded by governments around Europe and Asia to mobile phone carriers. At the same time, a formal WRC 2000 Spectrum Review of 3G Phase 2 spectrum took place. Table 2.1 provides an overview of the timetable.

3G trials and integration will commence worldwide in 2001. Japan will be the first country to introduce 3G to the population. In summer 2001 we will see the first commercial deployment of 3G services, which will be available in Japan and Europe. With the beginning of 2002, simple 3G-capable terminals will begin to be available in commercial quantities. Later in the year, network operators will launch 3G services commercially and roll out 3G throughout Europe. Special vertical market applications and end user services will be introduced. Early adopters will begin using 3G regularly. For the first time, more data communication will be transmitted by 3G than by voice communication. 3G will establish itself for for nonvoice mobile communications.

In the third quarter of 2002, new 3G specific applications will be designed. A greater network capacity will make new solutions possible, and more capable terminals will become available. 3G usage will take off.

By 2004, 3G will have arrived commercially and reached critical mass in both corporate and consumer sectors. Carriers still won't be profitable, but they will be on the right track. By 2005, the 3G Phase 2 spectrum will be available. What Phase 2 will contain is subject to WRC decisions and the experiences that have been conducted by then.

2.4   Mobile Applications

This section describes four major applications: mobile Internet, m-commerce, mobile location services, and mobile entertainment.

Year	Action
1999	3G radio interface standardization
2000	Continuing standardization
	Formal approval of the IMT-2000 recommendations
	Award of 3G licenses in Europe and Asia
	WRC 2000 Phase 2 spectrum review
2001	3G trials and integration in Europe
	3G launched in Japan
	Commercial deployment of 3G services
2002	Production of 3G terminals in commercial quantities
	Commercial launch of 3G services
	3G take off phase
2004	3G will reach critical mass
2005	Move toward 3G Phase 2 spectrum

Table 2.1. 3G Timetable

2.4.1 Mobile Internet

The Internet by definition is mobile since the IP addresses are connected to devices and not to locations. Moving a server or a mobile phone won't change how the system works. On the other hand, the Internet does not provide any means to detect the location of an object. Any Internet-enabled device could be anywhere. If Amazon.com were hosted in France, Iraq, or Indonesia, nobody would notice or care (from a networking point of view). So, moving the traditional Internet to the mobile devices is rather easy. Exploiting their potential means that an additional layer needs to be introduced.

Adding this functionality can be done either at the IP level or on the application level. Adding location-based information at the IP level would mean a major redesign of the whole networking infrastructure. Since this is not really acceptable, location awareness was introduced at the application level, which can be more easily changed. This is described later in this section. Besides location-awareness, other aspects are important for mobile Internet connectivity. A browser that makes the best of limited resources is a necessity. And today's solutions in the mobile market are not really good. They try to emulate standard web browsers as well as possible without taking the limited resources into account. The same applies to web designers; they build their sites with standard web browsers in mind, that is, sites are often not designed for small screens with few colors.

Once these display issues have been resolved, mobile devices will become part of the everyday Internet. People will create web sites with mobile phones and other mobile devices in mind. In Japan, imode took off because it enabled anyone to create web pages that looked good in standard web browsers and mobile phones. The next generation, called iAppli, is based on Java and will allow the creation of Internet-based applications that can be executed on iAppli-enabled mobile phones and standard web browsers.

Moving the Internet to mobile devices means expanding its reach but requires a redesign of the existing web sites. Many web sites today are badly designed and can hardly be used with a normal web browser. With mobile devices, even well-designed web pages can have problems because they were not created with small displays in mind.

2.4.2 Mobile Commerce

As e-commerce enables and forces today's managers to rethink their current business practices in this new virtual world, so will m-commerce soon create a similar revolution in how and when tomorrow's businesses serve their customers. Innovative use of technology will soon enable a greater level of accessibility and portability through the mobile phone than any Internet-based PC allows today, and to a significantly larger customer base. In addition to voice-based services, nonvoice applications through a mobile phone have rapidly become widespread and are generally accepted by both business and personal markets.

By the end of 2001, the Internet will be accessible through a mobile phone as well as through a stationary computer. Internet phones will become low cost commodities, packaged with cheap prepay services and available from a wide range of retail outlets. Mobile Internet access will therefore be available to all.

In the near future, new technologies such as Bluetooth (allowing any wireless electronic device to communicate to any other) and the next generation mobile networks (due in 2003), will significantly improve the capabilities on offer. For customers, their mobile phone will become central to their personal lifestyle.

The vision of the future is a personal "lifestyle portal" offering mobile subscribers access to a rich range of services and content while on the move. Those organizations responding to their customers' needs will be the winners in the mobile world, for it is to them that customers will be inclined. The portal of tomorrow will process requests for a customer across multiple delivery channels, with information tailored to meet the characteristics of the customer's device.

In an area such as mobile commerce, the convergence of industries has become apparent. Experiences in both the vertical industries and mobile operators industries have shown us that it is best to develop a tailored road map for m-commerce, identify the business goals, and determine how these will support a customer proposition.

Once the road map is negotiated, the program structure can be implemented. In most cases this means production of a validated business case and quantifying the benefits and costs of the proposed services. Depending on the primary business goals, the business case might focus on cost reductions, customer retention, revenue enhancement, or a combination of these and other factors. In identifying a viable service proposition, the business case will also define a plan and schedule to allow the program to move forward.

2.4.3 Mobile Location Services

Mobile location services provide context-aware services based on the location of the user. In many countries in Europe, location-based services are becoming apparent. Finland, which is one of the most advanced countries regarding mobile services, is also very strong in mobile location services.

Accuracy

Different location-based applications require different levels of accuracy. Clearly, it is important for ship captains to know exactly how far they are from shore and the water depth, whereas for people, location accuracies of a hundred meters or so are often acceptable.

Driving directions, roadside assistance, and tracking of fleet, packages, and people will each become more prevalent with the availability of improved location accuracy. Although some early adopters in vertical markets will be satisfied to know in what part of town their trucks or packages are located, most customers in the horizontal market will want to know exactly where their assets, or even their children, are. Similar dynamics surround roadside assistance. Roadside assistance providers can improve their efficiency by knowing in what part of town motorists are stranded, but most subscribers feel safer if they are located within 125 meters. Turn-by-turn driving directions, the most complicated location service, require even higher accuracy and frequent updates.

The key to incorporating accuracy into a network-based location service is to combine improved location-finding technology with less accurate methods such as cell of origin data, so that network operators can achieve scale quickly. In addition, operators can market the services broadly to existing customers instead of targeting only subscribers with enhanced phones. Customer care, billing systems, and switches can be integrated with the location applications without waiting for network-wide coverage or complete handset penetration. Finally, customers can immediately use their new location services in 100 percent of their coverage area and receive service 100 percent of the time, regardless of the inherent inconsistencies in location accuracy and availability.

The Finnish Connection

Helsinki, Finland, is one of the most wirelessly wired cities in the world. It is almost impossible to find people without at least one mobile phone. Some of my Finnish colleagues have more than five phones, which seems a bit ridiculous, but good for demonstration. They use one phone to control the lawn mower, the second one to switch on the light, the third one to control the heat, the fourth to buy food, and the fifth to browse the Internet. Today, it is difficult to do all five things at the same time on one device. In the near future my colleagues will create a device capable of doing these five things, and more, in a single device. Depending on where you are the device will provide you with different services.

At the Helsinki airport, you can buy a can of soft drink with your mobile phone. Just walk up to the vending machine, type in the phone number of the machine and select what you want to drink; a few seconds later a can is released. Party people in the city center of Helsinki can use the Party Finder Service to locate a nearby party. The mobile phone either directs them to the party or the phone informs the phone owner that he is walking by a house with a party.

Sonera,[32] Finland's largest telecom operator, launched a commercial location service for cellular users; it will tell them where to find the nearest outlets for selected services. Initially, users will be able to find the location of the nearest pharmacies, gas stations, and tourist facilities. Later, customers will also be offered a facility to locate other mobile telephone users, provided the latter have given the necessary authorization for this.

WAP users will receive a map showing the location of the nearest outlet for the service they require. Other users will receive SMS or voice instructions. Sonera says that the strength of its system is that existing handsets can use the service without any modification. It claims that the only change is to the network, requiring no more than the installation of new Sonera-developed software on a server.

When a user makes a call to the service, the call is routed to the server. The server knows the location of the base station that handled the inquiry, so it knows which cell the customer is using and can supply the location of the nearest outlet for the requested service. This approach is known as Cell ID. The system's accuracy can be enhanced through the use of probability. Users tend to be in certain locations within an individual cell, and the operator can use this information to tweak the accuracy when offering directions. The service is accurate within about 100 meters to 500 meters in cities, to within 500 meters to 1,000 meters in suburbs, and to up to 1.5 kilometers to 2.0 kilometers in other places.

For many purposes this will be sufficient. If you are looking for the nearest McDonald's[33] and it is 10 meters away, you can see it. But if it is half a mile

---

[32]http://www.sonera.com/
[33]http://www.mcdonalds.com/

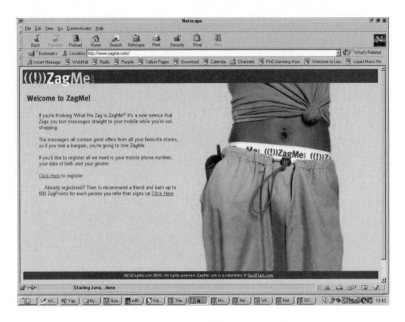

Figure 2.2. Location Service provided by ZagMe

away, you might need the telephone. The information depends on the application and on what you are looking for. Many other location-based services are in development in Finland.

Europe's Answer

Other European countries are trying to catch up. If mobile phone users cross a country's border, they are greeted in their native language by the local phone company. In early December 2000, I flew to Luxembourg and was informed about the local events in December. I was informed, for example, that the local Christmas market was on Place de Paris and from the 4th of December until the 22nd. When users drive to Italy through Switzerland, the Swiss and Italian telecom providers inform them about the cheapest way to make international phone calls.

Shoppers at the Lakeside Shopping Centre, near London, England, receive promotional messages on their mobile phones, alerting them to special time-limited offers available from stores in the mall. The service named ZagMe (see Figure 2.2) is operated in partnership with 150 retailers, including major retail chains such as Pizza Hut, Debenhams, The Gap, Argos, and Top Shop.

The ZagMe service allows retailers to send promotional text messages, using SMS technology, to the phones of registered consumers, alerting them to special time-limited offers in stores in the shopping center.

The good news is that, for ZagMe at least, digital mobile phone users won't be bombarded with unwanted messages, since the service is completely opt-in. GSM phone users must sign up for the ZagMe service, either in-store or in-mall, or through the firm's web site.[34] Nor will customers be deluged with messages, because the service is limited to no more than two messages an hour. In the future, users will be able to control the rate at which they receive messages.

To persuade shoppers to sign up, mobile phone users will get 5 UK pounds in "ZagPoints" when they sign up, as well as five pence for every message they receive. The points can be exchanged for prepaid mobile phone vouchers or store vouchers. ZagMe expects to see significantly higher response rates from the program than from traditional forms of advertising, especially among young adults aged 18 to 24.

Current and Future Events

The Wireless Location Industry Association (WLIA),[35] founded by companies in the United States, Europe, and Asia, provides information about wireless devices, applications, services, and software. One reason this association was founded was the decision by the U.S. Federal Communications Commission (FCC)[36] to have all mobile phone locations identifiable for 911 services. Wireless enhanced 911 (E911) rules need to be met by U.S. cellular companies, with E911 requirements divided into two phases. Phase 1 requires wireless carriers to deliver the telephone number of the handset originating a 911 call and the location of the cell site or base station receiving the 911 call. Phase 2 requires carriers to deliver more specific latitude and longitude location information. The FCC's E911 program mandates that U.S. cell phone companies be able to locate their callers within 100 meters by October 2001.

NeoPoint,[37] creator of NeoPoint smartphones, has announced a "location-based wireless portal" called myAladdin.com.[38] This portal site is a smart-information service that integrates wireless devices with the Internet; it adds intelligence to "raw" data services to provide mobile users a truly enhanced experience. The service is available not only on the NeoPoint smart phones but also on a variety of other WAP-enabled wireless handsets, using CDMA, GSM, TDMA, and iDEN technologies. The service is being marketed to carriers as well as to vertical markets, including banking and online trading, and the company has a number of content distribution agreements in place.

Another company, E-blana,[39] is to launch a series of location-based services in Ireland. These services will encompass location-based billing, location-based emergency services, dispatch services, and information services.

---

[34] http://www.zagme.com

[35] http://www.wliaonline.com/

[36] http://www.fcc.gov/

[37] http://www.neopoint.com/

[38] http://www.myaladdin.com/

[39] http://www.e-blana.com/

Location-based billing will allow mobile operators to offer different price ranges depending on location, for example, calls that are 10 percent cheaper than those from land lines when the user is at home; information services will include positioning systems, maps, and "buddy lists." E-blana wants to create an application infrastructure on which people can roll out real business applications in a wireless environment. Anyone with a business will be able to create location-based services based on E-blana's infrastructure.

2.4.4 Mobile Entertainment

As world moves toward the mobile information society, entertainment is going along. Soon it will be you against your best friend from the other side of the globe. That thought is not only thrilling for the player, there's also added revenue opportunity for operators, and service and content providers. Entertainment on the move means great opportunities for mobile business minds.

Solution providers such as Nokia[40] have created mobile entertainment service solutions for providing entertainment over wireless networks. These solutions help operators and service and content providers to implement and run mobile entertainment solutions. The universal network is not just a business network, it can also be a huge amusement park connecting like-minded people all over the world.

Today's most popular electronic games are already network-connected. Playing chess across the Internet is more fun than playing against a computer; car races on a network are more fun than racing against a single player; quiz games played in a group are more fun with more players. This means that introducing games to the mobile world is not a great risk, but a huge opportunity. There will be a variety of entertainment applications, such as board games, word games, quiz games, and adventure games. And the market will be constantly craving new applications. It's time for content providers to grasp these opportunities. The consumers are waiting to be entertained in a new, exciting, and easy way. There will be more users, more traffic, and more revenue.

Current mobile devices, such as mobile phones, have a limited graphical display and low bandwidths, meaning that the quality of games will be rather low in the initial phase, but through the connectivity, people will still like the games as they get in touch with people with the same interests. In the near future we will see mobile devices that have capabilities similar to the Gameboy Color;[41] mobile entertainment will become more important than stand-alone devices, such as PlayStation,[42] that cannot as yet be connected to the Internet. It is just a matter of time until PlayStations and other devices will be part of a gaming network on the Internet. Mobile devices will still play a more important role since they can be used whenever the player has a few extra minutes, such as in a traffic jam, on a train, or while waiting for someone.

---

[40]http://www.nokia.com/

[41]http://www.gameboy/

[42]http://www.playstation.com/

Digital Bridges,[43] a mobile entertainment company, claims that 100,000 games have been played through its WAP site. The games were played during a six-week period, via WAP phones connecting to Wirelessgames,[44] the gaming content channel of Digital Bridges.

The majority of players are subscribers to Omnitel,[45] Digital Bridges' first live-operator customer. Omnitel is Italy's second largest mobile phone network, with more than 12 million subscribers. Subscribers can access 18 games, ranging from quiz games, puzzles, and card games, to two-player board games. All of the games are designed specifically for WAP users, "lasting around 5 minutes to provide a short, contained, and enjoyable experience," claims the company.

Another example is the union of In-Fusio,[46] a games and animation developer for the mobile phone, and Webraska,[47] a provider of real-time mapping and guidance services for WAP mobile phones. They are joining forces to create location-based games for mobile phones in an attempt to mimic the popular pocket games consoles (such as Nintendo's Gameboy). In-Fusio brings to the party its expertise in developing, customizing, and animating games for mobile phone; Webraska's adds its know-how in real-time mapping displayed directly on a GSM telephone screen, space search, and guidance services. The companies hope to break new ground in mobile phone interactive entertainment.

Besides games, gambling will play a major role in the universal network. The opportunities for the gambling industry will grow explosively in the mobile world. Two minutes of blackjack on the way to work, five minutes of roulette in a work break. No need to load a game, no need to start up a computer. It will also be harder for law enforcement agencies to track illegal gambling, since people on the move are not easily traceable. What happens if you start playing while driving from Las Vegas to San Francisco? While you are in Nevada everything may be legal; once you are close to San Francisco, gambling may be illegal.

2.5 Mobile Business

In the mobile world, different business models are emerging; most of them are known from other platforms, but in the following sections we discuss the basic mobile business models and their differences from the physical and computer-based world. Availability, mobility, and scalability are issues that are unique to the mobile world. Another issue is the variety of devices and applications that arise in the mobile world. To tailor business models to the mobile world, companies need to take these and other prerequisites into account.

Mobile business can be subdivided into four different types of services: pico, micro, macro, and wide area services. The picoservices deal with the immediate

---

[43]http://www.digitalbridges.com/
[44]http://www.wirelessgames.com/
[45]http://www.omnitel.it/
[46]http://www.in-fusio.com/
[47]http://www.webraska.com/

surrounding environment. This could be, for example, a parking lot availability service in a car park or mapping services of a building. Microservices go a step further and include information that is geographically more distributed and may include the city, as well as information that is not so immediate. Services would include train and bus station information and local traffic information. Macroservices are from the region and are of more generic interest, for example, weather information and local news service. Wide area services are the information that can be found on the Internet and that are not directly linked to the immediate vicinity of the user; for example, stock market information or world news.

2.5.1 Mobile Advertising

The fragmentation of media has affected advertising in many ways, and the Internet has changed the advertising world significantly. Understanding media and media characteristics is one of the most difficult issues today. Interactive media has become the hardest media of all to characterize because it is so fast-moving.

Advertising has always tried to affect the buying process of the consumer. The buying process has, depending on the situation, several phases: from the recognition of the need to the actual purchase decision to the experience of consuming the product. The objectives of advertising have been to get the consumer in front of the door of the store where the products are sold. When he steps in, other issues, such as the price, point-of-purchase promotion, and the sales personnel, start affecting the consumer.

Advertising tries to reach objectives that are not directly linked to the sales of the product. Brand awareness, positive attitude, brand identity, personality, and image have been the objectives of advertising.

Advertising on Wireless Devices

Various studies in the year 2000 have shown that consumers are willing to think of their wireless Net devices as sponsored deliverers of information, much like newspapers or television. Just like the World Wide Web, the wireless market is moving toward advertiser-supported delivery of free services.

Most wireless users are ready to treat their phones as advertiser-sponsored sources of information. More than half of the wireless users would prefer an advertising-supported model over a monthly or per-use fee-based model. According to a study, on the advertiser side, interest levels of local businesses in advertising on wireless devices jumped in the last year from about 8 percent to 30 percent.

Advertising on the Internet tries to more directly affect the behavior of the consumer. The computer-mediated environment can guide the consumer all the way from brand awareness to purchase decision and the purchase itself.

Practically, the consumer can conduct the whole buying process—from need recognition to purchase—on the Internet.

Closing the Time Gap

But in many product groups, the consumer has not yet adapted to the computer-mediated environment. The lack of trust regarding e-commerce is still an issue for many consumers. To have an effect, advertising needs to be lodged in memory. Consumers face an information overload. Commercial messages are everywhere and not necessarily always in a useful context from which they can be easily remembered. If the consumer does not remember the advertisement, its message, or the company, advertising is a waste of money. Advertising does not happen when a consumer is buying the product. There is a time gap.

Mobile devices in the near future will be able to close the time gap. These devices acknowledge that the consumer is remembering certain information only for a short period of time. Mobile media advertising can be used to take the advertising message closer to the actual purchase decision. Although it will revolutionize how advertising is presented in the future, it will not replace today's advertising efforts but will add a new service on top of it.

Mobile advertising is more effective because the consumer does not have to remember so much and for so long. The device takes into account the consumer's memory and preferences. Advertising closer to the purchase decision becomes more effective and has more power. Mobile devices can remind people about advertising they have experienced in other locations.

An image cannot be created at the front door of the store; it is something that needs to be built up over a longer period of time. Image is closely related to trust. Unfortunately, many things are absorbed unconsciously and are not available when the advertising company wants them to be. Location-aware technologies will enable companies to take advertising closer to the purchase decision.

Advertising for Context

Using context awareness, advertisers can detect whether a certain customer enters a shop to buy a certain product. When customers enter a shop, they could receive advertisements about the new or cheap products at that particular shop. Depending on the current needs of the customer, the advertisement would show different products, of course. Someone who owns a DVD player will not necessarily want to buy another one but might be interested in add-ons and DVD discs. Studies have shown that about 70 percent of purchase decisions are made in the shop at the last moment. This means that the consumer can be affected near the purchase decision.

Mobile devices take the messages to this moment. A more integrated marketing and communications strategy becomes apparent. Through mobile computing, the computer-mediated world of the World Wide Web can be integrated to the physical world of brick-and-mortar shops.

It is highly unlikely that people will buy books from Amazon.com while walking down the street. The whole buying process does not have to happen in mobile media and in many cases won't. Consumers will buy from the brick-and-mortar world because they are accustomed to doing so, but mobile devices can help the consumers in their decision-making. This is a step ahead in bringing the Internet and the physical world together. Consumers can take the computer-mediated world with themselves to everyday life.

In a recent study, Ericsson[48] showed that mobile users are not only receptive to mobile advertisements delivered to their phones, but respond to them as well. In the survey, users were given the option of receiving a free SMS if they would accept text advertising. The users completed a demographic profile and received mobile advertisements targeted at their demographic group.

According to Ericsson, more than 60 percent liked receiving the targeted advertising, and almost 40 percent found the advertising compelling. About 20 percent sought more information after seeing the SMS advertisements. If you give the mobile users something in return, they are more than happy to receive mobile advertising.

Addressing Advertising Issues

Although I can see a great future for mobile advertising, there are some limits that need to be taken into account. Online-banner advertising is not always profitable and failure is possible in the mobile world as well. Hype will drive the business in the early years, so the real-value proposition will not be evident.

Advertising is the one revenue model that many companies are going toward, because it is the easiest. This has happened on the World Wide Web and it is likely to happen in the mobile world. It is an existing business model, easily understood by everyone. The major problem is the display screen of today's mobile devices. Many people will try to apply traditional approaches to these mobile devices and will most likely fail. To succeed, the physical dimension will require new approaches. The average phone has two to four lines of text. In a newspaper or on a web site, advertising and regular information share the same page. On a mobile phone with four lines, it is difficult to display a corporate message plus regular text on the screen. If the advertisement covered a quarter of the screen—much more than in other media—it would still only be one line of text. With newer models, text can be replaced with graphics, but it is still difficult to differentiate between advertising and regular information. There are a lot of issues as to how to make that model successful. Customization and personalization are some of the key features to make mobile advertising work.

---

[48]http://www.ericsson.com/

Positioning Advertisements for Success

Wireless advertising needs to be positioned as additional content. Through customization and personalization, advertising can become valuable information. This means, for example, that a stock quote might carry with it a link to an online trading site. The link does the promotional work of advertising and is paid for like an ad, but the user perceives it as content.

And it seems to work. fusionOne,[49] for example, displayed personalized Father's Day gifts to selected customers. Of those people who received those ads, about 9 percent bought the displayed product. In this case, the campaign was permissions-based and highly personalized, meaning that only people who gave their permission would see advertising based on their profiles.

To make mobile advertising successful, it is important that advertising is not unobtrusive in the mobile space and does not disturb people on the move. Therefore, mobile advertising should be used carefully. Sending advertisements and coupons to the mobile phone every few minutes without consent and particular reasons will ensure that you lose customers faster than you can generate new leads. A revenue model based on advertising can push a message into the hearts and minds of individuals, but if it becomes too obvious or intrusive it will fail. Advertising in the wireless world must be unobtrusive, must offer value to the user, and must complement, not interrupt, what the user is doing at that time. Mobile advertising will blur the line between advertising and service, to the point where the user no longer really perceives the pitch as advertising.

Japan is a bit ahead of the rest. With imode, Japan has had some time to experiment in the mobile advertising arena. The major difference between European and Japanese mobile devices is that Japanese can fit at least 256 colors and 200 characters on one screen. Graphical displays and animations are also possible. Most important is not to think in terms of the Web. Images and text ads will work provided they are not too long. M-Commerce is about simple ways of providing promotional and personalized information and not about sophisticated graphics or complex text messages.

Advertising in the Future

Imagine going out on a weeknight while on a business trip in a foreign city and having no clue where to go. The mobile phone could provide you with information about pubs in your area and provide a discount voucher for the first round of beers. This information can be sent to colleagues you would like to meet in the evening. Everyone would receive a map showing how to get to the pub and would receive the same discount.

Although many ad agencies talk about delivering advertising dressed up as content, not very many have been able to deliver it. But this market is matur-

---

[49]http://www.fusionone.com/

ing and will grow explosively over the next few years. Mobile advertising will allow agencies to produce tailor-made campaigns that target users according to where they are, their needs of the moment, and the device they are using.

While technology to create this advertising will be expensive, it is easy to imagine that the investments are worthwhile. Through personalized information, the interest of consumers is much higher than with any other technology and therefore mobile advertising will create a compelling alternative to traditional advertising.

2.5.2   Mobile Banking

Bringing the Internet and the associated banking and commerce opportunities to mobile phones will drive new levels of intense competition in the finance industry. A mobile phone removes the traditional restrictions of geographical location and high entry costs and will be the latest weapon in the assault on financial services.

Existing financial institutions now face a consistent set of market issues. Servicing costs for customers are increasing. Customers are less loyal than before. Customers expect to have multiple channels to access the bank. The margins are driven down by new low-cost Internet banks, which are new niche players that have a large effect on the whole market.

Banks cannot afford to ignore the real competitive threat of mobile operators offering financial services and the new revenue opportunities mobile-based commerce offers. With annual sales doubling and penetration approaching 70 percent in countries such as Finland, the mobile phone should be recognized as a significant element in devising a successful remote channel strategy.

Within two years, a rapid expansion in new electronic delivery channels will support a range of transactional services. These channels include digital TV, game consoles, mobile phones, and PDAs.

The mobile phone is unique among the customer devices expected to dominate remote access to financial services. It is personal, timely, and usually switched on. These attributes provide new service and sales opportunities for banks and therefore should not be ignored.

Customer Demands

The convenience and immediacy of these applications will appeal to customers, and this will push banks to seriously consider providing new services. Failure to provide these services will mean risking the loss of key customer segments to competitors that do provide them.

Meeting customer demand for greater convenience, choice, and access to banking services requires an investment. The return on investment in an innovative electronic channel is predicted to be significantly higher than supporting existing brick-and-mortar channels, as illustrated by the experience gained in Internet-based services. Banks failing to incorporate remote channel strategies will have an overall higher operating cost than competitors. Mobile banking complements other remote channels by providing immediate access to financial services for customers on the move.

Banks must be ready to take full advantage of this profitable new customer access channel. New strategies, pricing models, and revenue opportunities provided by offering location-specific, timely, and personalized services will be exploited by players that invest early in this market.

Customer Services

Some new entrants to the financial services market will be mobile operators, who already have access to a large percentage of banking customers through the communication services they provide. This entry represents a major challenge to the financial services industry in retaining existing customers. Operators are launching a range of new services, including Internet access via the mobile phone, and the addition of their own financial products into the offering is the next stage. Opportunities for banks go far beyond providing basic financial information. Outside the financial hub, customers will use other services such as checking the latest traffic news, stock prices, news headlines, and sports results, or even playing games. Such a combination delivers a level of customer service superior to that possible from a single delivery channel. It affords both retail and corporate banking customers the opportunity to have a closer relationship with the bank, tailored to their specific needs.

Customers will always have specific requests that need a rapid response, for example, checking a balance, authorizing a payment, or buying and selling stock. However, the personal nature of the mobile phone means the bank can contact the customer as important events happen. For instance, a customer could be notified if approaching overdraft limits, if bill payments were due, or if interest rates had changed. While customers are unlikely to pay for notification of account balances, they may be prepared to pay a premium for being warned of being overdrawn, especially if immediate action could save penalty fees from being levied.

If banks restrict themselves to core services such as account balance and bill payment facilities, customers will quickly move to new entrants offering a wider range of services.

Banks must develop and launch initial offerings in mobile banking and commerce services as soon as possible, to remain competitive and prevent further disintermediation. The recent release of WAP as an accepted global standard on which mobile Internet services will be delivered will revolutionize the industry. With WAP-compatible devices expected to reach 20 percent penetration of the European market within two years, there is no time for banks to delay if they are to provide the services their customers will demand.

Threats from new entrants into the market, competition from outside Europe, and increasing demands by customers, mean banks that fall behind at these early stages will struggle to catch up. Banks must go beyond simple mobile banking services, offering a full portfolio to customers, tailored to their customers' lifestyles.

Customer Security

Security is a key issue. Many different components are needed to perform a transaction (handset, SIM card, mobile operator infrastructure, bank infrastructure), and both the customer and the bank must be satisfied that each of these is as secure as possible. The WAP protocol defines standards for secure transactions, and these are being further developed in each release of WAP. Eventually, the phone will act as a personal authentication device, using an electronic signature to authorize and protect transactions. The signature can be stored on the handset itself or on a separate smartcard.

A study by IntelliQuest[50] shows that consumers are reluctant to use mobile banking if the bank cannot show that it is secure. And 75 percent of the respondents indicate that they would refuse to use the mobile services if they were not personalized. As banks and brokerages add wireless Internet services, they need scalable and reliable transaction systems to meet the anticipated m-commerce growth.

A Mobile Banking Example

The Chase Manhattan Bank[51] uses Tantau's[52] Wireless Internet platform as a main component of its wireless infrastructure. With this technology, Chase can enable its wholesale and retail customers to conduct financial transactions over a wireless device. Functions will include account access, e-mail, web access, and location-based services, such as locating convenient ATMs.

Tantau's Wireless Internet platform is the major building block in the effort to seamlessly integrate Chase's wired and wireless online transaction infrastructure and will help provide the most secure and convenient banking experience to their customers. Chase customers can transfer data to and from any WAP-enabled cellular phone, laptop computer, or PDA, using any wireless carrier. The Tantau platform enables Chase to maintain a direct link with its customers and provides Chase with many additional benefits, including an uninterrupted relationship with its customers, a secure transaction environment, the ability to develop personalized user services, and ultimately the establishment of a stronger foundation for customer loyalty.

Tantau's Wireless Internet platform offers specialized and interactive modules that provide enterprises with the tools necessary to conduct mobile e-commerce transactions. Features such as proactive messaging, content conversion, and profile management enable companies to send, transform, and

---

[50]http://www.intelliquest.com/
[51]http://www.chase.com/
[52]http://www.tantau.com/

personalize content to end-users through a variety of mobile devices such as cellular phones, pagers, and PDAs, including Palm products. The ability to control the content delivered to its customers' wireless devices allows businesses to build and maintain strong customer relationships. In addition, Tantau's technology features multiple protocol support (WAP, SMS, and standard HTTP) as well as gateways for integration with back-end applications and data sources. It also addresses the most critical requirements for high-volume Internet transactions: scalability, availability, transaction integrity, and security.

2.5.3 Mobile Devices

Mobile devices present a huge paradigm shift for all parties involved: the market, the industry, and the user. Most people think of the Internet as the World Wide Web that can be accessed through a high-tech browser. These browsers consume a lot of disk space and memory and require a high-resolution screen to display the content of a web page. In the mobile world, all resources are restricted; therefore, it is not possible to guarantee all the prerequisites will be fulfilled. The industry therefore has to create new devices and applications, and the users have to accept a different approach to the Internet.

The most profound change is that mobile devices are not about the physical device anymore but rather about their specific utility. The "appliance" in Internet appliance is only needed because of simple physics. So far nobody has found a method to connect to the Internet without a physical medium. To make the best out of the appliance, it should focus on its role as a "vessel" and nothing more.

Positioning a Device

Looking at the mobile phone industry, you can see that the winning manufacturers are those that enable the most services. Motorola[53] lost market share because it focused too much on technical details, such as battery life and size, and neglected the easy use of the mobile phone. Nokia[54] and Ericsson[55] invested in design of the phone and its interface. Therefore, the positioning of future mobile devices should not be about the physical product itself, but about the tasks users can complete or the experiences they can gather by using the product.

When positioning a mobile device, a company must be aware of the target audience. Both the uninitiated Internet user and the Internet professional should benefit from the device. The mobile device should provide a general Internet access option for any consumer and additional context-aware features. The mobile device will become for many people the only way to access the Internet in the future.

---

[53]http://www.motorola.com/
[54]http://www.nokia.com/
[55]http://www.ericsson.com/

Creating a Simple Interface

Once the positioning is right for the devices, it is important to create a good experience for the user. The right experience is about the task, not the product. To deliver the right experience, the device should be invisible to the user. The built-in user interface and hardware design should be a mere messenger of information and services. To make the use as simple as possible, all elements of the user interface should be easily accessible and understandable without computer experience. Complicated options menus as provided in Outlook, for example, are a no-no. Even menus and hidden windows should not be taken into account. Just as Nokia phones provide only context-relevant menu-points on screen, these devices should never show functionality that does not make any sense at that given time.

Look at Word 2000; it shows only relevant menu items. But relevant in Word means that it has been used often in the past. This is not context relevant. If I opened 10 documents in the past, there is still a good chance that I want to create a document or save a modified document. If I haven't done this in the past, it won't show up in the menu immediately. Good idea, bad approach, good example.

Buttons and other elements of the user interface that are part of the hardware should be easy to operate and clearly signed. If the interface is done properly, there will be no button at all. Everything will be handled through the display. This makes it easier to extend the functionality of the hardware.

Predicting the Future

Good mobile devices will be able to automate many tasks and save the user of the device valuable time. This timesaving can only be achieved if the device can save preferences for every user. Once the users have authenticated themselves, their preferred information and services should appear on screen and anything they might need should be available with no more than two clicks. The services need to be context sensitive. If you watch a football game on television or in the stadium, for example, the mobile device could provide additional information on the players and the teams.

With the appropriate positioning and user experience, a mobile device will be more readily perceived as exactly what it is: a simple solution that accesses the Internet for the user to complete day-to-day tasks. Addressing these issues facilitates content, commerce, and communication tasks achieved through a new wrapper. Mobile devices add increased convenience for users if done properly.

2.5.4 Mobile Payments

Payments in the mobile world are quite easy. Every mobile user has a billing relationship with a telecom provider, unlike the traditional Internet, where there was not a unique billing relationship between user and provider. Some users accessed the Internet through a friend's connection, others at a university, through AOL, T-Online, or at work. It is difficult to identify the person and the billing provider.

In the mobile world, users have their own smartcard and personal identification number (PIN) that make identification easy. The PIN and the smartcard are not only tied to a certain person, but also to a certain telecom provider. Different business models are possible in this area; credit solutions are strong in the United States, but the rest of the world is oriented toward debit and prepaid solutions. In the mobile world, credit solutions do not work well.

For wireless technology and m-commerce to catch on in the United States as they have in the rest of the world, service providers must introduce debit and prepaid solutions that fit small budgets, not just corporate executives. For example, payment is done in the United States in a completely different way than in Europe. Your satellite television contract, home phone landline, gas bill, and wireless phone are probably all credit accounts. In Europe, a company to which you owe money can deduct what you owe from your bank account at a monthly, weekly, or yearly rate. In other cases, you prepay an account, that is, you pay before you use something, such as telephone or gas; once the prepaid amount has been used up, the service will not be usable until you pay again in advance.

The concept of direct debit means passive approval of all outgoing payments. This approach does not open a way to deduct an unlimited amount of money from your account, as you may fear. Only authorized people and companies are allowed to debit from the account, and you can disapprove each payment until six weeks after it has been executed. The advantage is that you don't lose time writing checks or going to a cashier to pay a bill. Everything is done automatically and electronically. No manual or physical processes are involved, making prepayment suitable for the digital world. The physical and manual billing and check process looks very old-fashioned to the rest of the world and it is rather unsuitable for the payment of mobile services.

Prepaid is the most common option for mobile phones in Europe, although it is not necessarily the best for the consumer at first sight. It is less convenient and more expensive, but it definitely is the best for mobile providers. The prepaid model is best for consumers too, because it guarantees that they don't pay more than initially planned. Prepaid options guarantee a steady and foreseeable income, especially for startup companies. Phone carriers don't want to be in the credit, billing, or collections business.

For wireless technology and m-commerce to catch on in the United States as they have in the rest of the world, U.S. carriers must design offerings around the budgets of individuals. What does 300 minutes mean to an individual? It is not only five hours of air time, but a potential liability if she exceeds her allowed minutes. People on budgets want to know what it's going to cost them up front. Wireless carriers should figure out how to allay concerns about

---

Payment Models for Wireless Devices

There are several payment models in the wireless world.

- **Credit** – The callers get bills and pay the bills with bank transfer or checks.

- **Debit** – The callers have the amount deducted regularly from their bank accounts.

- **Prepaid** – The callers pay before they use the device.

---

unlimited costs of the average consumers in order to bring them on board. Critical mass is still the name of the game, and no one is going to win without offering plans (prepaid or flat rate) that average consumers will embrace.

In Europe, most people have a least one mobile device that is connected to a carrier, because the device, such as a mobile phone, is available for nearly free. In the United States, unless mobile devices are connected, most of them are stand-alone PDAs.

One of the most interesting technologies in connection with billing is Bluetooth. Ericsson,[56] for example, is partnering with Scandinavian retailer ICA Ahold[57] in one of the first tests using Bluetooth wireless technology in retail stores. The system being tested will enable consumers with phones enabled for Bluetooth and WAP to pay for items, check their accounts, and learn about current items on sale.

The initial trial is being conducted at an ICA shop near Stockholm, Sweden. The store is equipped with multiple Bluetooth access points and a Bluetooth networking server that connects to a cash register server and a payment processing system. If customers enter the shop with a Bluetooth-enabled phone, they are greeted by the shop and presented with information that helps them navigate through the shop. Once the customers have selected all the goods they want to buy, they can pay through their mobile phone at the shop's cash desk. The amount will be put on the phone bill.

2.6 Portals

Portals today play an important role on the Internet. They aggregate content and services. They are starting points for users who want to explore the World

---

[56]http://www.ericsson.com/
[57]http://www.icaahold.com/

Reasons for Portal Success

In this new highly competitive marketplace, a variety of factors will drive wireless portals in the near future.

- **WAP standard** – All handset vendors have announced that all future models are to be WAP enabled.

- **Operator adoption** – Operators are adopting increasingly aggressive promotions and marketing strategies to encourage end-users to upgrade their handsets.

- **Future of WAP** – Further upgrades of WAP will support enhanced graphics and animations.

- **Early deployment** – Commercial deployment of 2.5G and 3G infrastructure and handsets is on its way, earlier than anticipated.

Wide Web. Introducing pervasive computing will increase the number of content and service providers significantly, therefore making it even more difficult for users to find what they really want.

Portals will therefore be even more important in the future. They will go beyond today's possibilities of portal technology and introduce a set of new paradigms, complementing the existing ones to form truly pervasive portals. Two of the most prominent solutions are presented in this section: device portals and personalized portals.

The Delphi Group[58] developed a set of services that will be in the first wave of mobile services (see Figure 2.3). E-mail is still the most important service; it always was and will remain important in future networks. CRM and Content Management Systems (CMS) become even more important in the future than they are in today's portals. Because of the pervasiveness of technology, it becomes harder to convince a customer to stay with a certain service provider, so it is important to collect as much information as possible about customers and try to create a good profile that will serve customers next time they use the service. CMS is also a very hot topic since content needs to be displayed on different occasions in different ways. Groupware applications play an important role in making internal business processes pervasive. ERP and consolidated data warehouses are also important services that will profit from being avail-

---

[58]http://www.delphigroup.com/

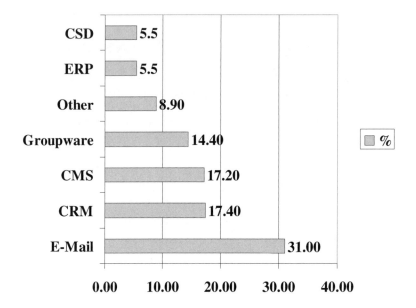

Figure 2.3. First Wave of Portal Services

able not only on computers, but also in production environments and on the road with sales people.

The Strategis Group[59] released a study in 2000 that predicts that almost 17 million users in the European Union will be using mobile portals regularly. The level of freedom and the choice of services available through the portal will be key factors in the differentiation of one cellular operator's offering from that of their competitors.

As a consequence, Strategis expects that by 2005 the number of portal end users should top 183.7 million in the European Union alone. Portal-based services are very much about the personalization of the end-user's experience since they are meant to add functionality and relevance to ownership of a mobile phone. Although preferring localized content, portal users always want full access to all information.

Cellular operators will launch portal-based applications for use by any cellular phone user, scrapping the previously used "walled garden" content model, which restricts subscribers' access to third-party portals. That model was also very common in the early years of the World Wide Web, when AOL[60] and T-Online[61] created content and services that were accessible only to subscribers

---

[59]http://www.strategis.com/
[60]http://www.aol.com/
[61]http://www.t-online.de/

to these particular online services. Today, almost all services are open to anyone with a web browser.

2.6.1 Device Portals

A device portal is the concept that any individual device has its own portal. This means that information and services relevant to that device can be exposed through links on a single site. My car's portal would provide information and services related to it. It would not be a generic car portal but an individual portal for my car, filled with information related to it.

Personalized device portals are dynamic web sites that use information about the device, along with information about the device's context, to generate a web site with information and services tailored to the ownership, use, and maintenance of the device.

Although every device of the same make is sold with the same status, its configuration and use make it unique over time. A personal car portal would have information and services relevant to the current state and configuration of my car. The device portal contains information how the car is actually used, whether the driver drives it to work, in town, or on long-distance travels. Based on that information, the system could provide additional services and information. If the car is used daily for driving to work, traffic jams could be located and alternative routes provided. If the car is used for driving in town for shopping, the system should provide offers from local shops and convenient car parks located near the shops. If the car is used for long-distance travels, a hotel planner could allow the user to select hotels and restaurants near the target location.

The information on the portal should be provided not only on the Web, but also directly in the car, by WAP mobile phone, and other channels. The same applies to all types of device portals. A personal printer portal should be accessible through the Web and through the front panel of the printer, for example. A refrigerator, operated from a mobile phone, could notify a supermarket shopper about needed food supplies.

The advantage of organizing information related to devices in the context of the device is that it allows users to access information and services associated with the device they are currently concerned with, whether they are using the device, maintaining it, or performing some other task. Furthermore, the device holds a great deal of information that is useful in determining what information and services might be of interest, based on its current state or historical information of usage, repair, and purchase, for example.

Device portals are already popular for mobile phones, and they are a natural extension. Other devices will follow the trend in the near future, since selling the actual devices won't create a lot of revenues. The margins for all devices are falling, so companies must sell many more devices to compensate for the loss in margins. It is quite clear that there is a natural limit for the number of devices, so companies need alternative revenue streams. Device portals are

Services of Device Portals

The following list shows the standard services that every device portal should offer, regardless of the type of device.

- **Autobiographer** – The device should store information about itself for future use.

- **Availability** – The services of the device should be available anytime and anywhere.

- **Configuration** – Every device should be configurable over an easy-to-use web interface.

- **Extensibility** – The device should be able to learn new features over time.

a good strategy to compensate for lower margins: they tie the customer to the company.

If possible, a single billing method should be provided for the device, that is, all services and information provided through the portal can be billed through the maker of the device. The manufacturer should be open to third-party service and information providers, but should run all billing in-house to generate additional revenues.

2.6.2 Personalized Portals

Personalized portals are the logical extension of today's horizontal portal idea. Today's personalization is limited; My Yahoo! or similar web sites afford slight, on-site organization of contents, services, and presentation, but they are a long way from personalization.

True personalization means that the service knows the context, such as time, location, and reason. Only if this is the case can the system respond adequately without having to disturb the user with unnecessary and repeated questions. The service also requires some sort of "intelligence." I don't want to introduce a new concept of artificial intelligence—maybe "behavior" would fit better. The system needs to know how to behave in certain situations.

Let's imagine that I have to fly to London for a business meeting. Everything connected to the travel is handled by a personal portal called "Danny's Travel to London." My personal portal is connected to the flight information at the airport in Stuttgart and London Heathrow. It can communicate with the

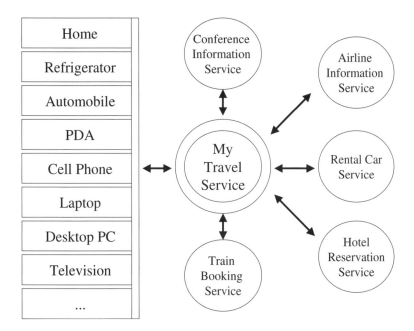

Figure 2.4. Design of a Personalized Travel Portal

rental car service at the airport in London, knows the address of the hotel in Central London, and is aware of the meeting duration and content. Have a look at Figure 2.4 for a view of the personal portal idea. All service and information providers are connected to the personal portal and can be accessed by devices that I may have around me.

To be truly personal, the portal can react in certain situations according to the preferences of the user, in this case, me. The portal could, for example, receive information about a late arrival of the plane and inform the rental car company and the hotel. The personal travel portal should also be able to pass on the hotel address to the rental car's navigation system. And the hotel could be informed about the number plate of the car, to reserve a parking slot for the car in the hotel garage.

The user of the services does not need to worry about the airline, the rental car, the hotel, and so forth. Based on the preferences and other indicators, such as frequent traveler cards and schedules, the travel portal will create the optimal travel for me. The travel portal will not go for the cheapest airline or the cheapest rental car, but for the cheapest solution, for example.

If the arrival of the plane conflicts with the schedule of the meeting, a system in the far future could decide, based on the agenda of the meeting, whether the meeting needs to be postponed or whether it is suitable to start the meeting without the missing participant. If the meeting is to be postponed, all participants must be informed and their personal travel and meeting portals must arrange to accommodate the changes.

This intelligent network is secure and accessible only to the person who is traveling. No one else can change the underlying parameters and preferences. And only trusted service providers will be allowed to view certain information that is required to process the service. A different traveler with the same requirements, for example, will have his own personal travel portal. The other traveler may have different flight preferences or preferred hotels.

These personal portals can create a personal business or leisure network that accommodates the needs of the users and acts on users' behalf.

2.6.3   Situated Portal

In the first step we will see a lot of specific personal portals that will deal only with one aspect of life, such as travel, health, meetings, or shopping. They will be costly to implement and probably not too flexible. The real power will come later, when these portals are able to handle all aspects of life. These "in between" portals are called situated portals.

Turkcell,[62] for example, the leading provider of mobile communications services in Turkey and one of the largest and fastest-growing mobile communications operators in Europe, announced the launch of the "My Colleagues" service, Turkcell's new subscription-based service exclusively for corporate customers. "My Colleagues" allows medium-sized Turkish companies with three to nine Turkcell lines to save up to 30 percent on their GSM bills. For a fixed monthly fee, "My Colleagues" subscribers receive a 30 percent discount on all calls made to five Turkcell numbers they select and various discount rates on all other calls.

It is just a matter of time until a "My Colleagues" portal will be opened that will allow the exchange of information and services among colleagues. New colleagues, for example, will automatically receive information on all colleagues in a team, their phone numbers, e-mail addresses, and so forth. All this information will be stored automatically in their mobile phones and laptops.

Researchers at Andersen Consulting's Center for Strategic Technology Research have developed Online Medicine Cabinet (OMC). The OMC is a prototype of a computerized bathroom cabinet that greets you, checks your blood pressure, communicates with your health care provider, and reminds you to take your Prozac.

The goal of OMC is to support health care without disrupting daily activity. It combines special sensor technology, embedded computers, and the Internet to create a situated portal, a smart appliance that monitors a person's health needs and responds with customized services.

OMC is intended as a consumer device that can provide a single point of access for health services, but one that will also work for hospitals, doctors,

---

[62]http://www.turkcell.com.tr/

and pharmacies. The immediate market for OMC is people who have chronic diseases, like diabetes or hypertension, and the elderly. The OMC interacts with service providers by allowing home users to monitor their conditions and send up-to-date information to their health care providers.

OMC integrates technologies such as face recognition, voice synthesis, flat panel displays, and smart labels. The device uses facial geometry recognition to identify each member of a household. When someone enters the bathroom, the computer initiates a dialog by greeting the person through voice technology. Using the flat panel display built into one of the cabinet doors, the computer will offer health information for the day and a list of personalized reminders, such as doctor's appointments and medication alerts.

For example, at the end of the day, it could alert a woman who takes birth control pills that she hasn't taken hers yet, or it could prompt a heart patient to check his blood pressure. Once he does, the results can then be sent from the bathroom via the Internet to the doctor. Special sensors detect when a medicine bottle is lifted out of the cabinet and when supplies are running low. Once OMC detects that a refill is necessary, it sends an automatic e-mail request to the pharmacy.

By using smart labels, OMC even warns users if they pick up the wrong medication. The OMC can keep track of how often the medicine is consumed, who picks it up, and how often it should be taken. It communicates with the embedded computer in the cabinet. Although just a prototype, it is already impressive and can be expected to trigger many other portals, eventually leading to truly personalized portals dealing with every aspect of life.

Chapter 3

Home Automation Systems

Today, more than 50 million American homes have more than one PC, and family members often vie with one another for access to the Internet from the den, the living room, the bedroom, or the kitchen. The importance of the Internet for communications and commerce is expected to soar, and home networks are suddenly a practical necessity for many people, not just a project for electronic tinkerers.

3.1 Introduction

We are rapidly approaching the day when a much broader array of home devices will be sharing data, not just PCs and peripherals, but also television sets, stereo systems, smart land-line telephones, cellular phones, digital cameras, and even kitchen appliances. A consumer might download music from the Internet through a computer and play it on a home stereo, for example, or play a DVD movie on the home-office computer but watch it on the big television set in the living room.

Your washing machine will talk to your local electricity portal to negotiate the price of energy for washing trousers. The oven provides you with a selection of menus, based on the ingredients of your fridge. By simply pointing a digital video camera at the television, you can cause the two devices to instantly recognize each other. A signal sent from the computer in the car could arm the home security system or turn down the thermostat. A computer in the master bedroom could display images beamed from the camera in the nursery or over the front door.

The refrigerator could know it was low on milk and eggs and place an order with the local supermarket, and a microwave oven could check a database that listed the allergies or eating habits of family members and issue an alert if an unwanted ingredient was detected when a package's bar code was waved in front of it. All the clocks in the house would set themselves by linking to the PC, which would set its own internal clock from the Internet checking with an atomic clock.

One of the hottest markets in the near future will be home automation that will allow you to connect every device in your home to every other device and control them over the Internet from your office or on the road.

The idea of integrating all electronic devices at home has several advantages. It allows the exchange of information between these devices, thus reducing some overhead for the user. It also allows the devices to communicate with external entities. If the dishwasher breaks down, the home network could automatically call a technician and negotiate the date for him to come. If the home network is intelligent enough, it could also tell the technician what is broken and which parts need to be replaced. The whole transaction becomes more efficient for the owner of the broken dishwasher and for the technician.

Many people think of these developments as the future, but they have arrived in the present. In Italy you can already buy washing machines that are connected to the Internet and have a web server built in. In Switzerland, a company is working on a home-automation system that connects existing domestic devices and consumer electronics with each other and with the Internet.

The concept of home automation is to connect all of electrical and electronic systems and devices in a home together on a network so that they can be controlled with a common interface and react to each other. For example, if you start a movie on the VCR, the lights dim and the telephone directs calls to the answering machine.

Home automation is currently defined by the Home Automation Association (HAA)[1] as "a process or system (using different methods or equipment) which provides the ability to enhance one's lifestyle, and make a home more comfortable, safe, and efficient."

Why would anyone not want home automation? The technology to create all such fancy networks exists today. But to many consumers, home automation seems like a complex solution in search of a simple problem. These attitudes and economics will be overcome once the standards in home automation become stable and the convergence of technologies and service providers is established. The transition to a new age of the "automated home" will become commonplace, and the dynamics of lifestyles, technological advancements, and societal factors will be absorbed.

3.1.1 Advantages of Home Automation

Home automation has several advantages over a nonwired and a nonconnected home. If done properly, home automation can make life easier and simpler. It can provide instant access to resources in the house and personalized control over the environment. (A personalized environment means that different people will have different settings and experiences in a room.)

Home automation allows proactive maintenance and servicing of existing devices. If the central heating breaks down, for example, e-mail could be sent

---

[1]http://www.haa.org/

to the technician, who in return would check the calendar of the homeowner to find a suitable time and date for an appointment. Communications and security also play an important role; through home automation, it is possible to create single communication and security infrastructure that allows for easy management. Since need, societal influences, industrial standards, and economics all play a part in the establishment of a market, a consideration of these factors will help our understanding of the real benefits gained by implementation of a whole-house automation system.

The home-building industry is changed right now by several factors, such as new technological standards, building codes, and public needs. Traditional wiring of houses for electricity and phones do not suffice for the needs of the next generation of personal home devices. Electricity and communication are required everywhere, anytime, and by anyone. And not only at certain spots within the house. A home built on traditional wiring standards is becoming incomplete; the subsystems and devices the home contains are smarter, and services cannot be obtained through these older standards. The lifestyles of people are so diverse and different from those of past generations that the needs of people have become dynamic. Society has become more complex, resulting in more sophisticated tools that can be used in simple ways. With home automation, homes can be mass-customized for the wishes of large populations.

The benefits of implementing a whole-house automation system can be seen from the practicality of what the system will do for a particular home owner. New devices will be installed easily with minimal, if any, configuration. Installing a DVD and configuring it to run with the receiver, speakers, and television can be difficult for nontechnical people. The creation of an underlying communication and application layer enables all devices to be connected in the same way. One cable per device will be the maximum in the future. Although we will see many devices connected by a wireless connection, it will take some time before we see devices that receive power through the air.

By providing a single infrastructure, we will see also a significant step in simplifying the usage of the single devices. It will also reduce the number of remote controls. I have currently four remote controls at home. And why? Because my television is from Sony, my DVD player from Yamakawa, my amplifier and tuner from Pioneer, the other stereo from Akai. If I had bought all devices from a single company, the number of remote controls could be reduced, but when most people buy a new device, the features, price, and other things play a more important role than the brand. You can already buy remote controls that work on various devices, but as soon as a new device appears, you can be sure the remote control won't work. Philips[2] has created a remote control for all devices; instead of having buttons to press, it provides an LCD display that recreates the buttons on every single remote control. The user specifies the device to use, and the appropriate interface appears on the display. The

---

[2]http://www.philips.com/

disadvantage is that new devices need programming. The devices currently cannot transmit the required information to the remote control.

As a bonus, virtual services from various Internet and home automation providers will be added without additional installation or configuration. Access to information will be instantaneous and ubiquitous. These benefits can be achieved when a whole-house automation system is implemented correctly.

3.1.2 The First Generation

The first generation of integrated devices works only passively, meaning that existing services can be controlled by other devices, such as a TV remote control. Today, we can use a remote control and a television set to check and control domestic devices. A dishwasher could, for example, send a short message to the television that it has finished washing the dishes. Just as the Web developed in three phases—information, communication, and transaction—so will home networks develop. The first step is to let these devices provide information about themselves and their status. The next step will be to allow communication between these devices, and in the end, the devices will be able to do automated transactions.

In the second generation, once the communication works, users can ask for certain information and react to it. If the stove sends a message that the water is boiling, the user could respond by reducing the heat under the pot.

In these early years of home automation, many companies work with different technologies to achieve their vision of the universal network. To connect a fridge with the stereo, the heating with the movement sensors, and the surveillance camera with the lighting in the garden, industry must have standards. The problem is not that standards are missing, but that there are too many. Home-PNA, R7.3, Home-RF, Home-Plug, Universal Plug and Play, Jini, HAVI, and CE-BUS are only a few examples of how to control the communication of home automation systems. At the moment, therefore, there are two factions: one faction tries to establish company-independent standards, and the other faction is building point solutions to make as much money as possible as soon as possible.

3.1.3 Existing Technologies

Startup companies especially do not want to wait for a standard, so they create products without a polished standard. They need to establish themselves in the market before the big companies start to divide the market among themselves, making market entry for startups difficult. One such example is the company Starseed[3] in Switzerland. It provides a proprietary solution called Personal James (see Figure 3.1).

---

[3]http://www.starseed.ch/

Figure 3.1. User Interface of Personal James

Personal James combines hardware and software that allow owners of Windows-based PCs to remote-control their homes. The product does not support any standards but can be bought today and works quite well.

Starseed's Personal James can feed the goldfish, make coffee shortly before the owner arrives home, or open and close the window shades to simulate activity in the house while the owner is away. The heart of the system is software for the Windows platform (currently only Windows 95 and 98) that enables interaction between the members of the household and sensors and actors in the house. Starseed wants to release Mac and Windows 2000 versions of its software to support as many home owners as possible.

Besides the software, Starseed supplies all the accessories. One important accessory, for example, are the sensors that measure temperature and light and detect movements. In addition to sensors, Starseed also provides a selection of actors, such as cameras or power switches that allow simple remote control of any electronic device. Through the switches, the devices can be switched on or off.

The people that live in a particular home can see the output of the sensors on the Internet through a web browser and can direct the actors to change settings within the house. The sensor status messages can also be distributed by e-mail or SMS if something changes. A movement sensor could send an SMS if detecting a movement; a head sensor could send e-mail if the temperature rises above 80 degrees Fahrenheit. The advantage of the Starseed system is

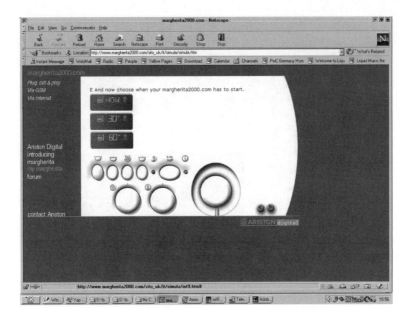

Figure 3.2. Controlling Margherita 2000

that the homeowner does not need to buy new devices. The additional sensors and actors can be controlled by a simple personal computer. The disadvantage is that only simple features of the existing devices can be used.

Another company that is building Internet-enabled devices is the Italian company Merloni Elettrodomestici.[4] Merloni sells the Margherita 2000, the first washing machine with an Internet connection. Every washing machine is accessible through the washing machine portal of Merloni.[5] The owners of the washing machines can log in to the site and check the current status of the machine or send commands to it (see Figure 3.2). The washing machines provide a web interface and an SMS interface to communicate with the mobile phone of the owner.

Although Merloni uses standard technologies, it is not easy to integrate this washing machine into a home automation network. Right now, it does not provide proper interfaces, just replicas of the front panel of the washing machine. The panel allows remote control of the device, but neither the display on the Web nor the SMS interface is standardized. Some integration will be required to support a home automation network, but because standard technologies are used, integration is more or less just a minor interfacing problem.

---

[4]http://www.merloni.it/
[5]http://www.margherita2000.com/

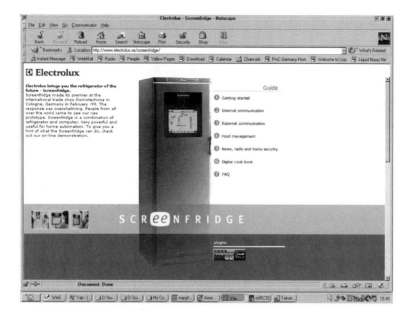

Figure 3.3. The Screenfridge Solution

Electrolux,[6] a Swedish company probably best known for its vacuum cleaners, has developed the Screenfridge,[7] an Internet refrigerator that manages a pantry, among other things (see Figure 3.3). It can e-mail a shopping list to a cybersupermarket and coordinate a convenient delivery time with the owner's schedule. At the time of this writing, Screenfridge was only a prototype. No release date has been announced.

The idea behind Screenfridge is that the fridge is considered to be one of the natural places for communication in every family. Many families post notes, display postcards, and attach other messages on the refrigerator door. Screenfridge supports not only Post-It notes (for which there is still a place) but also video-messaging between family members and online shopping, TV, and radio.

Screenfridge is a communication central where family members can communicate with each other by e-mail or video-mail. A touch of a button is all it takes to record a video message and post it to another family member. No traditional keyboard is attached to the fridge, but members of the family can use an on-screen virtual keyboard, similar to the virtual keyboards on PDAs. The screen is a touch screen that accepts all entries made by tapping the screen. Since video-mail is possible, however, only a few people are likely to use the text-mail option, anyway.

The virtual keyboard will probably be used more for traditional e-mail that can also be received and sent from the Screenfridge. Family members have

---

[6]http://www.electrolux.se/
[7]http://www.electrolux.se/screenfridge/

their own mailbox where both e-mail and video messages are stored. The Screenfridge creates a convenient environment, especially for people who are unfamiliar with e-mail programs, operating systems, and computers in general. The interfaces also allows the family members to surf the Web.

Screenfridge offers an additional set of features, called food management, that deals with storage (tips on storing food correctly), handling (ways to ensure safe procedures), and preparation (a cookbook with hundreds of recipes suitable for the food currently stored in the fridge). Users can even reorder needed food directly from the grocery store.

Screenfridge is also equipped with a TV and radio receiver so the home-owner can get rid of the bulky television set in the kitchen and watch the news on the refrigerator instead. The TV can be connected to a DVD player, to a surveillance camera that watches the garden, or to a baby-cam that looks after an infant in the crib.

Another company that has already introduced Internet connectivity into its products is Lavazza,[8] the world's largest maker of espresso machines. The Italian company has already manufactured more than 10,000 of their E-Espresso-point machines and shipped them to their largest distributors. This first generation can only send e-mail back to Lavazza to provide information about servicing and reordering of Espresso coffee. From this regular feedback, Lavazza can learn more about the use of the coffee machines and use the results to create machines that serve the coffee drinkers even better in the future. The next generation of espresso machine will not only contain feedback e-mail to Lavazza, but also a full Internet connection and a touch screen to allow users to go online. The idea was actually developed by E-Device,[9] a small startup company that worked with Lavazza.

South Korea is playing an important role in home automation. LG Electronics[10] presented a microwave at the Housewares Show[11] 2001 in Chicago, Illinois. The microwave, called Intello@chef, uses a modem and a touchscreen to connect to the Internet. This allows the consumer to download information about cooking and the use of the microwave. In addition, the system allows users to download upgrades to the operating system and application installed on the microwave. Applications in this case are recipes, cooking times, and microwave power control. LG Electronics plans to cooperate with big supermarkets to allow online ordering through the microwave.

As you can see from the numerous examples, many companies provide devices with Internet connectivity. But few provide interhome connectivity functionality. No one wants 30 devices with modems connecting to the Internet. Something has to change soon; otherwise, the technology will become unnecessarily complicated. We can also expect that some devices will provide a 56K

---

[8] http://www.lavazza.it/
[9] http://www.edevice.com/
[10] http://www.lge.com/
[11] http://www.housewareshow.com/

analog modem connection, others will provide ISDN, some will have asymmetric digital subscriber line (ADSL) connectivity. Other devices may connect through mobile connectivity to the Internet. This situation makes operation difficult and security problematic. Every device will have its own configuration and security standards.

Many other companies do not want to wait until a certain standard has been universally accepted. Smaller companies are trying to push their own open standards, for example, Echelon[12] with its Lonworks product. While most of the bigger companies are involved in standardization processes, smaller companies try to establish open standards to grow their market share. These open standards propose an Internet gateway device that connects all devices to the Internet through a single connection. This ensures that security can be implemented easily and that maintenance of the whole system is under control. Through an Internet gateway device, access to the different in-house devices can be restricted, for example.

On the other side, a number of companies are trying to establish standards that are device and company independent. Sun[13] with its Jini[14] technology is perhaps the best-known promoter of standardized technologies. Besides Sun, Hewlett-Packard, IBM, Lucent Technologies, and Microsoft are working on similar technologies that will enable home automation and the universal network in general. At the moment, each company follows its own strategy and technology. They are already defining and implementing interfaces to connect to the other technologies, however, knowing that a single technology will not create a universal network, neither in-house nor worldwide.

3.1.4 Basic Architecture

In most homes, five groups of electrical and electronic devices can be found; they are rather similar and can be added to a network to provide more convenience for the homeowner.

In the first installation of home automation networks, we will most likely see components and devices that already form a network or that are easy to connect to a network and have some sort of remote control. Lighting, for example, is already connected to the power circuit of the house and can be controlled through switches that are located wherever the homeowner wants to put them. The same applies to appliances and climate control devices that may be used in the house. These devices have additional logic to support the needs of the user and may have remote controls, timers, and sensors already built in.

If the house is already equipped with electronic security systems, such systems are most likely to become part of the home network. The alarm is already connected to the local police station, for example, and video cameras may be in

---

[12]http://www.echelon.com/

[13]http://www.sun.com/

[14]http://www.jini.org/

Components of a Home Network

In the first generation of home networks, we are most likely to see these five groups of electronic and electrical devices connected and forming a local home network:

- **Communication systems** – Telephone, intercom, and Internet

- **Data systems** – Computers and other data devices

- **Entertainment systems** – Audio, video, theater equipment located throughout the home

- **Lighting, appliances, and climate control** – The traditional home automation and control network

- **Security systems** – Traditional security components plus video monitoring, etc.

---

use to watch over the surroundings of the house. Most likely the video camera input will be redirected to a web site, allowing the homeowners to monitor their houses remotely. The alarm could be extended to send an SMS to the user's mobile phone, informing the user about irregular activity on the grounds.

Another networked environment in the house is the entertainment system. Digital radio, DVD player, television, and other pieces of equipment are connected to provide the ultimate experience. These components can be easily integrated into the home network and can be used as the control center for the home automation system, since they are based on a sophisticated hardware platform and allow input by remote control and output by speakers and the television, for example.

The traditional communication systems, such as telephones, intercom devices, and the connection to the Internet can be used by other devices as well, if connected, and can create a richer experience.

Existing laptops, desktop computers, PDAs, and calculators are already often connected in most homes by modems, hubs, or similar devices to each other and the Internet. To connect these devices to a home network is relatively easy; most of the devices have the necessary software installed and the sockets to allow the physical connection to a network.

For these devices to communicate with each other, they must connect either through a wire of some sort or a radio signal, the so-called wireless network.

Creating the Communications Infrastructure

Once all devices are network enabled, they need to exchange information and service. To do so they need some sort of communication platform. The following list shows the most common networking platforms for homeowners. Often, more than one is used to accommodate all the needs of the owner.

- **Phone lines** – Communication runs through the existing phone lines with outlets throughout the house.

- **Power-line** – Communications run through the existing electrical system with outlets throughout the house.

- **Structured wiring** – Modern wiring systems connect devices to networks.

- **Wireless** – New radio signal standards enable communication of all devices without wiring.

Different devices have different requirements for speed and volume of communication and different software and hardware components, so different types of media are required to connect the devices. Communication also depends on the application or service you are expecting from a certain device. A device that is moved around a wire connection is not really suitable.

The easiest and maybe cheapest way of wiring all devices together is to use existing phone lines. Most homes have several telephone outlets already in place. This wire is suitable for voice communications, data, and even entertainment networking with new technologies and applications developing swiftly. The advantage is that most networking software and hardware infrastructure devices can use phone lines to communicate.

Power-line technologies gain importance as they are increasingly used for Internet connections, promising high-speed access. Less known is that the same technology can be applied to in-house services. The home's traditional electrical system already connects lights and appliances and has outlets throughout the home. Until now, the electrical lines were limited as a network medium because of low speed and volume. Therefore, they are currently used for lighting and appliance networks and some security applications. New developments in technology are introducing communication and data to the power-line network. Nortel Networks,[15] for example, is running several tests throughout Europe and Northern America to make sure that the network components do not interfere with the devices. In the first run of tests, the frequencies of the network interfered with microwaves and other devices. As soon as data was sent through the network, the microwave switched on or the mobile phone was unreachable. The second and third round of tests were run on other frequencies to stop interference.

3.1.5   Home Automation Futures

New standards and technologies are evolving in wireless solutions: from the traditional lighting, appliance, and security networks to communication, data, and some entertainment systems. Radio frequencies are being dedicated to home networks. Today, DECT and IEEE 802.11 are probably the most common standards. DECT is about to phase out because it allows only transmission of 64 kbit/, which is not enough for a home network anymore. IEEE 802.11, which is described in detail later in this chapter, provides a bandwidth of 11 Mbit/s and is more suitable for home networks with a connection to the Internet.

New or renovated homes should use modern wiring systems to provide the capacity for current and future networks. A typical wiring system will include RG-6 (coaxial) wire for multiroom entertainment systems, CAT 5 wire for data and communications, and special wiring for speakers and home controls. Fiber optic cable is also being installed in some homes for future capacity. Very likely, wireless solutions will also be introduced into these homes for mobile devices. Either IEEE 802.11 or Bluetooth will be probably used.

Once the network is installed and the devices can talk to each other, we need a device that allows the home to communicate with the rest of the world so that the homeowner can reap the benefits of this electronic era. A solution, sometimes called "Residential Gateway," is just such a device; it ensures the secure connection of the home network with the Internet. A broadband connection to the Internet through this gateway will enable the control and observation of the home from a remote location and will also download entertainment and information to the home instantaneously. The gateway will probably be supplied and installed by the homeowner's telephone or cable company as an add-on service or perhaps by a systems integrator as a cabling hub. The gateway will require a firewall to protect the home from the outside.

Finally, home network needs an interface by which a homeowner communicates with and controls the network. Traditional networks use touch pads or remote control devices. The telephone is becoming another interface of choice, allowing both manual and voice control in some instances. Of course, the PC keyboard and mouse are also popular human interfaces. As technology advances, new interfaces are being developed, for example, a control screen included in the door of a refrigerator or intelligent light switches that not only switch a light on or off but also allow the exchange of information.

---

[15]http://www.nortel.com/

It becomes obvious from this discussion that the possibilities and permutations are endless when it comes to networking at home. If you want to create a networked home today, you will probably have several different networks using different media and languages to communicate internally and with each other. So far no standard home network technology is available. Homeowners must become involved in the design of their network, since each individual has different needs and wants.

3.2 Technologies

The following sections provide information about some of the most promising technology. Which technology will be used in the end cannot be said at the moment, but an overview of what can be done today will enable you to envision the home network of tomorrow.

3.2.1 HomeRF

HomeRF[16] is another wireless technology that is beginning to be used in homes. HomeRF differs from Bluetooth in that it was designed to solve a different problem than that targeted by Bluetooth. Whereas Bluetooth is a cable replacement, HomeRF is about getting midrange wireless technology for network use. Able to travel a distance of about 165 feet, HomeRF transmits at 2.4 GHz spectrum, putting it at the same operating frequency as Bluetooth. HomeRF is actually able to get 1.6 Mb/s out of the frequency, making it a bit faster than Bluetooth.

HomeRF has its origins in the 802.11 wireless Internet protocol and DECT voice technology, which means that HomeRF can not only transmit data packets but can also support up to four voice phones. By dynamically allocating bandwidth to voice transfers if necessary, HomeRF wirelessly solves not only computing communication but all forms of communication in general. The system works with one device acting as a control box, sending out signals to other HomeRF devices in the area. This control box can be any HomeRF device and will typically be the first device installed in a HomeRF network. The control can send out packets that wake up other devices from a low power state, making them ready for communication. This approach allows many devices to use HomeRF, even ones, such as Internet appliances, that will remain idle for the majority of the time. Most HomeRF devices will be laptops, desktops, printers, modems, and the like, forming a personal home network.

HomeRF has a range of 165 feet, so its developers knew that other devices outside of one Power Area Network may interfere with other PANs. Take an apartment building, for example. The vast majority of apartments will not span a sphere with a radius of 165 feet from a HomeRF source, meaning that

---

[16]http:/www.homerf.org/

HomeRF devices in one apartment could potentially interfere with another apartment's HomeRF system. To prevent this from happening, HomeRF incorporates a unique learn feature. Essentially, this feature teaches all existing and new HomeRF devices that the user defines the information for the user's PAN. It does this by setting one existing HomeRF device to the "teach" mode and a second, new, device to the "learn" mode. That way, devices within a given area can only communicate with the HomeRF devices that they have been taught, preventing conflicting PANs.

A few HomeRF-based devices already exist, such as the Intel AnyPoint wireless home network and the Motorola AL 200 Multi-User Wireless Modem. With HomeRF transmitter/receiver units running about $25 in parts and about the size of a compact flash card, HomeRF looks like it will be both cheap and small. The $25 mark still makes the device too expensive to be found in every laptop; however, look for system integration to come in higher-end laptops. In addition, some low-cost PC cards will be sold shortly, allowing HomeRF technology to extend to many devices.

One interesting thing is that HomeRF can withstand interference from none other than the microwave oven. The 2.4 GHz radio frequency range is very susceptible to interference from a microwave oven, which throws out a myriad of frequencies when it is operating. HomeRF deals with the interference by altering the frequency at which it transmits; that is, by hopping, which all but eliminates any data interference. In addition, each packet sent to a device on a HomeRF network must be acknowledged, so even if a packet is lost because of interference, the sending device knows this and resends the lost packet before proceeding.

3.2.2   IEEE 802.11 Wireless LAN

IEEE 802.11 is one of the most used wireless LAN network technologies on the market. The reason it is almost unknown is that every vendor sells it under a different title. Apple[17] has maybe the best-known brand for IEEE 802.11: AirPort. Lucent[18] calls the technology WaveLAN.[19] No matter the name, all devices based on IEEE 802.11 are compatible. This means that someone with an Apple iBook and the AirPort card can connect to a WaveLAN station, and vice versa. IEEE 802.11 is a noncellular network, unlike other standards such as the GSM mobile phone standard.

IEEE 802.11 is a wireless LAN technology offering a limited coverage for LAN users. Cell radius is usually from a few tens of meters to some hundred meters. The coverage area consists of small islands, and the purpose is certainly not to offer a large coverage network like GSM. The coverage area is often tailored according to the user's own need and can also be temporary.

---

[17]http://www.apple.com/
[18]http://www.lucent.com/
[19]http://www.wavelan.com/

The specification of wireless LAN outlines two possible modes of operations: client/server and ad hoc mode WLAN. In the client/server WLAN—often called an infrastructure configuration—terminals communicate with base stations or access points (AP), which form the coverage area. The APs are further connected to the wired network.

The coverage area of the client/server type WLAN network usually borders on a building or a campus and can therefore be comparable to a single GSM inside cell. The main difference between the GSM and WLAN technologies is that to cover the whole building with the WLAN technology, several access points are required, depending on the building architecture, wall materials, and so forth.

The specifications of WLAN also define an ad hoc mode. In this mode, mobile terminals themselves build the network. The coverage area is built with the help of wireless adapters and is limited. In the ad hoc mode, the whole network is seen as movable and is independent of any infrastructure, unlike GSM or the client/server type or WLAN. It is also isolated, because it has no interface to the wired network. WLAN supports only data communication and therefore can be seen as a potential alternative or an extension to the wired LAN.

The standardization process of IEEE 802.11 began from the need to connect wirelessly to the wired Ethernet-based data communications network and thus to offer mobility for the LAN users within a rather small area. One of the main advantages of WLAN is that it provides LAN users access to real-time information anywhere in their organization. Further, one aim was to reduce installation costs and thus achieve short- and long-term cost savings. Installing a wireless system can be fast, and the need to pull cable through walls and ceilings can be eliminated. Wireless technology also allows the network to go where the wire cannot go.

Specification of the standard IEEE 802.11 started in 1990 and was completed in 1997 by the Institute of Electrical and Electronics Engineers (IEEE).[20] The first phase of the standard IEEE 802.11 supports only 1 Mbit/s and 2 Mbit/s data rates. The first phase standard was followed by an extension IEEE 802.11b, which supports data rates up to 11 Mbit/s with the RF technology direct sequence spread spectrum. However, the user does not have to purchase a radio operator's license to use the frequency band 2.4–2.483 GHz, which is dedicated to WLAN use but is also known as an ISM band (band for industrial, scientific, and medical use). This means that anyone with access to a WLAN can buy and install an access point.

The noncellular WLAN does not require an infrastructure when using the ad hoc mode of operation. Thus, the complete system can be seen as movable.

The specifications of IEEE 802.11 define two layers: the Physical Layer (PHY) and the Media Access Control (MAC) layer. The PHY layer one specifies

---

[20]http://www.ieee.org/

the modulation scheme used and the signalling characteristics for the transmission through the radio frequencies; the MAC layer defines a way of accessing the physical layer. The specifications of the IEEE 802.11 layer two (MAC layer), also defines services related to the radio resource and mobility management.

The standard defines three different physical layer characteristics for a wireless LAN. One layer is based on infrared technology, the other two on RF transmission methods: direct sequence spread spectrum (DSSS) and frequency-hopping spread spectrum (FHSS). However, because of operation in an unlicensed RF band, the spread spectrum modulation must meet the requirements set by each country.

The chosen modulation techniques for the DSSS are differential binary and quadrature phase shift keying (DBPSK and DQPSK). However, the FHSS uses 2-4 level Gaussian frequency shift keying (GFSK) as the modulation schemes. Depending on the modulation scheme used, both DSSS and FSSS support data rates of 1 Mbit/s and 2 Mbit/s. As mentioned in Section 2.1.2, the data rates of 8 Mbit/s and 11 Mbit/s with the DSSS can be achieved with WLAN that supports the standard IEEE 802.11b. The operation frequency of both RF methods is 2.4 GHz.

For WLAN devices to be interoperable, they must have the same physical layer standard. Therefore, DSSS equipment cannot communicate with FHSS-based equipment.

A typical user of WLAN infrastructure mode might be a doctor seeing a patient, and then writing patient information directly to the patient register in the laptop. Other users might be students at universities or people participating in conferences who could use their laptops as a notebook. Ad hoc WLAN offers no access to the wired network; instead, stations can share files, which could be useful, for example, in conferences. These are indoor solutions, but the specifications do not preclude WLAN coverage from being built outdoors as well. Anyway, in cases like these, WLAN users do not need to move within the network to the extent they would move in a GSM network. Perhaps because WLAN does not support speech transmission and data service, users are not expected to move on a large scale. Thus, a typical WLAN user would be one who moves from location to location but uses the WLAN equipment only at a fixed location, so no complex mobility scenario is needed. Next, we briefly look at the basic services supporting mobility.

Association is a basic service that enables the connection between the station (STA) and the AP in an infrastructure WLAN. An AP is basically a radio BS that covers an area of about 30 to 300 meters, depending on the environment. An AP and its associated clients form a Basic Service Set (BSS). Though no handover mechanism is specified in the standard, the standard introduces a service called reassociation, which is related to the roaming from one BSS to another. Two adjoining BSS together form an Extended Service Set (ESS) if they share the same ESS identity (ESSID). This is the case when roaming is possible. Thus, the parameter ESSID is analogous to the concept of a neighboring cell in a GSM network.

An independent BSS (ad hoc mode, IBSS) is the most basic type of IEEE 802.11 WLAN. At the minimum, it consists of two stations. The network is often formed without preplanning and is alive until either station is moved away from the other's coverage area.

3.2.3 X10

Another (older) standard that has been adopted by many companies is X10. It is a communications protocol for the remote control of electrical devices, designed for communications between X10 transmitters and X10 receivers that communicate on standard household wiring. Transmitters and receivers generally plug into standard electrical outlets, although some must be hardwired into electrical boxes. Transmitters send commands such as "turn on," "turn off," or "dim" preceded by the identification of the receiver unit to be controlled. This broadcast goes out over the electrical wiring in a building. Each receiver is set to a certain unit ID and reacts only to commands addressed to it. Receivers ignore commands not addressed to them. Thus, a user can control all sorts of devices in a house without having to consider rewiring the house and need not buy new devices to support this standard.

The simplest X10 transmitter is a small control box with buttons. The buttons select which unit is to be controlled and which control function is to be sent to the selected units. There are also clock timer transmitters that can be programmed to send X10 commands at certain times. Some of these can be programmed with buttons on the timer; some must be connected to a computer to select the times. Other special-purpose transmitters send certain X10 commands at sunup or sundown, upon detecting movement, or as commanded by tones over a telephone.

The simplest X10 receiver is a small module with an electrical plug (to connect to a standard wall outlet), an electrical outlet (to provide controlled power to the device it's controlling) and two dials (to set the unit ID code) on it. An appliance module has a relay inside that switches power to its outlet on or off in response to X10 commands directed to it. A lamp module is similar but has a so-called triac element instead of a relay and will respond to dimming commands as well as on or off commands. Other receivers can be wired into wall outlets or into lamp fixtures.

X10 specifies a total of 256 different addresses: 16 unit codes (1–16) for each of 16 house codes (A-P). Normally, a transmitter is set to a certain house code (generally selectable by means of a dial) and so can control at most 16 unit codes. There is no restriction on using multiple transmitters each set to a different house code on the same wiring. Also, several receivers could be set to the same house code and unit code so a single command issued by an X10 transmitter could control multiple receivers in parallel.

Although one of the oldest and most used technologies in the United States, X10 is not very popular throughout the world, because it is tied to the power system in the United States, meaning that it works fine with 120 volts and 60 hertz. Converting devices to support other power systems is neither trivial nor cheap. It remains to be seen if X10 will succeed in the future.

3.3   Business and Home Automation

Although the home automation technology seems intriguing and useful, it is necessary to think about possible business cases for which it is a successful solution. Very few people buy technology just because they want to play with it. To be successful, a product must be rolled out to the mainstream. Therefore, a product or solution has to be cheap enough that everyone can afford it and must be easy to use. These two aspects are difficult to perfect, especially in the home environment, where there are still too many people with blinking clocks on their VCRs. Home automation products need to be invisible to be successful. Their functionality needs to be easily accessible without being vulnerable to configuration mishaps or software bugs. Anything based on a "standard operating system" will fail in the long run. Simple operating systems will operate most devices in the house; the less code used, the fewer bugs to worry about. A minimalistic approach in technology is required, with a lot of effort put into the user interface. Creative planning for affordability and ease of use will make the product successful.

Security and confidence are extremely important; it is generally accepted by everyone involved in the development of these devices that the added-value online services will be the driving force behind widespread adoption of the technology. To make widespread adoption easier, manufacturers hope that the way these appliance networking devices are sold will change. The model is mobile phones, which are cheap because service operators subsidize purchase of the phone to get a sufficiently large user base and volume production; the real money is made by providing the phone service.

This model has been successful with mobile phones; it will be used in other areas as well, and the home appliances market will be one of the first to embrace the concept. Supermarket chains are likely to subsidize the sale of high-tech fridges if they are directly connected to the online shop of the supermarket and enable the automatic reorder of food. A network-enabled washing machine might be subsidized by a service from a soap powder company, which uses a bar code reader to determine the best configuration of the washing machine for the clothes that have been loaded into the machine. The real opportunities, both for the consumer and the manufacturer, will come when companies start launching associated online services or dedicated device portals.

3.3.1   Home Automation Applications

Many applications are possible with home automation, and we have already seen quite a few throughout the chapter. To make home automation interesting for homeowners, it needs to become much easier. A new device should autoconfigure itself once it is switched on at home. Video recorders are slowly being enabled to do so. You switch them on, and they try to obtain the channel program from the television set. This works only if the television set and the VCR are of the same make, since every company uses its own proprietary technology.

To make home automation useful, industries must introduce infrastructure applications that enable the free exchange of information between all devices within the boundaries of a house. This requirement poses the first problem. What are the boundaries, which walls or which fence? One of the first applications, therefore, should define these boundaries through an easy-to-use interface so that it is easy to recognize devices that belong to the same home. With a login/password procedure, only authorized devices are connected to the local network; otherwise, people could walk into the house and steal information from the home network.

The first applications of the home network will be the connection of the various devices to the Internet. According to surveys, the main reason to build a home network is to share Internet access, whether through a conventional dial-up modem or, increasingly, through a high-speed cable or digital subscriber line (DSL) modem. A network enables two or more computers to share the high-speed connection at the same time, so family members don't have to take turns. Once the computers have been connected, other devices will follow. A family can read e-mail from any device in the house.

The second most common reason to build a network, the surveys found, is to enable two or more family members to play multiplayer games together instead of one family member playing against the computer. Playing games, by the way, is the second-fastest-growing use of computers, after surfing the Internet. If family members are not available, a player can select a friend over the Internet to play with.

The next step will be that all devices can download software updates and device-related information from the Internet. With the device-related information, knowledge can be created within the device. At the same time, we will see more devices communicate with their environment.

3.3.2   Techniques for Home Automation Profitability

Home networks will become much more interesting and complex in the next few years with the growing deployment of new digital devices like television set-top boxes, smart telephones, and wireless Web pads that connect to the Internet through radio waves. The trend will accelerate as consumers begin buying digital entertainment—like music, videos, and books—over the Net. This is downloaded on one device, probably a powerful PC acting as the household's Internet gateway, and the files are then transferred to another device that can handle them better. That device might be a stereo with a better speaker system, a television with a larger screen, or some sort of specialized digital device, like an e-book that can be carried to the comfortable couch in the living room. In the short term, money will be made by selling high-tech devices. Service providers will have a difficult time in the beginning. A hype phase initiated by the hardware manufactures will be followed by a short depression phase that will mainly eliminate the unsuccessful service providers. After the depression phase, everyone will know about home networks (either through good or bad press) and the market will stabilize to enable the creation of successful home automation service providers.

To make money with home automation services, providers must check the paradigm of the intelligent house. Most people spend more than two-thirds of their time in their house or apartment. To understand the value of the business case is to understand which technology is superfluous. Superfluous technology can generate money in the short run, but it is highly likely to be replaced very soon with something different. Providers must question whether it makes sense to control the washing machine from the refrigerator. People are not willing to spend money on things that make life more complicated without any additional benefit. Automatic reordering of food by the fridge is also a questionable benefit, since it removes the social component of shopping. Maybe the first step would be to hand out mobile devices to all shoppers to make shopping more efficient. The device could locate food in the shop and provide the shopper with additional information on discounts and special promotions.

To make life easy, usage must be easy and useful and installation must be simple. Because few people want more cables on which to stumble, local area home networks should not require additional cables. In most cases they can use existing infrastructure, for example, to exchange information through a wireless LAN, or they can use power plugs to connect to each other. As long as no single standard has been established, people will be reluctant to buy new television sets or central heating devices, since the interfaces may not be compatible in the future. The installation of new software needs to be managed centrally in a transparent and simple way.

To be innovative, let your creative developers design new appliances, but always get feedback from your customers and let other people involved in house building, such as plumbers and architects, discuss the need and the usefulness of the proposed designs. To make the "intelligent house" work, you need an economy, an ecology, and an ethos of the home automation network.

Chapter 4

Technologies of the Future

Pervasive computing is slowly becoming reality. The concepts have been available for several years, and the companies who drive the Web are recognizing the value of an extended Internet: a universal network. Some companies already fear the end of personal computer-based computing. That won't happen, but the growth rates will drop. Not everyone wants to have a personal computer with Windows or MacOS sitting on their desktop. In many cases, people would like to have access to the Internet through their mobile phones or their TV sets. The Nokia Communicator[1] offers web access, e-mail, and file transfer. Many companies have started to provide access to the Internet through set-top boxes, allowing users to view web content on the television screen and write and send e-mail without having to know what a device driver or a dynamic-link library (DLL) is. These Internet appliances have been around for quite a while, but basically they just take the functionality of a PC into another device.

4.1 Internet Services

Pervasive computing goes a step further. It replicates the standard functionality of the Web into embedded devices and offers services provided by the device to other entities on the Internet. The idea is to reap the benefits of ever-broader networks without having to deal with obtuse, unwieldy technology. The first generation of embedded devices were passive, meaning that they relayed existing services to other devices, such as the TV. The second generation of embedded devices is more intelligent and looks for services on the Internet, collects them, and bundles them into a metaservice.

4.1.1 Enabling Technologies

Today, companies are forced to build their entire offering virtually from scratch. Online businesses provide all services required for the complete solution; they are not able to outsource parts of it. Amazon.com,[2] for example, sells books to

---

[1]http://www.nokia.com/
[2]http://www.amazon.com/

its customers. All services required for selling books have been implemented by Amazon.com and are maintained by them, making the web site proprietary, massive, and costly.

Inventory management, distribution, billing, and web store management are all services required by most online retailers to implement the service of selling goods on the Internet. Although not part of the retailers' core business, these services need to be implemented, maintained, and operated by the on-line retailer. Next-generation online retailers will be able to outsource these services to inventory management, billing, distribution, and web store management solution providers, which can provide the services at a lower price and a better quality.

To make the outsourcing of services feasible on the Internet, every service needs to be able to communicate with the other. The concept of service is, on this level, rather abstract. The service of billing can be further divided into several simpler services. One will be physical printing of the bill. The bill is printed on the local printer of the retailer and then sent to the customer. The bill could be printed at a local billing office, to reduce the costs of shipment. If the printers of the customer have a direct web connection, the bill could be printed at the customer site, to eliminate shipping costs for the billing company. Additional costs could be reduced even further if the bill is entered directly into the ERP system of the company and paid automatically.

To make this new paradigm work quickly and efficiently, service providers must integrate all levels of service. The Internet enabled the communication between different services and HTML/XML enabled data exchange between different services. Nevertheless, a new layer needed to be added on top of these layers to enable services to accept other services to connect and create new metaservices or simply broadcast the availability to the network.

As today's networking capabilities are too cumbersome or limited for the next generation of applications that are about to appear, several companies have created technologies that connect everything from light switches to super-computers in one ubiquitous network. The race is on to create the standard for the next generation of the Internet and, as often happens with high-technology efforts in their infancy, companies will compete to establish their own vision of the universal network.

Sun and its Jini technology are probably the best-known promoters of the universal network or pervasive computing vision. But many other well-known companies have started to create similar technologies and have incorporated the idea of the universal network into their corporate vision. Hewlett-Packard, IBM, Lucent Technologies, and Microsoft also have technologies and paradigms to take their customers to the next level of computing: pervasive computing.

This chapter gives an overview of the available technologies and the visions of the companies behind the technology. The race has just started and it is impossible to say who will win in the end.

The technologies are part of the corporate vision or company strategy, so we cannot expect them to spread rapidly throughout the world. The tactical goal of these new technologies is, in most cases, to make the companies developing the software and architecture appear as innovative as possible and to drive sales of more traditional products such as operating systems, servers, and printers. The strategic goal will change many things in the long term, though.

Companies that use these technologies can reduce time-to-market significantly and reduce costs as well. This allows them to be more mobile, flexible, and modular and to react more quickly and precisely to changes in the market. These modular services can be used by anyone connected to the Internet. People and companies can take several modular services and form a new service or add their own components to the service to make it more valuable. Every company becomes a user and provider of services on the Internet.

4.1.2 Business Opportunities

The new paradigm of Internet services allows businesses and consumers to use the Internet as a cost-effective access to a wide range of high-quality, dependable services. Areas of services will include traditional Internet services such as financial management, procurement, marketing, travel, and data storage but will also create new digital services, such as partner collaboration services and health care monitoring.

The advantages for businesses using these services means that the time-to-market is increased, costs are decreased, and market changes are easier to adapt to. These advantages also mean a growing opportunity for businesses to become Internet service providers (ISPs) themselves. Software suppliers, for example, have already started to make their products available on a usage basis over the Internet, rather than through the traditional software licensing model.

Pervasive computing will take the Internet far beyond the one-way Web to a rich, collaborative, interactive environment. Pervasive computing will harness a constellation of applications, services, and devices to create a personalized digital experience. It constantly and automatically adapts itself to personal needs and those of family, home, and business. It means a whole new generation of software that will work as an integrated service to help people manage their lives and work in the Internet Age.

Consumers will experience the simplicity of integrated services: unified browsing, editing, and authoring; access to all their files, work, and media on-line and off; a holistic experience across devices; personalization everywhere; and zero management. It means, for example, that any change to your information, no matter if you used your computer, your mobile phone or your television, will instantly and automatically be available everywhere that information is needed.

Knowledge workers and businesses will benefit from unified browsing platform, editing, and authoring; rich coordinated communication; a seamless mobile experience; and powerful information-management and e-commerce tools that will transparently move between internal and Internet-based services and support a new era of dynamic trading relationships.

Independent software developers will have the opportunity to create advanced services for the Internet Age—services that are able to automatically access and leverage information either locally or remotely, working with any device or language, without service providers having to rewrite code for each environment. Everything on the Internet becomes a potential building block for this new generation of services, while every application can be exposed as a service on the Internet.

4.1.3   Internet Services Standards

To make Internet services just as successful as the World Wide Web, it is necessary to create standards that are just as widespread and accepted as HTML. The standards include protocols and APIs for accessing and deploying services on the Internet that need to be added to these content-oriented Internet standards.

The standards must support the core functions of electronic services, such as the description and virtualization of the Internet services. On the Web, catalogs, icons, files, and entire web pages represent actual products, databases, or organizations. The creation of virtual representations of web objects is proliferating rapidly, yet there is no standard means of creating virtual representations. Many of the methods are homegrown or less than functional. A component that virtualizes web objects lies at the center of many current and new commerce, content, and collaborative services.

Internet services must support tracking and monitoring. This functionality is crucial to the commercial viability of Internet-based services and must be built into the core components to allow a quick deployment of intelligent web services. Results can be observed easily, and the quality of service can be guaranteed by adjustments to the usage of the service and changes in business and technology.

The third important point that needs to be provided by the core functionality of an electronic service standard is secure and private service. A core Internet services platform must support building blocks for rapid security and for privacy-enabling the service.

These core functions provide the Internet service engine that are required to operate a service on the Internet. They support and integrate with the services and embed core capabilities within the services themselves. It is, for example, possible to create services directories that allow users to track activities, virtualize objects, and identify service components, access types, and participants. By monitoring and adjusting QoS, service providers guarantee SLAs. Another important feature that becomes available instantly is billing. It supports secure transactions and authentication of the participants. Giving service customers and service providers tools for the interaction enables them to negotiate SLAs and transactions. Access can be virtualized and service delivered.

Virtualization means that a service, such as a file, that you want to be visible to certain people gets a virtual name on the computer of every person who is allowed to view it. The source name and target name are therefore different, making it possible to move the original location of the file without changing the file name at the destination or even notifying users about the change.

4.1.4   The Migration of Applications to the Web

The first step in pervasive computing has already taken place as more and more services and applications are available on the Web. Popular services like online e-mail and calendar services will soon be a standard web offering. Any device that contains a web browser can then access these services. For example, e-mail will be accessible anywhere from a cell phone, a handheld computer, a notebook, or a desktop computer.

The problem is that not all files are on the Web right now. A text written in StarOffice, for example, is usually saved in most cases on a local hard disk and is not available from other computers or embedded devices. If applications such as word processors were moved to the Web, files could easily be saved on an Internet web server so that customers could access their data from any Internet-enabled device.

Moving a word processor to the Web is no trivial task, so companies are looking for other ways to access documents through one of the web interfaces. fusionOne,[3] for example, has built an Internet-based technology that recognizes and updates information across a personal network of unrelated devices of different sizes and platforms. A traveler using an Internet-connected kiosk, for instance, could call up fusionOne's site and access documents residing in that personal network.

fusionOne has developed software, called Internet Sync, that enables customers to specify which files they want to access on their personal network and seamlessly synchronizes the digital information. Internet Sync enables customers to access the most recent updates to almost any file on their own personal hard drive back at the office, including word processing documents, spreadsheets, MP3 music files, browser cookies, and calendar and contact information. Content, but not aplications, can be moved to any device the customer is using at the moment.

Sharing files over the network is fine, but it does not help to have a certain image file if the device you are using cannot display or change the image. Pushing applications to the screen of any device will require changing the paradigm of programming to allow automatic detection of the capabilities of embedded devices. A framework for programming applications for different devices needs to be established as a standard to allow the creation of such an application without additional overhead for the programmer.

---

[3]http://www.fusionone.com/

4.1.5 Open Internet Services

By using open standards, businesses can offer their Internet-based services to as many people as possible. At the same time, the single service can be combined to work with other services to create an even more valuable service. Services providers will also benefit from the lower costs of standards-based products.

In the past, there have been no clear standards on how to provide the core functionality for Internet services. Putting an additional layer on top of traditional standards such as HTML will not help the effectiveness of the proposed services and will make them dependent on these other standards. The new standards should propose a way to provide basic features without requiring intensive technology engineering, to shield the user from the pain of learning proprietary solutions.

Although the Internet and Web are clearly based on layered protocols, the profusion of nonstandard technology and engineering to adapt proprietary solutions to generic usability are all-too-familiar themes to the computer industry. The Web's accelerated growth and continued success continues to be an opportunity to change industry patterns. In fact, the rapid pace of adoption often rules out time to architect the complex solutions of the past. New services have to be deployed instantaneously. They must be done with the assurance that core functions will be in place to support them.

With deployment of a standards-based Internet service solution, customers will experience a more valuable and more personalized service and businesses will be able to provide more efficient and mission-critical services to their customers without the overhead of complex technologies. Service providers can create new services much faster when core functionality is already provided. These new standards will drive more traffic to the electronic services, as more people are able to use and find services and will allow faster, lower-cost deployment of value-added services with or without partners.

This is the ultimate goal of pervasive computing: making service the prime directive on the Internet while reaching out for devices not yet connected to the Internet. Several companies have started to build technologies and visions to reach this goal; the rest of this chapter describes which companies have done what and how they have implemented it.

4.2 Programming Models

To allow any types of devices to communicate with each other, developers must create a whole new environment. Part of this environment is a new programming paradigm that allows all these devices to share information and services. In this section, we look at some of the most important issues around pervasive or nomadic programming.

There are a number of ways to connect devices, but depending on what is to be done with the devices, different approaches should be taken. First, it is important to find out whether a device is to display information only or whether it is part of the service chain, meaning that it also provides services to other devices and humans. Another important factor to determine is whether a device is connected constantly to a network or whether it is connected only as necessary. If the latter is true, the device needs to contain some memory to review cached data. Information display is therefore one of the first problems that must be resolved. Most devices do not provide a 1024 × 768 resolution as most computers provide today. To display the information correctly, it is therefore necessary to create a device-independent data model that can serve all existing and future devices. Such a model would support current devices, as well as all older models with limited display capabilities. Therefore the user need not buy the latest version of all devices but can use adapters for older devices to view the same content. This device-independent model requires an intelligent, render-device-oriented translation mechanism, called transcoding, to provide the optimal output for all devices.

The problem is simple to express but difficult to resolve. In the past, most applications were written for a certain target system and nobody cared about running them on other systems. But in the world of pervasive computing, all business-processing systems should be as deployment transparent as possible. If the consumer accesses a system through a connected computer or a web browser with high resolution and rich color, we want to take advantage of that. Conversely, if access to the systems is through a voice recognition system or a palm-computing device, the service should take advantage of the strengths of that device. The most important feature is therefore to provide transparency of access to computing systems. Today, most companies understand that a web presence is not enough for survival in the digital jungle. Many companies have started to provide WAP access to their services and a call center. These additional channels to their service have been costly. In the future, based on a new application paradigm, this cost can be reduced greatly.

One of the easiest ways of achieving this level of presentation independence is the use of XML, XSL (Extensible Stylesheet Language), and HTML/DHTML (dynamic HTML). This type of independence would move the presentational elements to the client device, with the more advanced mechanisms providing a level of client-side edit checking and list selection. The various client-side rendering technologies would handle presentation and simple edit checking. The service provider would not be responsible for the rendering of newer devices that support content-rendering and could focus on providing a rendering engine for older devices that need to part of the service chain.

One can use DHTML to define a presentation layout that rivals that of traditional client/server computing and have it all execute within a browser frame. If our pervasive device is capable of this type of rendering and processing, this is a powerful way of extending application functionality to the focused device.

Many DHTML-aware devices allow users to work offline, drawing content from the browser's page cache. This would allow a limited form of roaming with the portable device, which, though imperfect, is the first step to a pervasive environment.

A rich component specification will help a lot in this scenario. It could provide input to a transcoding engine for use as a template in defining the source material. By using advanced Unified Modeling Language (UML) concepts to model the specifications, one can export those specifications through one of the XML-based UML schema expressions, such as XMI.

With that approach, the component specification can be converted into a machine-readable format. This conversion allows the transcoding engine (transcoder) to understand the format and the behavior of the interfaces and their operations. If a device executes operations of a given interface only and views the results, there is little additional work to do.

If the portable device is better served by the implementation of more involved processes, then script code can be written to execute on the application or web server(s) to facilitate the collaboration of multiple operations or components, with the results provided to the transcoding engine in an expressive fashion.

Previous programming models have focused on a single system, even attempting to mask interactions with other systems to look like local interactions. Pervasive computing technologies need to be explicitly designed to allow the integration or orchestration of any group of resources on the Internet into a single solution. With today's technologies, this type of integration is extremely complex and costly. New programming models will have to make all software development intrinsic.

4.2.1 Manufactured Component Objects

As most devices will not be permanently online, a more powerful programming model is required. This means that bandwidth and connections are reduced to a minimum and the device becomes network transient. The user can then roam freely, meaning that the user is not restricted by wires or certain mobility providers anymore. To support free roaming, a richly specified component-based solution becomes an especially powerful ally.

Component-based development requires a formal separation of specification and implementation. If that separation can be achieved, a device using a certain component can use any implementation of a component because all implementations adhering to the given specification are feature-compatible with each other. The user can go anywhere in the world and access the same services.

A system designed to execute with one set of topological constraints, such as a traditional client/server system, could be rehosted to different devices with minimal impact on the overall system. Likewise, given a component with multiple implementations, each implementation could provide the same output given the same set of input conditions. The key point of contention with all of this is the location of the persistent data used to disconnect the life cycle of a given component object—an instance of a component—from the life cycle of an application's execution. The persistence issue must be solved to restore the node independence we require in nomadic computing.

The basic premise of the architectural pattern is that one component object—referenced by a number of different consumers—is responsible for the manufacturing and management of many individual component objects that are of interest to consumers. More importantly, the architectural component object manages the persistence of the overall collection of component objects, while the manufactured component objects manage the processing of business rules against their individually encapsulated state value. This sharing of responsibility ensures that the node responsible for management of state may be different from the node(s) responsible for enactment of business rules. The prudent application of a pattern or two means our portable devices are once again free to roam.

4.2.2 Design Advice for Developers

Introduce component-based development guidelines and apply them to pervasive computing so that the programming model separates the "process" from the "persistence." If you want to review these types of component dependencies, have a look at the UML specification and how it is implemented in the modeling tools, such as Rational Rose.

To create a good pervasive computing service, concentrate on defining behavioral interfaces that achieve business goals, independent of the persistence. Do not assume that each boundary represents a disparate node; instead, initially view the separation as a delineation of roles.

More importantly, look to fully resolve one or more business goals in a consistent package. Ensure that there is a single interface, factored to one or more components, capable of satisfying the needs of each use case identified during analysis. Although consistency is difficult to achieve, it can still be helpful when you are designing interfaces. This single goal will ensure that your business components are both detached from the persistence issues and supportive of the resolution of business, and not technical, goals. You may be concerned that implementing this type of architecture may cause performance problems. Keep in mind that network performance and computing capacity will continue to increase, while application design lasts for the life of the application. What may seem like a potential performance problem today will seem trivial in 18 months. But in a truly nomadic network, you don't know what type of devices will connect to your services. As you can guarantee neither bandwidth nor computing power in a distributed network, do not rely on these variables. Expect the worst and do your best.

4.2.3   Basic Building Blocks

By providing prefabricated components, developers can focus fewer resources on where or how an application runs and more on what it does, especially on the part that really adds value. Today developers spend more than 50 percent of their time on things that are related to the application they want to do, not on the core functionality itself. By using components, developers can address some of the biggest challenges they face today: the tradeoffs between functionality and manageability. Component use allows, for example, application hosting on a higher level, enabling the integration of hosted applications with other applications, whether hosted or not. It also makes it easier to customize applications and tailor them to the needs of the single user. Standard interfaces make it also easier to increase and enhance functionality and enable users to run applications both online and offline.

With a set of basic building blocks, developers can leverage and customize services in their own applications and services, reducing the effort required to create compelling products. These services need not necessarily be available in source code form for the developers; they could be rented or leased from service providers that develop and operate these basic services.

Some of the most important building blocks are the following: identification, notification, personalization, directory, unification, and availability.

Identification

Customizing a service to a specific user requires strong authentication and authorization of the user. This means that before using any service in the pervasive computing world, the user or a service needs to identify herself or itself. This can be done through simple login/password procedures, using one-time passwords or smartcards and biometric devices. The identification service should work on two levels: the identification itself and the interface between the device and the user of the service. Devices will have different ways of offering identification services. The television may go for an eye scan, the mobile phone for finger prints, and a kiosk for smartcards. This requires a good back-end database that offers all the required information to match against. These databases should be controlled by the government or a trusted third party. A service requiring identification should not need to have the complete database available. It should pass on the credentials to the identification service and receive only the required data back. By offering identification services, devices provide not only personalization but also privacy for their customers.

Notification

Notification works on several levels and with several objectives. It allows users to exchange messages over a network. Users will be notified of any communication as soon as it arrives at a certain device and the user is logged on. Any type of messaging can therefore be integrated. If you use, for example, a device with a text display, you should be able to convert an audio message into text.

On another level, notification can inform devices about automatic upgrades of their software and increased functionality of other devices connected to the same network, without user installation or configuration. Pervasive computing technologies proactively adapt to what users want to do on any of their devices. This inversion of the traditional installation-dependent application model is a necessity in a world where users will enjoy the benefits of services on multiple devices.

Personalization

Once a customer has been identified, personalization plays a big role. It allows the device to create rules and preferences that implicitly and explicitly define how notifications and messages should be handled, how requests to share data should be treated, and how multiple devices should be coordinated (e.g., always synchronize my laptop computer with the full contents of my storage service). It also provides a personal profile of what users like and dislike.

Directory

The service directory includes all available services on a local network and interfaces into other directories on the Internet and other local networks. Thus, users can find services and people with which to interact. These directories are more than search engines or Yellow Pages. They can interact programmatically with services to answer specific schema-based questions about the capabilities of those services. They can also be aggregated and customized by other services and combined with them.

Unification

Unification of information can only be achieved if the pervasive computing architecture foresees a universal language and protocol that describes the meaning of a particular piece of information. That universality enables data to maintain its integrity when being transmitted and handled by multiple services and users. The result is that services can interact and exchange and leverage each other's data. This also means that the pervasive computing platform needs to provide a unique and central storage for user-related information to maintain a correct set of data. Each of the devices can access this storage, optimally replicating data for efficiency and offline use. Other services can access the unique storage with the user's consent. Once data has been replicated for offline use, it should not be modifiable through a different device; to maintain data integrity, all other devices can only read the information and must wait for that particular device to upload the information again.

Availability

Availability information about a certain user can be stored in a calendar and accessed through different services, depending on the needs. This feature becomes especially important as people use more devices more of the time and as users and services interact more richly. The pervasive computing platform needs to provide the basis for securely and privately integrating a user's work, social, and home calendars so that they are accessible to all of the user's devices and, with consent, to other services and individuals.

These basic distributed services need to be available both online and off. A service can be invoked on a stand-alone machine not connected to the Internet, provided by a local server running inside a company, or accessed through the Internet. Different instances should be able to cooperate and exchange information, so organizations can run their own infrastructure or host it externally without compromising their control or access to services across the Internet or when not connected to the Internet. So, for example, a corporate directory service can associate with a service in the Internet cloud.

Today, only two companies offer the full set of basic functionalities that are required to set up a complete pervasive computing infrastructure: Hewlett-Packard and Microsoft. We examine their offerings later in this chapter. If their infrastructures are truly pervasive, they will also work with each other. I have my doubts regarding the Microsoft offering since it runs only on Windows, but if implemented in an open architecture, it could run as part of the E-Services initiative by Hewlett-Packard.

Sun and IBM are ramping up their offerings to match those of Hewlett-Packard and Microsoft, so we will see a fierce competition in the future. Someday, we might use Sun's directory service, Hewlett-Packard's infrastructure, IBM's personalization and identification features, and Microsoft's calendar, for example. But this would require all companies working together to make sure that the components are based on the same architectural design.

4.2.4 The Future

The move to pervasive computing, together with the convergence of digital technologies into devices of ever-changing form, will become predominantly important over the next few years. A shift in programming paradigms is necessary to support these new needs, and a new architecture that is free of today's limiting factors is needed to support the new business models and technological advances.

This does not mean that current investments are a waste of money, but that a shift will happen very soon. What we see today as foundation blocks of a given service solution will become in the near future building blocks for a new foundation to support any type of pervasive computing. New adapters will be required to support the translation of information and services to the new device-driven network, but most of the current Internet will be included in future offerings. The new foundation layer will ensure that the applications we build today are ready to support the topologies of tomorrow.

The components model enables use of different devices no matter where users are and what type of devices they are using. Pervasive components enable the building of services that meet the needs of users rather than requiring users to serve the services. There is bright future out there if programmers and solution architects adapt to these new paradigms.

4.3   Device-to-Device Communication

A set of technologies has been introduced to allow devices to communicate with each other. These technologies connect devices to an existing network, such as the Internet, and set up LANs for the exchange of information and services, for example in an office or at home.

This is the lowest layer in the pervasive computing technology architecture. It defines how communication is established, how information is transported and how a connection is terminated. It does not specify how the information needs to be structured or what a service is. Jini, ChaiServer, Inferno, and Universal Plug and Play are technologies that have been developed respectively by Sun, Hewlett-Packard, Lucent Technologies, and Microsoft. Bluetooth is a new company-independent standard that allows the ad hoc creation of WLANs.

4.3.1   ChaiServer

Hewlett-Packard contended the implementation of Sun's Java for embedded devices. The reason was that embedded devices have different requirements and that Sun's Java implementation does not take this into account. Embedded devices can be simple, for example, a palmtop that requires only minimal or no administration, or more complex, for example, a printer that requires administrative and management features.

Chai, the name of Hewlett-Packard's implementation of the Java virtual machine, means "tea" in many languages, such as Russian, Czech, Turkish, and Hindi, and "life" in Hebrew. Since tea is one of the most popular drinks throughout the world, Hewlett-Packard decided to call its virtual machine (VM) and embedded technologies family of products Chai to convey the notion of a world where virtually every device, process, or service is improved (that is, given life) just by virtue of being empowered by Chai. Another reason for calling the product Chai is the connection to Java, an informal name for coffee. With Chai, these devices, processes, or services can combine measurement, computing, and communications capabilities to attain a new level of local sophistication and intelligent interoperability.

Unlike Sun's embedded Java virtual machine (JVM), ChaiVM accounts for the differences in embedded devices and enables manufacturers of embedded devices to get the most out of the hardware. The ChaiServer[4] adds new functionality to the ChaiVM by extending it to allow web-based connections to other devices on the network. The connectivity is implemented with existing Internet protocols and technology standards and extends the capabilities of the embedded devices. ChaiServer has a scalable architecture that allows appliance designers to install only those portions that are required by the appliance. It provides a scalable, compact, robust web server with a very small read-only memory (ROM) footprint, ranging from about 200–400K, making ChaiServer perfect for embedded applications with footprint constraints.

The ChaiServer creates information appliances that can manage appliances and devices remotely through the World Wide Web. The appliance can download and run new diagnostic routines in devices remotely and receive notification of events in the devices and take action on them. The embedded devices can upgrade software dynamically in the devices with new releases.

Adding the ChaiServer to embedded devices adds capabilities to a device with little additional cost, since most of the existing infrastructure and software can be retained. Every device can have its own web pages that may contain information on the functionality of the device or that could securely manage and administer the device through a set of dynamic web pages.

ChaiServer also provides an execution environment that allows users to update the appliance with platform-independent, dynamically loadable, plug-in objects called Chailets. A Chailet is an HP ChaiServer object written in the Java programming language. It performs functions ranging from creation of a home page to complex operations (such as diagnostics, measurements, or computations) based on input from remote devices. Chailets implement one or more methods that may perform some computations and then send information to, and retrieve it from, a host. A Chailet communicates with other network entities, using protocols like HTTP, SMTP (electronic mail), or through the ChaiServer Notifier Chailet. Chailets can be loaded at runtime with the Loader, and they can interact with the host device(s) through the I/O interface. Chailets have their own Uniform Resource Locator (URL) with which they can be directly accessed on the Internet by any web browser. Chailets can also include native code using standard Java Native Interfaces (JNIs). Chailets require the ChaiServer in order to run, which in turn runs on any Java-enabled platform ranging from a small embedded device to a large UNIX server.

Some of the main features of ChaiServer are the support for HTTP 1.1 (ChaiWeb is an HTTP daemon that enables a web browser to access the functionality of Chailets), the installation, update, and loading of remote Chailets, and event notification and propagation. Chailets can be used to generate dynamic web pages.

---

[4]http://www.chai.hp.com/

4.3.2 Inferno

Inferno,[5] developed by Lucent Technologies,[6] is one of the oldest technologies available. The first version of Inferno appeared in March 1997. The technology consists of a small-footprint operating system that can connect to networks or run programs within a virtual machine. It was designed with smart phones, Internet appliances, or set-top boxes, and it supports programs written in two languages: Limbo, developed by Lucent technologies, which translates Java applications on-the-fly, and PersonalJava, the stripped-down version of Java, developed by Sun for embedded devices.

Inferno can run directly on hardware platforms or can be hosted on standard operating systems such as Windows NT and Linux. It is a distributed architecture-independent network operating system that models all available resources as files. The virtual machine hides the differences in hardware, and the name spaces are personalizable. Security is one of the strengths of the Inferno architecture. Built-in security mechanisms enable encrypted communication between the devices and Limbo, making Inferno a good solution for enabling particular applications in the universal network. Inferno has been developed for the telecom world and is not a general solution for the converging universe of computers and information appliances. For the telecom world, it offers one of the best solutions by providing a common API, which enables the exchange of information and services.

The idea of treating all resources in a universal network as files may make it easier for users to access them but does require quite a lot of overhead and makes it difficult to exploit all the features of the single resource. Inferno is a good native operating system for embedded devices and network appliances. To make Inferno a full-blown implementation of a pervasive computing framework, Lucent must add, for example, dynamic extensibility, scalable lookup and brokerage services, identity through attribute descriptions, and an inter-machine trust and interaction model.

Another problem with Inferno is that almost nobody knows about it. Although the technology is well-designed and works very well in its niche markets, Lucent has spent no time marketing the solution. Inferno fits well into today's view of things but lacks the vision for the future of the Internet. It enables embedded devices to participate in a network without allowing other services or applications to exploit the resources of these embedded devices.

Lucent has three target sectors for its Inferno technology: the network element manufacturers (such as Cisco[7]), the consumer electronics manufacturers (such as Philips[8]), and network service providers. Inferno allows these sectors to introduce a wide array of new devices and new customer-focused

---

[5]http://www.lucent-inferno.com/

[6]http://www.lucent.com/

[7]http://www.cisco.com/

[8]http://www.philips.com/

service offerings. Inferno-based services could increase customer satisfaction and strengthen customer loyalty. The Inferno system is backed by a complete infrastructure that supports highly interactive applications. Lucent has developed scenarios for sending and receiving e-mail on mobile phones or receiving pay-per-view films over a set-top box that can be connected to any type of network.

Lucent has introduced a new firewall concept, based on Inferno technology, that allows network devices to talk to the firewall software on a server, making it easier to detect intruders and prevent attacks. Philips introduced the first Inferno-enabled mobile phone, the IS-2630, which connects to the Internet. Intel and UMEC[9] have also announced reference designs for a web phone, a telephone with a web browser and e-mail program built in.

The advantage of Inferno is its maturity. Lucent has released version 2.3 of the Inferno software package, making it a stable solution. It runs on most personal computer operating systems, making it easy to develop applications for; every developer receives a CD-ROM with a reference manual and many examples, so it is easy to build new services. The downside of Inferno is that the software and the CD are not free. Within the three target markets Lucent has a long list of well-known partners, which will help to guarantee the success of the product. Another factor, which will help to bring Inferno to a broader audience is the well-organized "University Partners" program, which ensures that many students will have access to the technology and so will be able to develop applications for it. A seed financing program for Inferno projects tries to get independent software vendors on-board.

Inferno is a device-centric software solution, and complex services, which require the coordination of several types of devices and their services, are difficult to implement.

4.3.3 Universal Plug and Play

Universal Plug and Play (UPnP) by Microsoft is another technology that allows the creation of networks for the exchange of services and information. It is an extension of the plug-and-play hardware recognition system, which was introduced with Windows 95 (and is also known as plug and pray), allowing people to tie devices together without needing a computer. Devices announce themselves and their capabilities when plugged into a network.

UPnP works with "smart objects," such as light switches or volume controls, and intelligent appliances, such as web-enabled telephones or computers: devices that are currently not connected to a network. Unlike the other approaches described in this chapter, UPnP is an evolution of an existing technology, taking on the burden of the underlying technology. This makes UPnP more complex, less innovative, and less elegant. Microsoft calls this approach more secure because it builds upon a heritage of existing technologies and brings In-

---

[9]http://www.umec.com/

ternet technologies into a new class of devices. The conservative approach is typical for Microsoft.

UPnP only works with devices that are based on one of the Microsoft operating systems, making the system not truly universal as the name tries to suggest, but tries to further the market reach of Microsoft products into the embedded devices market. Microsoft has found support from Compaq, Intel, ATI, 3Com, AMD, Kodak, and others.

UPnP, which is conceptually related to Jini, works nicely as a complementary technology to Jini, because UPnP could handle much of the grunt work required to secure blocks of IP addresses, for example. This would allow Jini to concentrate on the interaction between the intelligent appliances themselves and the network.

4.3.4   Jini

Jini[10] is perhaps the best-known component of the pervasive computing technology thanks to the marketing efforts of Sun.[11] Jini is part of the pervasive computing initiative by Sun Microsystems, which allows all types of devices to be connected into so-called impromptu networks. Jini allows access to new network services and creates a network consisting of all types of digital devices without extensive planning, installation, or human intervention. Each device broadcasts the services it offers to all other devices in the community; the services can then be used by all members of the network.

An impromptu community is created when two or more devices create a network to share their services. They do not need to have prior knowledge of each other in order to participate. The communication is established dynamically and does not require the devices to exchange drivers to offer their services to the other devices in the community. Jini is designed to bypass computers altogether. The only thing that is required is the Java platform someplace on the network.

Other than traditional networks, an impromptu community will most probably consist of information appliances, such as mobile phones, television sets, and PDAs. Every electronic device handles information and contains a certain type of microprocessor. Jini adds the functionality to connect to a network and exchange information and services. It enables the discovery of any device or program on the network and makes that device or program seamlessly available to authorized users.

Jini makes it possible to associate devices, such as printers and scanners, with people and places. Imagine you need to print out a text in another office; just press Print and the text will be printed on the printer that is next to you, no matter what type of printer it is and to whom it belongs. Jini allows instant access to any network program or service by providing an object-oriented approach to distributed computing.

---

[10]http://www.sun.com/jini/
[11]http://www.sun.com/

The most significant feature in Jini is the Federations (a reference to Star Trek), which consist of a bunch of loosely connected devices that are regulated in a decentralized manner. It is assumed that every device connected is friendly. This concept makes it easy to integrate new devices into the impromptu network, but also creates security issues. The first release of Jini did not include distributed security features.

The benefit of Jini is that no investment in new equipment is needed to enable the vision of pervasive computing. Jini runs on all types of devices that can be fitted with a JVM and allows dynamic change of the network. Jini heavily depends on the existence of an underlying operating system in order to work, requiring embedded devices to install and load an operating system, which in turn requires a certain amount of memory. Since Jini works as an add-on, it is rather easy to program applications and services on standard personal computers with Java and Jini installed. If users connect Jini-enabled devices to their personal computers, no drivers need to be installed in addition to the Jini software on the computer.

One possible application of Jini could be to tap multiple processors across a network to work in parallel and resolve highly complex computations. This type of clustering enables computers on the network to use the available capacities to the utmost. Imagine 20 computers connected to each other; a user starting a computing-intensive application on one system will broadcast the request for processing power to the other computers. Every computer that has processing time available will be able to donate it to the application. This, of course, requires a rewrite of traditional single-processor applications.

Scalability is one of the major issues with the current implementation of Jini. It can run in workgroups of up to 200 objects only. This makes Jini a workgroup solution in which participants share the same security model. Jini does not scale well to a wide area network (WAN), nor does it provide functions to cross firewalls, which protect company networks from the rest of the Internet. The reason for the lack of scalability is that all changes are expected to be consistent. An additional drawback to scalability is that all members of an impromptu network need to share a single clock at which they operate. If one device gets out of sync, it needs to be resynced in order to share its services and data. This takes time and resources. Devices in such a network cannot drop out and reconnect whenever they wish; they must be online all the time to share their information and services.

Less of a problem is Jini's dependency on Java. It is difficult to enable devices that are not Java enabled to talk the Jini way of network communication, but Java is available for almost any type of hardware. It may be more of a problem to introduce Jini into a company with zero knowledge of Java. The metadata system of Jini requires suppliers and consumers of services to agree on a common description of the services and devices so that they can find each other. Java supports only a global namespace, making it impossible to create local names for devices and services that are located elsewhere. Therefore, the whole name needs to be used to address such a service or device.

Jini can work as an extension to CORBA (Common Object Request Broker Architecture), as can most solutions presented in this chapter. Actually, most of the solutions presented here were built at a time when CORBA was not as powerful as it is today. Jini can be viewed as a Java directory and lookup service, which nowadays is also available in CORBA. But this can also be said of most solutions provided in this chapter. The difference is that for the first time, all types of devices can exchange information and services in a standardized manner.

Jini is a good device architecture through its installable interface, and many companies have started to license the technology to create new devices and services. Cisco,[12] for example, has created a Jini-powered cable modem, and Quantum[13] demonstrated a free-standing Jini hard disk.

4.3.5 Bluetooth

Bluetooth[14] was first introduced in May 1998 as a result of several companies—Ericsson, IBM, Intel, Nokia, and Toshiba—working together to provide a solution for wireless access to computing devices. Each company helped develop Bluetooth into the product it is today. Ericsson was instrumental in developing the Special Interest Group (SIG). Since its inception in 1998, more than a thousand companies are involved with the SIG.

The codename Bluetooth traces back to 10th-century Denmark. Harold Bluetooth, King of Denmark, was raised as a Christian boy by his mother. When his father died, Harold became ruler of Denmark. In a time of war and destruction, Harold found himself in charge of rebuilding churches and propagating the belief of Christianity throughout Denmark. In doing so, Harold Bluetooth was credited with uniting the provinces of Denmark under a single crown. Just as Bluetooth technology unites different computerized devices to one standard, Harold united a country in a belief.

The concept behind Bluetooth technology is to allow wireless communication between two entities without the hassle of connecting wires. Cellular phones will automatically be able to send e-mail to your computer when you come within 10 meters of the computer.

Bluetooth is the specification for small form-factor, low-cost, short-range radio links between mobile PCs, phones, and other portable devices. From its cable replacement to radio link and data transfer times, Bluetooth is actually simple to understand. Bluetooth consists of a 9 × 9 mm chip that is inserted in two different devices so that they can communicate with each other. Bluetooth uses the frequency band of 2.45 GHz and switches among 79 channels in this band at 1,600 hops per second. The rate at which data is transmitted and received is 1 Mb/s. The Bluetooth baseband protocol is a combination of circuit

---

[12]http://www.cisco.com/
[13]http://www.quantum.com/
[14]http://www.bluetooth.org/

and packet switching. Each packet is transmitted in a different hop frequency. This band is available globally except in a few countries. The fact that this frequency band is free and unregulated precedes the availability of global expectations by the FCC. The range in comparison with its competitors can reach 10 meters or 40 feet. Bluetooth can be outfitted to make longer connection distances if desired.

Bluetooth contains a maximum of three voice channels and seven data channels per piconet. Security is administered at the link layer. Each link is encoded and protected against both eavesdropping and interference. Bluetooth can be considered a secure short-range wireless network, using encryption of up to 64 bits. One of the main advantages of Bluetooth is that it provides a universal bridge to existing networks. Installation of Bluetooth has grown from just PCs and mobile phones to many others devices, like fax machines, keyboards, mouse devices, and joysticks.

There are different reasons for considering Bluetooth for future uses. There is also question of why to use Bluetooth in the first place. The problems foreseen with Bluetooth are cost, privacy, accessibility, security, and future. Future aspirations for Bluetooth are unstoppable because of the acceptance it has received from many big companies. Concerns over privacy are whether transmissions will be secure. Security on transmissions has been questionable since the evolution of Bluetooth.

Business solutions can be one of the most important reasons why Bluetooth will take off so well in the business market. Checking e-mail without the hassle of connecting wires will be second nature, as will printing from across the room without having to plug in a cable. All of these simple solutions will help businesses perform at higher quality. There is no limit to what Bluetooth can help the average business with. As long as both a PC and cellular phone have Bluetooth technology inside them, they can "talk" continuously.

Imagine receiving e-mail when your computer is not even on; with Bluetooth this is possible. When someone leaves voice mail on your cell phone, Bluetooth automatically sends it to your PC for e-mail availability. Bluetooth allows easy access to any or all electronic devices that can send or retrieve data. Other items involve printers, keyboards, mouse devices, and fax machines—all can work with Bluetooth.

Widespread adoption of Bluetooth will eventually determine whether or not it becomes global. Already used globally in devices, Bluetooth must rely on marketing strategy to become a worldwide phenomenon. Bluetooth will allow other countries to have the same business success that the United States will have if Bluetooth is incorporated properly in the business world.

E-business will definitely benefit from Bluetooth, for example, buying and selling stock while out of the office. Bluetooth can also link e-wallet to POS terminals for payment in e-cash.

Nokian,[15] the Finnish manufacturer of tires, has developed a new business model for Bluetooth. In the future, sensors built into the tires can send warning messages to the mobile phone of the drivers. This development was done in conjunction with the Finnish manufacturer of mobile phones, Nokia. They plan to roll out the first generation of tires in 2001; these tires will work with all mobile phones that support Bluetooth. The first generation was developed especially for trucks and race cars. Later versions will perform additional measurements, for example, to prevent aquaplaning.

Sales of Bluetooth technology are likely to exceed 2 billion dollars/euros by 2005, according to research carried out by Allied Business Intelligence.[16] The report concludes that Bluetooth technology will replace cables, joining user devices with a short-range radio link that is universally compatible. Bluetooth will enable a wireless connection between virtually any electronic device over a distance of up to 10 meters. Broadcasting at the 2.4 GHz ISM band, Bluetooth microtransceivers take advantage of the recently formalized IEEE 802.11 specification for wireless LANs. The sales projections are based on the assumption that Bluetooth will be used in many user devices including notebooks, desktops, handheld computers, PDAs, cellular/PCS handsets, pagers, printers, fax machines, modems, wireless LAN and LAN access devices, headsets, and thermostats. Early adoption is likely to be highest among business users of mobile phones and notebook computers.

4.4   Information Exchange

The bottom layer of the pervasive computing architecture connects the devices, and the top layer connects the service providers with the service customers. The middle layer is responsible for the exchange of data between devices and for the flow of information between service provider and service customer. By defining standards, Hewlett-Packard with JetSend, IBM with T Spaces, Lucent Technologies with InfernoSpaces, and Microsoft with Millenium offer solutions for solving the problem of inconsistent data types. The problem with data is that it is saved on every device in a different format, making it difficult to transport the information to another device that does not understand exactly that format. The middle layer provides a means for devices to negotiate the appropriate format in advance. For example, it would be possible to choose the JPEG format for the communication between a scanner and a printer. The middle layer also creates a device-independent format that can be understood by all participating devices. XML, for example, could be used for the communication between a word processor and the hard disk. The following technologies promise to solve the problem of data incompatibility.

---

[15]http://www.nokianrenkaat.fi/
[16]http://www.abi.com/

4.4.1   JetSend

Hewlett-Packard[17] introduced the JetSend[18] technology in 1997 to reduce the complexity in handling different document formats. The technology complements most of the solutions presented here, such as E-Speak, Jini, and UPnP.

The idea behind JetSend is to allow devices to negotiate the best way to share documents. A JetSend-enabled scanner could send images to a JetSend-enabled printer directly, for example, without interacting with a personal computer. Another example is a cable television operator who sends out video on demand to its customers and does not need to worry about the format of the film.

The JetSend-enabled devices at the operator and the customer automatically determine the right format. The two devices will negotiate through the JetSend protocol, a format known to both of the devices that can be used to interchange information without losing it.

Hewlett-Packard offers a wide range of printers, scanners, and digital cameras, so naturally these devices were the first that learned the JetSend protocol. Now that HP computers also support the protocol they can handle JetSend communications for devices that are not JetSend enabled.

Hewlett-Packard positions JetSend as the Esperanto of the computing world, promising universal viewability of content. The JetSend technology already has been licensed by several companies, including Panasonic, Minolta, Siemens, Xerox, and Canon, all of which produce printers, scanners, and cameras.

4.4.2   T Spaces

T Spaces,[19] developed by IBM,[20] works on a Java-based technology that lets computers and embedded devices share data, such as e-mail or database queries. T Spaces is just one of IBM's many projects that applies to the future and tries to complement Sun's Jini to achieve the common goal of pervasive computing.

As IBM puts it: T Spaces allows you to connect all things to all things, where a thing is a chip-based device. It is a network communication buffer with database capabilities and enables communication between applications and devices in a network of heterogeneous computers and operating systems. The technology makes it easy for resources such as printers, scanners, fax machines, and software services to be shared across networks with many different kinds of computers. T Spaces is designed for the LAN and will help to reduce the hardware costs in homes and small offices first. T Spaces has not been designed with thousands of devices attached to a single network. There is also no way to cross firewalls without compromising the security.

---

[17] http://www.hp.com/

[18] http://www.hp.com/go/jetsend/

[19] http://www.almaden.ibm.com/cs/TSpaces/

[20] http://www.ibm.com/

Unlike Hewlett-Packard, which tries to create a global pervasive computing vision, IBM is targeting the home market with its T Spaces product, thus creating a local vision of pervasive computing. Pervasive computing in every household requires a dedicated server, which controls the flow of information and services between devices, and IBM hopes to be the company that sells these hubs into the house of the next century. IBM is looking at a way to provide a virtual terminal and a broker between resources, but so far only on a local level.

T Spaces has many advantages over other technologies. Data is decoupled from programs, meaning that data can outlive its producer (because once it's produced, it lives in tuple space) and can be produced before the receiver exists. The communication is anonymous, and the sender does not need to know anything about the receiver, and vice versa. Sender and receiver only need to know about tuple space, which mediates all communication. The communication is also asynchronous, whereby the sender and receiver have to be on the network at the same time to communicate. The producer produces when it's ready, and the consumer consumes when it's ready.

T Spaces is implemented in the Java programming language and consists of a very small core that can be loaded into most embedded devices with very little memory on board. The persistent data repository and the database indexing and querying capabilities are the strengths of the T Spaces implementation. New operators can be defined dynamically and used immediately, making the whole system very dynamic and interactive. Event notification is also integrated into T Spaces, so it reacts immediately to changes on the network.

T Spaces has been available for some years and has matured over time, but some flaws are visible. So far it does not perform well on Windows NT, and the built-in HTTP server will fail if there is no network connection, for example, on a laptop that has been disconnected from the network.

4.4.3   InfernoSpaces

The InfernoSpaces technology provides a framework for building distributed computing applications. It extends many of the Inferno namespace capabilities to non-Inferno platforms and allows application deployment across a heterogeneous environment, independently of the hardware platform, the network protocols, the programming languages, and the operating systems. InfernoSpaces contains of a set of software libraries that allow, for example, legacy applications to take advantage of a distributed computing environment. An application created with InfernoSpaces will be able to interoperate with other Inferno or InfernoSpaces applications.

InfernoSpaces is a flexible, scalable, and distributed computing technology that allows any device to be connected seamlessly and easily with any other device. The creation and the sharing of network services and devices becomes much easier. InfernoSpaces can be used to create any type of distributed application in a network and can be used with any programming language and operating system. This last promise is not yet true: InfernoSpaces only supports C, Java, Limbo, Windows, Solaris, and InfernoOS at the time of this writing. Other than the Inferno package, InfernoSpaces is free of charge, making it accessible to anyone with an Internet connection.

The advantage of InfernoSpaces is its simplicity; it can be learned in days. It is based on a file model that is known to all developers. Its flexibility allows developers to separate application design from the underlying network configuration. The software scales well from the smallest embedded device to large network elements and servers. The design model allows anyone to write networking application without writing specific networking code. The simple-to-use and elegant framework allows even beginners to develop networked applications.

Some of the applications that can be written with InfernoSpaces are the following: IP telephony, distributed call processing, Internet games, instant messaging solutions, directory services, and online billing solutions.

InfernoSpaces is a highly sophisticated technology, which will work well in conjunction with other pervasive computing products presented in this chapter.

4.4.4   Millennium

To complement Microsoft's pervasive computing strategy, the company is working on a next-generation distributed operating system called Millennium. Millennium lets computers share tasks across a network, automatically adjusting to new components being added or removed. The goals of this technology include seamless distribution, worldwide scalability, transparent fault tolerance, security, resource management, and resource discovery.

Several prototypes have been implemented so far: Borg, Coign, and Continuum. Borg (another reference to Star Trek) is a stripped-down version of the JVM (using the Microsoft flavor of Java) that can create a cluster of computers that looks like a single computer when running Java programs. The discovery of new devices in the network is based on a notification-oriented system.

The second prototype, Coign, is an automatic distributed partitioning system (ADPS). It can automatically convert local Componet Object Model (COM) applications into distributed client/server applications without access to source code. Using a scenario-based profiling system, Coign discovers the internal structure of an application and divides the application into client and server components, choosing a distribution that minimizes communication between client and server. Coign supports the Microsoft flavor of Java, as well as Visual Basic and C++ based on the distributed COM architecture written by Microsoft. When a program is started, Coign decides how to distribute a program and automatically accomplishes that task in a way that maximizes the network performance. This is combined with a discovery protocol that measures bandwidth availability, latency, and the speed of the available CPUs.

Continuum (again a reference to Star Trek) has the same functionality but will work with any application. The designers of Continuum had the ambitious goal of distributing the Windows API to create a single computing environment (i.e., one single system image) across multiple machines. The goal of Continuum is to provide a distributed single-system image environment to a large class of applications regardless of their source language.

The advantage of this system is that it allows application designers to continue with their existing applications and trust the underlying Millennium component to take care of it and distribute it. The distribution is handled automatically after the application has been written. This approach is far easier than that of Jini or CORBA, for example, which require the application to adapt to the new paradigm during the development.

The downside of the system is that it is still only released as developers' prereleases and the prototypes run only on Windows. Millennium is built on top of Microsoft's COM, and future releases will rely on COM+, which will be strictly limited to the Windows platforms, making it a homogeneous environment with a central server.

4.4.5 InfoBus

InfoBus, just like Jini, is part of the pervasive computing initiative of Sun. InfoBus allows applets or JavaBeans to exchange data. Components written to the JavaBeans API can become data providers and data consumers, which are defined in the InfoBus architecture. A bean that acts as a provider connects to a database and offers data through the InfoBus. Beans that act as data consumers retrieve the data from the bus and process it. The advantage of InfoBus is that participating objects do not need to understand data formats and can concentrate on the implementation of the data processing. This segregation of provider from consumer is extremely powerful in that it enables applications to be independent of their data.

The InfoBus specification provides a set of interfaces that allows the sharing and exchange of dynamic data. It is possible to create so-called data flows between cooperating components. The semantics of the data flow are based on the interpretation of the data content, which flows across the InfoBus interfaces as opposed to responding to names of parameters from events or names of call-back parameters.

InfoBus complements Jini, which allows device-to-device communication, by implementing a way to exchange data over a standard interface. Through Jini and InfoBus, the functionality of the Web can be extended to other devices without introduction of a new paradigm, such as the E-Services strategy of Hewlett-Packard.

4.5   Service Broadcasting

The top layer of the pervasive computing architecture is the service layer, which allows the exchange of services over a network. Services that reside on a device can broadcast their existence and offer them to other devices, business objects, or human beings. Although Jini offers some basic functionality for local service exchange, it lacks the scalability and the security to make it a product for the Internet. The only product that is able to scale well on the Internet is the E-Speak product by Hewlett-Packard.

4.5.1   E-Speak

Jini's vision is not unique to Sun. Many in the industry today and over the last several years have had a vision of interconnecting devices. Hewlett-Packard also has a similar vision of connected devices working together to provide services to end users; HP announced it in March 1998 with ChaiServer.

HP's E-Speak technology, code-named Fremont, takes this vision even further by adding new, dynamic capabilities such as scalability, security, and heterogeneity. Jini is an architecture for device interaction in a small, trusted workgroup (LAN) or home environment, whereas Fremont is an architecture for service interaction in a large, unsafe, distributed environment, such as the Internet. Fremont offers services, including computing resources, information, and even access to applications on a pay-per-usage basis, similar to the way in which information is now available on the Web.

The difference between the old Web and the new infrastructure is that the availability and the quality truly become the most important aspects of the service. It is not necessary to know how the service is managed, who provides it, or where it is installed and configured. The Fremont technology will take care of the basic issues with services on the Internet.

Fremont is a network middleware layer that lies on top of operating systems, making services independent of the operating system. One could call this type of solution "install once, serve anywhere"—a variant of Java's "write once, run anywhere."

Fremont makes any computing resource, such as disks, files, Java objects, legacy applications, and device drivers available as services over the network. It also allow these electronic services to advertise their capabilities and discover new capabilities as they are added or become available anywhere on the network. Fremont provides unique mechanisms and protocols for negotiation, brokering, bidding, and billing between these electronic services. The management, the monitoring, and the fine-grained, dynamic access controls and security make it easy to create service solutions that are not only powerful, but also secure. The Fremont architecture makes it easy to combine electronic services, thus creating a new service in a modular way.

These metaservices do not need to reside on a single device. It is possible to combine services from different devices to create a new service. Imagine a

E-Speak (Fremont) Overview

Hewlett-Packard's E-Speak technology offers very interesting features.

- **Independence of language** – Unlike other pervasive computing implementations, Fremont does not depend on a single programming language, such as C++ or Java.

- **Metadata system** – Fremont supports attribute-based lookup, making it easy to exchange information and services.

- **Name virtualization** – The virtualization of resources makes it easy to move the original resource without reconfiguration of the clients.

- **Revocation of privileges** – Fremont can configure itself to revoke access to materials lists and other secure information.

- **Scalability** – Unlike Jini, for example, Fremont can handle resources on the Internet, not just on an intranet or closed network.

weather report service that uses different devices such as a thermometer and a barometer. If each of these devices were Fremont enabled, users with little programming knowledge (mainly HTML) could present the actual weather data on a web page.

Fremont links services, not just repositories of data, making a real leap into the future of computing. It has been designed to be a universal language and protocol for electronic services. Hewlett-Packard sees Fremont as a technology platform for open services. An open service is a state where services can be dynamically composed of best-in-class, competitive service components, and resources, using standardized, nonproprietary interfaces.

To put the features of Fremont into a nutshell: It is a federated software infrastructure that runs on top of an operating system, similar to the Web. It is a living system, similar to an operating system, but unlike middleware such as CORBA, which consists basically of a set of tools. It simplifies and secures the creation, management, and access of services over the Internet.

Most pervasive computing technologies enable device-to-device connectivity, but this is not sufficient to enable electronic services. ChaiServer allows devices to talk to each other, but it does not specify how to do this. To create electronic services, companies must advertise, broker, compose, and maintain the service. The broker, for example, can handle sets of services, sets of data types, and sets of access devices.

Fremont allows the creation of instant extranets, providing business partner collaboration. On a case-by-case basis, businesses can allow partners to access single services on their intranet without compromising security. The ability to connect services spontaneously allows people to collaborate in a far more direct and efficient way than we know today. The creation of an extranet takes months to decide and implement, since an extranet opens access to a company's intranet. With Fremont, particular services can be relayed in a secure way to the Internet, making the service available only to the partners who are allowed to see and use it. This reduces the risk of someone being able to break into the corporate network.

Partners that use the Internet to share services need to start up a client application. It represents an interface to the originator. This interface allows the originator to choose a file from a directory on his machine and make it available to a partner who is running the client application. A gateway process, running on the originator's machine, presents the client application with its interface to the FireScreen service. The FireScreen gateway is responsible for pushing shared information to the external FireScreen connector and for retrieving requests found at the connector site.

A connector process, running on a separate host somewhere on the Internet, will allow gateway processes to post information. Gateway processes will post one of three types of information to the connector: availability messages, which represent sharing authorizations; consume messages, which represent file transfer requests; and the actual contents of a file. A second gateway process, running on the consumer's machine and acting in much the same role as the gateway process on the originator's machine will provide consumers with information about file availability. This gateway will also post consume or fetch requests as directed by the consumer's client application. A second client application, running on the consumer's machine, will allow the user to see the files made available with his identity and retrieve those files. This application will actually be identical to the application run by the originator. The consumer and originator simply use different features as they exchange roles.

This concept allows businesses to create next-generation portals, which are also called electronic service brokers (ESB). The ESB allows online services to charge other systems for its resources and creates a new business channel for the delivery of electronic services in the following ways.

ESB creates additional revenue opportunities for telephone companies by allowing them to provide services beyond basic connections to consumers, and it creates new business opportunities for companies desiring to deliver electronic services to their customers. Consumers can gain access to a wider range of functionality without having to purchase or install applications on their own, and ESB lowers the cost barrier for access to sophisticated capabilities. This allows customers to access services without having to pay for the underlying infrastructure. Instead of buying applications that need to be installed locally, for example, you rent them over the Internet for the time you need them.

Fremont, aka E-Speak, sits on top of other consumer-device focused technologies, such as Jini, ChaiServer, or UPnP. While Sun is promoting Java everywhere and Microsoft is doing the same for Windows, Hewlett-Packard does not care about the operating system or the implementation language for accessing the electronic services. It can use any of the mentioned technologies to implement these services.

Several E-Speak pilots are under development, at Uniscape,[21] Captura,[22] and Helsinki Telephone,[23] among others. At Uniscape, for example, E-Speak finds translators and allows them to bid for services. Customers can select translators based on speed, quality, and price.

4.5.2 Salutation

Salutation is a service discovery-and-session management protocol developed by leading information technology companies. Salutation is an open standard that is independent of operating systems, communication protocols, and hardware platforms. Salutation was created to solve the problems of service discovery and utilization among a broad set of appliances and equipments in an environment of widespread connectivity and mobility. The architecture provides applications and services and formulates a standard method for describing and advertising their capabilities, as well as finding out the capabilities of other aplications and services. The architecture also enables applications, services, and devices to search for a particular capability and to request and establish interoperable sessions with them.

The Salutation architecture defines an entity called the Salutation Manager (SLM) that functions as a service broker for services in the network. Different functions of a service are represented by functional units. Functional units represent essential features of a service (e.g., fax, print, scan). The attributes of each functional unit are captured in the functional unit description record, for which Salutation defines the syntax and semantics (e.g., name, value).

The service discovery process can be performed across multiple SLMs. An SLM can discover other remote SLMs and determine the services that are registered there. Service discovery compares a required service type(s), as specified by the local SLM, with the service type(s) available on a remote SLM. Remote procedure calls are used to transmit the required service type(s) from the local SLM to the remote SLM and to transmit the response from the remote SLM to the local SLM. The SLM determines the characteristics of all

---

[21]http://www.uniscape.com/

[22]http://www.captura.com/

[23]http://www.hpy.fi/

Discovery of Services

Salutation Manager can be discovered by services in a number of ways:

- **Static tables** – Using a static table that stores the transport address of the remote SLM.

- **Broadcast** – Sending a broadcast discovery query, using the protocol defined by the Salutation architecture.

- **Inquiry** – Querying the transport address of a remote SLM through a central directory server. This protocol is undefined by the Salutation architecture; however, the current specification suggests the use of Service Location Protocol (SLP).

- **Specification** – Directly specifying the transport address of a remote SLM.

services registered at a remote SLM by manipulating the specification of required service type(s). It can also determine the characteristics of a specific service registered at a remote SLM or the presence of a specific service on a remote SLM by matching a specific set of characteristics. Salutation, unlike Jini, is a lightweight protocol and makes the least assumption of the underlying protocol stack and computing resources. Hence, it can easily be ported to low-power handheld devices.

4.6   The Vision

Although pervasive computing is being implemented by several companies, as we have seen in this chapter, it can only be successful if the company has a vision. The vision aligns all organizations within the company to ensure that the vision becomes reality. So far, only Hewlett-Packard, Microsoft, and Sun have tried to present a complete vision of the future of computing.

4.6.1   E-Services from Hewlett-Packard

Hewlett-Packard has created a unique vision based on the previously discussed products: their e-services strategy. Hewlett-Packard forecasts an explosive growth of specialized, modular electronic services that pervade the fabric of life, and Hewlett-Packard is aligning all of its organizations, resources, and expertise to help their customers take full advantage of the e-services vision.

It's no longer only web sites or portals that matter, but of importance are electronic services that are integrated into all kinds of devices and utilities and made available through brokers. An e-service is a service or resource that can be accessed on the Net by people, businesses, and devices such as computers and mobile phones. Several e-services can be combined automatically to perform virtually any kind of task or transaction.

Hewlett-Packard is working on the mass proliferation of e-services. These services will be modular and will combine and recombine to solve problems, complete transactions, and make life easier. Some will be available on web sites, but others will be delivered via TV, phone, pager, car, e-mail Inbox, or virtually anything with a microchip in it. Some services will even operate behind the scenes, automatically working on the user's behalf.

Hewlett-Packard sees three trends becoming important in the near future: apps-on-tap, e-service portals, and dynamic brokering of e-services. The proliferation of apps-on-tap will enable companies to take full advantage of pay-as-you-go software for many key functions: accounting, payment systems, payroll, ERP, and purchasing. The birth of new e-services portals will create vertical portals, such as OpenSkies[24] in the travel industry, and horizontal portals, such as Ariba.com's[25] procurement portal. The dynamic brokering of e-services will enable consumers and businesses to send out requests for services via the Net. E-services will bid to fulfill those requests, giving companies the opportunity to reach their customers anywhere.

To better understand the new opportunities, we can look at today's business on the Internet. Most Internet business is based on web servers and browsers that communicate and exchange information and follow predefined processes. The web-enabled startups rock whole industries by reaching out for customers that were not accessible to small companies before. Amazon.com is the perfect example of a startup that nobody took seriously in the beginning and suddenly was the biggest fish in the pond. Traditional book companies, such as little bookshops, large chains of bookshops, publishing houses, and large resellers suddenly had to start up their own online ventures to counterattack the attacks of the Internet startups. Slowly, companies have started to think about their businesses differently. They must adapt the rules of the startups and redefine their customer service. Customer-centered business has become more important, and customers have been enabled, through the Web, to serve themselves.

Extranets have helped to unify communities of partners and have saved the participating companies a lot of money. New services start to appear on the Internet every day. But the problem with today's web sites is the fact that each

---

[24]http://www.openskies.com/
[25]http://www.ariba.com/

E-Services

The first set of e-services provided by Hewlett-Packard will most likely include the following services:

- **Storage e-services** – Providing storage on demand over the Internet

- **MIPs on demand** – Providing computing power whenever it is necessary

- **Payment processing e-services** – Independent payment processing service that supports e-business

- **Imaging and publishing e-services** – Making printing and publishing easier through specialized e-service providers

---

company has built its services in a proprietary, massive, and costly way. The companies were forced to create their entire offerings from the ground up.

The open service paradigm developed by Hewlett-Packard makes electronic services more modular and thus allows them to be assembled on-the-fly because they are based on the open-services interface. They can easily be combined to offer new types of services. The paradigm of "do it yourself" evolves into "do it for me," through which the open-services interfaces the services talk to each other without human interaction. The interface allows integration of any type of device into an e-service.

It is expected that the shift in paradigm will be followed in the business world and in the IT area. Web sites will become less important. The automated services will work in the background. Most people would rather only think about the things they want to get done and not how things get done. With e-services, this expectation will become reality.

Implementing e-services has made it possible to offer traditional services, such as banking, to more people through a wider variety of devices and to implement new services. Business-to-business web sites will profit from the new paradigm as it becomes easier to implement billing systems, automated supply-chain management, procurement solutions, and a modular ERP system. All kinds of business-to-business transactions can now be handled by combinations of intelligent e-service systems.

The IT department will also benefit from the introduction of e-services. Certain services, such as processing power, data storage, and data mining, that are not required daily and are not part of the core business can be outsourced. E-services will help to ensure the availability and security of these services. They will give companies much more flexibility in the way they manage their IT infrastructures, making more efficient use of resources both in-house and outside the organization. The IT department will become a service provider and will use outsourcing strategically to lower costs and gain flexibility. It will enable e-services of all types and plan profitable e-services solutions, such as extended supply chains, and ensure the quality of service and the consistency of the user experience. Everything on the Net (both inside the enterprise and the outside world) will be treated as an online service.

The most important battle is the long-term one. In an e-services world there will be more choice and thus more competition. Customer loyalty will be based on the reliability of systems, how easy they are to use, and how useful they are.

Another interesting field for the paradigm of e-services is the pay-per-use service. All types of consumers will pay on demand for services such as software, video, or audio. Pay-per-use e-services will be tightly woven into daily life. People will plug into them through e-service utilities, such as corporate networks, phone companies, and ISPs, using a variety of devices. And they can take advantage of a much wider range of services because they'll pay only for what they use.

E-services are highly modular, making them attractive to a large group of customers who do not want to buy enormous, monolithic systems. Customers are able to subscribe to the specific services they want to use. This reduces the initial cost for accessing a service, and companies will generate more stable profit streams as money comes in more regularly and more customers subscribe. The basis for profit is broadened, and by streamlining whole chains of transactions, companies save costs. Another advantage of the e-services is that they can be developed, tested, and put on the market much more quickly because of their modular architecture.

E-services make it possible to focus on the real work and neglect the underlying technology and processes. Users will be able to take advantage of much more sophisticated services because they don't have to buy the whole package: they just subscribe to the services they need, paying for some of them on a pay-per-use basis. The aim of Hewlett-Packard is to turn any service or computing resource into a building block for e-services.

4.6.2 Microsoft .NET

Microsoft[26] is another company that provides a comprehensive vision of the future of the Internet. Microsoft is creating an advanced new generation of software that melds computing and communications in a revolutionary new way, offering developers the tools they need to transform the Web and every other aspect of the computing experience. Microsoft .NET will allow the cre-

---

[26]http://www.microsoft.com/

ation of truly distributed web services that will integrate and collaborate with a range of complementary services to serve customers in ways that today's Internet companies can only dream of. Microsoft .NET will be an important player in the next-generation Internet. It makes information available any time, any place, and on any device.

The idea behind Microsoft .NET is to exploit the focus shift from individual web sites or devices connected to the Internet to constellations of computers, devices, and services that work together to deliver broader, richer solutions. People will control how, when, and what information is delivered to them. Computers, devices, and services will collaborate with each other to provide rich services instead of being isolated islands where the user provides the only integration. Businesses will offer their products and services in a way that lets customers seamlessly embed them in their own electronic fabric.

Microsoft .NET will help drive a transformation in the Internet that will see HTML-based presentation augmented by programmable XML-based information. XML is the key to the next-generation Internet, offering a way to unlock information so that it can be organized, programmed, and edited; a way to distribute data in more useful ways to a variety of digital devices; and a way to allow web sites to collaborate and provide a constellation of web services that will interact with each another.

.NET includes the .NET platform from Microsoft, .NET products from Microsoft, and third-party .NET services. The .NET platform includes .NET infrastructure and tools to build and operate a new generation of services. It offers a unique .NET user experience to enable rich clients, .NET building block services, a new generation of highly distributed megaservices, and .NET device software to enable a new breed of smart Internet devices.

The .NET products from Microsoft include a new version of its operating system, named Windows.NET, that includes a core set of preintegrated services, such as MSN.NET, personal subscription services, Office.NET, Visual Studio.NET, and bCentral for .NET.

MSN.NET will become the new .NET platform by combining the leading content and services of MSN.[27] The new MSN.NET will enable consumers to create a single digital personality and will leverage smart services to ensure consistent, seamless, and safe access to the information, entertainment, and people any time, any place, and on any device.

The personal subscription services will add a set of premium consumer-oriented services on the .NET platform. These personal services are targeted toward the consumer market and will build on existing Microsoft entertainment, gaming, education, and productivity products. Today, these products are software applications that you buy on CD and install locally on your personal computer. In the future, these software packages will be online services that will give people the power of traditional desktop applications with the

---

[27]http://www.msn.com/

.NET Services

Microsoft will create a set of core services to support its .NET concept. These services will be treated as plug-ins or add-ons to the new Windows.NET operating system.

- **MSN.NET** – Internet platform for content and services

- **Personal subscription services** – Set of premium consumer-oriented services, such as entertainment, gaming, education, and productivity products

- **Office.NET** – Communications and productivity tools, including universal canvas technology that combines communication, browsing, and document authoring into a single environment

- **Visual Studio.NET** – XML-based programming model and tools

- **bCentral for .NET** – Subscription-based services and tools for small and growing businesses

---

flexibility, integration, and roaming support of the new .NET family of user experiences.

Office.NET will replace today's Office software package that includes Word, PowerPoint, Excel, Outlook, and other tools. Office.NET will provide an ever tighter integration of these applications by providing a so-called universal canvas technology that combines communication, browsing, and document authoring into a single environment, enabling users to synthesize and interact with information in a unified way. Instead of having separate applications for word processing and browsing, a single service will replace all of these applications. New collaboration capabilities provide the means to communicate and collaborate with people inside and outside their companies. This new service will be accessible through a new smart client that will replace the current browser technology to provide rich functionality, performance, and automatic deployments on any device.

Visual Studio.NET will provide a new environment for developers. This new service will support XML-based programming model and tools. They will be supported by MSDN, the Microsoft Developer Network, providing newsgroups and tools to support developers. This environment enables the easy delivery of highly distributed, programmable services that run across stand-alone machines, in corporate data centers, and across the Internet.

And last but not least, bCentral for .NET will provide a range of subscription-based services and tools for small and growing businesses. These hosted services include messaging and e-mail, enhanced commerce services, and a new customer relationship management service built on the .NET platform. These services will enable small businesses to better serve their customers online. The proposed functionality will include support for rich, hosted catalogs and the ability to track interactions with customers to enable personalized service.

The third-party .NET services are provided by a vast range of partners and developers that have the opportunity to produce corporate and vertical services built on the .NET platform.

The Microsoft .NET platform uses XML and standard Internet protocols. This concept allows the creations of XML-based web services. Whereas today's web sites are hand-crafted and don't work with other sites without significant additional development, the Microsoft .NET programming model provides an intrinsic mechanism to build any web site or service so that it will unite with and seamlessly collaborate with any others.

Microsoft is also creating an entirely new set of development tools, designed from the ground up for the Web and spanning client, server, and services. These tools will enable developers to transform the Web from today's static presentation of information into a Web of rich interactive services. Microsoft's Visual Studio allows the creation of Internet services in XML. Microsoft also provides tools for BizTalk, to visually program business processes by composition of services, enabling business analysts to develop solutions the same way developers do.

Microsoft promises that .NET services can be used on any platform that supports XML; unfortunately, .NET servers run only on Windows platforms, so not every device can become a service provider. Devices that do not run Windows need to create an interface to a Windows platform and use a proxy service to promote their services in a .NET world.

In the long-term vision of Microsoft, all applications software will likely be provided as a service subscribed to over the Internet. This will allow service providers to provide better customer service, transparent installation and backup, and a positive feedback loop into product development. Software delivered as a service also allows developers to respond more swiftly with backups and antivirus protection.

Thus, most software applications will become subscription services over time. These subscription services will be part of the next-generation desktop platform, Windows .NET, based on Windows technology. It will provide a tight integration with a core set of .NET building block services, it provides integrated support for digital media and collaboration, and it can be personalized. Another feature of the platform is that it can also be programmed by .NET services, meaning that existing subscription services can extend the platform easily without the need to install additional components on the platform itself.

Microsoft promises that its .NET platform will revolutionize computing and communications in the first decade of the 21st century by being the first platform that takes full advantage of both. The company from Redmond, Washington, promises to make computing and communicating simpler and easier than ever. It will spawn a new generation of Internet services and enable tens of thousands of software developers to create revolutionary new kinds of online services and businesses. It will put users back in control and enable greater control of privacy, digital identity, and data.

Microsoft's business philosophy has always been to produce low-cost, high-volume, high-performance software that empowers individual and business users and creates opportunities for customers, partners, and every independent developer. That philosophy is what sets Microsoft apart from its competitors, and Microsoft .NET takes it to a new level. As you can see from its philosophy and the services provided in the first generation .NET services, Microsoft's vision is targeted toward consumers and small-to-medium businesses. Large corporations are not mentioned once in their vision making. To make .NET a truly universal idea, several things need to change. First, it needs to take into account all types of individuals and businesses. It needs to extend its business model beyond its successful office products and support all types of platforms, whether or not they run Microsoft products. If Microsoft adapts its vision to become truly universal, it has a good chance of becoming a major supplier of services in the next Internet generation.

4.6.3 Brazil from Sun Microsystems

With other companies defining a strategy and a vision for the future, Sun[28] did not stand back; it defined a more complete vision of the future than that of Jini. This vision is called Brazil. The Brazil project is a web-based infrastructure that links people securely to information, computers, and other devices and leverages existing standards and protocols.

This framework enables stand-alone systems to work together within the web space. A strong authentication architecture allows extranets to access intranets in an open environment without compromising security. The approach extends the end points to new applications and smaller devices; yet at the same time it can adapt legacy applications to this architecture. Corporations can take advantage of web-based computing to dynamically control access to, and management of, corporate information systems and other digital data that represent for example: state in physical space, door status, room temperatures, and camera inputs. Each of Sun's initiatives tries to explore the possibilities expressed by this infrastructure.

The core component of the Brazil project is the Brazil web application framework. It began as an extremely small footprint HTTP stack, originally designed to provide a URL-based interface to smartcards so that the smartcards could

---

[28]http://www.sun.com/tech/features/brazil/

The Brazil Technology Architecture

The Brazil architecture is described by four main characteristics:

- **Toolkit** – A rich toolkit of powerful, reusable parts

- **Modularity** – Large applications achieved by combining simple parts in consistent ways

- **Simplicity** – Ease of building small applications

- **File-system neutral** – No preconceived notion or rigid structure of file systems

---

be accessed more readily from an ordinary web browser. Along the way it grew to provide a more flexible architecture for adding URL-based interfaces to arbitrary applications and devices.

The Brazil toolkit interfaces are based on the Java progrmming language for the advantages of its strong typing. However, the Brazil handlers communicate with each other with no type-checking involved so they can be reused for other purposes. The Brazil toolkit uses its own Brazil Scripting Language (BSL), to use the information communicated between handlers and for dynamic HTML generation.

BSL separates the Java handlers from the HTML web page look and feel. The handlers never generate HTML, and the page's HTML is just that. The advantage here is that making changes in the HTML doesn't require a programmer looking over the shoulder of the web developer to avoid or correct mistakes inadvertently made to the Java technology code in the process, and vice versa. No longer does the content server have to produce both the content and its presentation (look and feel). They're easily separable.

Although Brazil is strong on the technology side, it lacks a lot of the business vision the other two contenders offer today. It will be attractive to the IT departments because it uses standard languages and is based on reusable components, but without the business vision it will be difficult to convince the corporate world.

Device-to-Device Communication

- **Bluetooth** – Technology to create wireless local area networks

- **ChaiServer** – Java virtual machine extended to allow web-based connection to other devices on the network

- **Inferno** – Small-footprint network operating system to let any type of device plug into the network

- **Jini** – Devices that ran share services for "spontaneous networking" with other Jini devices

- **Universal Plug and Play** – Extends hardware recognition and connection of any type of devices

4.7 Comparison of Pervasive Computing Technologies

This section briefly summarizes the functionality of the different pervasive computing technologies. It is difficult to tell which technology will prevail. The technology that enlists the most companies for its vision will make it. Probably, two or three technologies will fight for the next few years to become the standard for pervasive computing. For pervasive computing, this does not really create a problem. Truly pervasive technologies will not only live side-by-side but also create many connections to eventually create a new technology built from the best components of every technology. If this reminds you of the Borg in Star Trek, you have understood the concept of pervasive computing. But other than the Borg touch, pervasive computing is not supposed to be hostile. Resistance is not futile if you do not like pervasive computing.

As we have seen, pervasive computing technologies can be divided into three layers. The bottom layer is responsible for the device-to-device communication, the middle layer is responsible for the exchange of data between devices, and the top layer is responsible for the exchange of services between devices. These three layers need to be present to make pervasive computing successful. The technologies we have discussed often represent more than one layer in the layer model. The layer model makes it possible to integrate technologies from different vendors. It is, for example, possible to use Jini in conjunction with E-Speak or T Spaces with ChaiServer. The reason is that most of the technologies are based on Java, with the exception that Microsoft has created a new programming language called C#, which everyone hopes will have interfaces to connect Java-based pervasive computing technologies.

Information Exchange

- **InfernoSpaces** – Framework for building distributed computing applications, independent of the platform

- **InfoBus** – Cooperation of applications across devices, which can exchange data through the InfoBus

- **JetSend** – Technology that lets networked devices negotiate common file formats for data exchange

- **Millenium** – Collections of computers that automatically divide up computing tasks across networks

- **T Spaces** – Java-based system that allows any type of device to share messages, database queries, print jobs, or other network services

---

Mobile phones, video cameras, CD players, car stereos, and other electronic mobile devices, all of which already use a lot of the technology, will most likely be the first devices connected to the Internet. Refrigerators, microwave ovens, and other household devices will later be connected to the rest of the world. The security measures that would allow every device to participate in the Internet are not yet in place universally. But companies like Hewlett-Packard and Lucent Technologies have strengthened security, resulting in a more secure infrastructure for any type of device.

A universal authentication module that is independent of the technologies used must be implemented; even more important, it should be independent of the authentication method. Retina scan, finger scan, voice recognition, login/password, smartcard, or any other technology should be connectable without problems. Only this device-independent approach will ensure that any service will be able to use the authentication module, no matter in which situation it is used.

The visions of Microsoft,[29] Sun,[30] and Hewlett-Packard[31] are mainly used to demonstrate knowledge in these technologies and business cases. It remains to be seen which vision will be realized, but I assume that all of them will be implemented since they are not that different. It is even probable that these visions will merge into a single strategy over time, once more knowledge and experiences about the technologies are available.

---

[29]http://www.microsoft.com/
[30]http://www.sun.com/
[31]http://www.hp.com/

Service Broadcasting

- **E-Speak** – Architecture for service interaction in a large, unsafe, distributed environment, such as the Internet

- **Salutation** – Service discovery and session management protocol

The various visions presented here imply that Microsoft and Sun are building a technology-driven vision with lots of good ideas in mind, but they don't offer a solution for the businesses. Technology is only a building block to being successful. A business, to be successful, needs a business vision, marketing vision, product vision, and many other parts of a corporate vision. Although HP does not target all of these parts, it at least addresses business with many business cases (see the HP web site). We will see which of these visions will prevail. My assumption is that all three of them will be accepted because they address three different target markets. Hewlett-Packard targets the business managers in the big accounts; Sun, the technology managers in the big accounts; and Microsoft, the technology manager small-to-medium enterprises. The big issue will be to transform these partial visions into a single vision about the Universal Network.

The Vision

- **Brazil** – Web-based infrastructure to link people and resources over the Internet

- **E-Speak** – Architecture for service interaction in a large, unsafe, distributed environment, such as the Internet

- **.NET** – Vision of next-generation operating system, using subscription services over the Internet

4.8 The Future of Pervasive Computing

Future opportunities are still wide open; because standards are just about to develop, it is hard to predict what the future of pervasive computing will bring. One thing is clear today: pervasive computing will change the way we use computers.

Software, for example, won't necessarily be installed on a computer. We will be able to use a certain piece of software on many different devices, meaning that software becomes a service that is paid for on demand. A request will be sent and the appropriate service will answer back. This paradigm will hold for any type of information or service. Information and services will be available whenever there is need for them. Imagine the car described in the preface. It does not need to have a gas station search engine built in. It is enough to know that one is available and how to get to it when the gas gauge low.

Pervasive computing will change the way we work: it will require many changes in the working world as everything moves to the just-in-time (JIT) paradigm. Products, for example, won't be built and then sold at a time when the customer is ready to buy. Products will be built when the customer is paying, and services will be offered at the time the customer needs them.

Pervasive computing may also change the way we see advertising. Why advertise for things not needed right now? Just as spontaneous networks can be created, advertising will be available on-the-fly to match the needs of the customer. With personalized advertising, consumers will perceive the ads as valuable information and feel less disturbed by the information flow.

Pervasive computing also makes it easier for freelancers (or e-lancers) to make money from worldwide contacts. Through pervasive computing, small building blocks in a highly specialized area can be delivered to other services, to make them more sophisticated without interfering with their business. This will also mean that we will move from software developers to service developers. The quality of the service idea becomes more important than a particular implementation.

Therefore, two types of new entrepreneurs will be around for the next few years: service developers and service providers. The service providers of today will eventually merge to the service providers of tomorrow, but startup companies will have a chance to take away market share from traditional service providers, who may be slow to move to the next generation of services. Because technology is changing very fast in these early days of pervasive computing, keep an eye on the book's web site[32] for updates on this topic.

---

[32]http://www.internetfuturestrategies.com/

Chapter 5

Applications in the Near Future

Besides mobile commerce and home automation, other applications and business models become visible. These areas have not been exploited and developed as much as the mobile commerce and home automation but will become more important as the underlying pervasive computing paradigms become more visible and persuasive.

The more devices that are pervasive computing enabled, the more business cases that will be developed. Don't assume that the list of applications and business models is complete. Every day existing ideas are extended and new ideas occur to innovators. Use the examples in this chapter to originate your own ideas. Some people call this process thinking out of the box, but that terminology is not radical enough. Think in new dimensions, forget about the box.

5.1 Wearable Computing

Most computers sit on the desk and interact with their owners for only a small fraction of the day. To date, personal computers have not lived up to their name—they are not very personal at all. Smaller and faster notebook computers have made mobility less an issue, but the same staid user paradigm persists. Mobile phones have not changed much about the paradigm either. Phones and PDAs have increased pervasiveness but still provide standard computer interfaces, making it difficult to provide the right service in a particular situation.

Wearable computing changes the way a computer could and should be used. A person's computer should be worn, much as eyeglasses or clothing is worn, and interact with the user according to the context of a situation. Context awareness becomes a necessity and simplifies use. Most of the data that is required to receive certain information or to invoke a certain service is provided by the context and does not require any user interaction.

New devices, such as heads-up displays, unobtrusive input devices, personal WLANs, and a host of other context sensing and communication tools, turn the wearable computer into an intelligent assistant, helping the owner reduce the amount of work, and making work safer. How it is done is of no concern through a remembrance agent (RA), augmented reality, or intellectual collectives.

5.1.1 Augmented Memory

The major difference between a wearable computer and traditional computing in form of desktops, laptops, PDAs, or mobile phones is that wearables are always on and have sensors that measure their environment constantly. Always on in this context means that not only are they always connected but that they are always ready to give information to the wearer, even when the wearer doesn't expect it. This opens the door to a whole range of augmented memory applications specifically for wearable computers.

Augmented memory means that wearable devices can store additional information about the wearers, their lives, and business-related topics. A simple example of augmented memory would be a traditional scheduling program that alerted you just before important meetings. The wearable device would flash an alert to a heads-up display or whisper the information in your ear.

More complex applications that are context based are far more interesting. Bradley Rhodes has been working on RAs, which monitor the actions of the user. As soon as a user types something into a certain device or walks around, the device continuously looks for documents with relevant content to the user's current situation. The file names or salient lines from these correlated documents are then continuously displayed at the bottom of the user's word processor in order of similarity. The system can find similarity based on the words currently being typed, people currently present, current location, and other physical information.

A wearable device could be equipped with various services such as GPS, indoor location systems, and face and speech recognitions systems. These systems act as sensors for the RA to provide the wearer with additional information, not only on what the wearer is typing but also based on physical environment. For example, if a person is meeting someone at a trade show or conference, the RA could remind the wearer who this person was, provide important information about that person, and display notes taken at the last meeting with this person.

The RA can also be used to create a "group mind" by sharing databases of files. In a meeting, everyone could share information provided by an individual, study documents of others more easily, and always see the relevant parts of the document for a certain discussion. Another example: the annotations and corrections one student makes over the course of a term can be valuable to another student. The RA can index other people's notes, and automatically bring up their notes and expertise whenever it is most relevant. This can be especially useful for knowledge transfer and on-the-job training for new workers.

Many more applications are based on augmented memory. They all try to help the sometimes limited memory of the human brain and simplify the lives of the people using it. These application do not provide people with additional services apart from temporary memory.

5.1.2 Augmented Reality

Another important service that will be offered in the near future is called augmented reality. Augmented reality refers to the combination of real and virtual services to assist users in their environments. To enhance the reality, a rich set of devices is being designed to support these services.

Augmented reality helps in many areas. For example in the area of telemedicine it can provide additional information to the doctor in a critical situation. During an operation, a heads-up device could provide important information about the status of the patient so that the doctor does not need to look up to manipulate other devices to get this information. In architectural jobs and construction sites, augmented reality allows the builders to see the 3D model of the completed building whenever they need it to make sure that they are still working within the predefined limits. The virtual model can be compared to the actual building and differences can be easily found.

Devices for the disabled help them live more easily. An interactive hearing aid, for example, will support additional information to the things said by other people. In a meeting the hearing aid will provide a transcript to a heads-up display and select certain symbols to reduce the amount of textual information. A blind person would use a minicamera to collect information about the surroundings; the information would be translated into audio information and a voice would present the most important facts to the person.

Several large, augmented reality systems already exist (for example, the Interactive Video Environment system), but a wearable computer with a small camera and digitizer opens a whole new set of applications. Some of the most prominent ideas for new applications are presented on the following pages.

Body Tracking

One of the most implemented solutions for wearables are body tracking devices, such as eye and finger tracking. These wearables contain a camera that tracks the movement of the eyes or of the fingers. Many pen computer users appreciate the pen interface for its drawing capability. However, given that a computer can visually track the user's finger, there is no need to use a pen. With such an interface, the user's finger replaces normal computer pointing devices. The user can control the operating system in this manner or digitize an image and virtually annotate it.

Even more interesting are eye tracking systems that allow people with severe disabilities to write e-mail and communicate with the rest of the world. After accidents some people are able to move only their eyes; using this technology, they are able to communicate. Although it is very slow, as you can imagine, it is a huge improvement over the previous situation where people had to guess what the person wanted.

But finger and eye tracking can also help to reduce work for all users. Laptops could be connected to a small eye and finger tracking device instead of to a mouse. The eye or finger tracking can also be used for many other devices besides a laptop; it could replace, for example, a remote control for the television or the dial on a phone.

Face Recognition

Over the past few years, much effort has been put into face recognition. The United Kingdom, for example, has cameras in almost all public places, to help combat terrorist attacks. The last few attacks by terrorists were quickly resolved by Scotland Yard because pictures from the cameras readily identified the terrorists. As a result, the number of attacks has been significantly reduced. On the other hand, camera surveillance could create a Big Brother country, in which the police control the movement of every single citizen in the country. Luckily, this is not the case, and hopefully, will never be the case.

This "mugshot" application allows a crime victim to search mugbooks much more quickly than ever before. An experienced user can find a particular person in the face database within a few mouse clicks. With the addition of face-finding software, this system is being adapted for use in wearable computing. The goal for the system is to overlay names on faces as the user moves about the world. The police could use the system in helmets during demonstrations or football games to find known troublemakers quickly and efficiently. Politicians could use it to gain additional information on their opponent and pass the information to consultants, who would return topics and ideas to the politician via audio streams.

Reporters could use face recognition to identify stars, very important persons, and politicians. Visually disabled people would profit from a face recognition system in combination with an audio interface; they would be able to "recognize" friends on a lively street, for example. Finally, face recognition systems could be a help for people with bad memories for faces—probably a mass market.

Language Translators

Another important and useful field for wearables will be their use for language translations in real time. The Office of Naval Research[1] announced in January 2001 that it will create a wearable language translator. In the first version it will be a flexible, belt-style computer—no bigger than a fanny pack—allowing the speaker's language to be translated in near real time for listeners.

---

[1] http://www.onr.navy.mil/

The idea is not to create a word-for-word translator as you may have seen on the web as a free service, but a system that understands the context in which a term or idiom is used to influence the resulting translation.

One of the features of the system will be a feature called "dictionary stacking"; for example, the world "click" means to most people a short sound, but for the military it is a measurement of distance (klick). By generating dictionaries for various situations and stacking them atop each other, it is possible to generate the appropriate translation for the wearer's circumstances.

Software is being developed to support all major European languages, such as Czech, German, English, French, Russian, Spanish, and Italian, and Asian languages, such as Korean, Thai, and Mandarin Chinese. As it is developed by the military, the initial use will be for the military, so they plan to include languages from regions in crisis, such as Bosnian, for example. It is hoped that a nonmilitary version will be released as well, for use by all sorts of workers, such as airport personnel, border patrol officers, customs agents, and phone operators as well as by tourists on holidays.

Such a device will help to translate what has been said, but to understand a person, one must grasp what was meant, and this won't be possible with a digital device for a long time. People will continue to learn other languages, because language and culture are closely related; translating words and sentences leaves behind many things a person wants to express that are hidden in the culture and not translated.

Visual Filter

Visual filters are another application that will have a great future in wearable computers. The basic concept is to process video images digitally in real time to assist the user in everyday tasks. People with poor vision could get additional information by applying a filter to their environment. By applying a filter, the device could reduce the world to lines, making it easier for these people to identify objects in their environment. Color-blind people could apply filters and attach numbers to colors to make it easier to identify the right color. Another application is to map around "blind spots" in the visually disabled.

Although current wearable computers do not have the processing power to do these manipulations in real time, the video image can be transferred to a base station computer that transforms the image and resends it to the user. Thus, experimentation can be done until wearable computers become powerful enough to manipulate video locally.

Navigation

One of the logical extensions of portable and wearable devices is GPS, which allows private users to find their position anywhere in the world to within 100 meters. One feature of the system is to guide the user through a city. Cars have incorporated this system for years now, but the resolution is typically inadequate. One hundred meters difference between the actual location and the calculated location could be the difference between being on a street, in the woods, or in a river. Cars have, therefore, additional built-in intelligence to keep them on roads: monitors of the direction and the speed of the car.

For wearable devices, this movement is called optical flow (comparing consecutive images to determine the direction of motion). Not only can the movement of a user's head be tracked, but warnings to the visually disabled can be given about approaching objects. By implementation a local beacon or a dead-reckoning system in the workplace, much more advanced applications can be developed.

Examples include virtual museum tour guides, where the GPS detects which object a person is looking at and provides additional information. Overlays of automatic wiring and gas lines in buildings and on streets could be checked with GPS-enabled wearables.

GPS also enables a new computing environment called the "reality" metaphor. The reality metaphor replaces the typical computer desktop metaphor by overlaying files onto real world objects. Thus, a filing cabinet can have a searchable index overlaid on it. Telephones can have virtual phone directories attached. Virtual 3D Post-it notes and movies can be applied to objects. Recent electronic mail messages can be rendered on a coworker's door (or the coworker) to remind the user of the last communication with that person. Again, such a system would help provide context-based information in a timely fashion.

Repair Instruction

There are plans to introduce a higher resolution of GPS navigation. This improved resolution could be used for repair instructions. Consider a large company with many devices installed. If one breaks down, the device could send out a message to a repair technician for help. The technician will easily be able to locate the device within the building.

Since manufacturers can control the markings on the inside of their products, they could add a wearable camera system to track the object in the user's visual field. By simply putting three distinctive marks at known distances from each other, manufacturer's can enable a wearable camera with known focal length to recover the 3D location of the plane defined by these three marks. By extrapolation from an online technical manual, the rest of the object's 3D location can be derived. Thus, when a repair technician walks up to a broken machine, the machine can transmit its diagnostics to the technician's wearable. The wearable automatically determines the problem, locates the 3D position of the object, and overlays specific 3D, real-time, step-by-step guidelines on the object for the technician to follow. This would quickly reduce the diagnostic time and reduce the cost for the repair operations.

5.1.3 Intelligent Clothing

Besides these more technical solutions around wearable computing other ideas directly relate to clothes. One of the first products, already available in Germany, is a coat that changes its behavior depending on the weather conditions around it. If you are skiing, the jacket will keep you warm. In summer, the same jacket will keep you cool while you are on the beach. When you are sailing, the jacket will protect you from the wind.

This invention comes from Starlab[2] in Belgium. What Starlab tries to do is to let clothes memorize certain conditions, a holiday condition such as wind on the beach or noise in a night club. If trousers can remember certain conditions they can be made to behave in a certain way. Starlab's idea is being used by many companies such as Adidas,[3] Samsonite,[4] and Siemens.[5]

So far, only limited applications have been developed. It is, for example, not possible to remove the smell from sweaty socks. But the industry has already developed clothing that can change according to the temperature. This solution of adaptable isolation is the first step to intelligent clothing.

More than 70 scientists from 28 countries come together at Starlab once a week to talk about their plans and research results. Starlab allows these scientists to work on anything related to the future of clothing. The only requirement is that the scientists keep the business aspect in mind. Starlab is becoming the European counterpart to the Media Lab at MIT[6] for dealing with new ideas.

Another idea Starlab has is to provide clothing with built-in identity chips. If a person with a certain piece of clothing sits in a car, that person will be authorized to drive it. Samsonite, for example, is trying to build a security system that makes it easy to identify luggage and sends off an alarm if a suitcase is opened by someone who cannot be identified as the owner.

Another idea is to implant a mobile phone into a shirt. A microphone would be in the front of the shirt and a speaker near the ears. Another idea is to include fiber connections in different types of clothing. Starlab is trying identify a new washing powder that can interact with the fiber connections and create energy when clothes made with fiber connections are worn in the sun. The clothes would contain chips and other electronics; no battery would be needed because the trousers or shirts would supply the needed power.

The first ideas would perhaps be caps with built-in mobile phones or pullovers with an Internet connection. Although these types of clothes would be of interest to limited target groups, many companies are willing to spend a lot of money to be first in the market. The market is still small, but it is just a

---

[2]http://www.starlab.be/

[3]http://www.adidas.com/

[4]http://www.samsonite.com/

[5]http://www.siemens.com/

[6]http://www.mit.edu/

matter of time until larger segments of the market become interested in special applications. In the future, we will see suits that keep the wearer warm and dry in cold and rainy weather, and maybe we'll see a dress that changes colors depending on the mood of the woman wearing it.

5.1.4 Standard Applications

Wearable computing will not only introduce new applications, it will also mean that standard applications such as word processors, e-mail applications, and web browsers will be put to new uses on a wearable. The difference between a wearable and a notebook is that a wearable can be used in situations where a person has no hands free or needs full concentration on something other than the computer. A laptop typically requires some table space to enable efficient work. Astronauts, geologists, doctors, and other professionals need the power of the computer but are not in a position to use a laptop. Imagine a space walk of two astronauts with laptops, maybe with Ethernet cables to connect them to a network. Not very practical.

Wearable computers can make standard applications available to people who can't work at a desk. It allows people to access information, communication, and transaction capabilities anywhere and anytime. Tax assessors, real estate appraisers, and insurance adjusters will have instant access to tables and codes. Commuters will be able to access online newspapers and office work on the train. Sportsmen such as cyclists, runners, and yachtsman can use a GPS to pinpoint their location. With wearable devices, they can communicate with their support team, learn the latest weather reports, track conditions, and get other information that will give them a competitive edge.

Almost all professions can profit from adapting standard applications to wearable computing. Stock brokers can access stock quotes, online trading, and alarms whenever they want or need to, on the beach, at home, in the plane. From a sociological point of view, continuous access may disturb private life, but there are people who live for their work. The military, for example, has introduced cybertroops that give the soldiers additional information about a situation; they can recall maps, plans, strategies, and information from their headquarters while holding a loaded weapon. In a more peaceful scenario rural doctors will be able to access online information and notes while visiting a remote farm.

Real estate agents will always have access to forms, maps, prices, and negotiation history when they are on site with a customer. A hotel concierge can easily verify if people walking into the hotel elevator have a room in the hotel or not. Decorators and designers can get online support for color matching and design decisions while being on site. Lawyers in courtrooms can verify new evidence when in court and change their strategy on the spot. They can review legal matters and ask for additional support in online chats with colleagues. Firemen and police will be able to locate an area of emergency much faster and more reliably, making a rescue operation more efficient.

Wearables will facilitate impromptu speeches, and future displays will allow a speaker to maintain eye contact with an audience while still reading notes, which is not possible with a notebook computer. With wearables connected to the Internet, a speaker can find background information on topics of the speech and get the right answers during the question-and-answer session to the people. Business people will use wearables for asynchronous and unobtrusive communication with family or company while in meetings, negotiations, or on business trips.

Another major function for standard applications will be as recorder of notes made anywhere and anytime for later word processing. Examples abound. Students will be able to use word processing, scheduling, and scientific packages in cramped lecture halls. Vendors could use wearables for taking notes at shows and conferences while conversing with potential customers. Geologists, botanists, and naturalists who work on the trail will be able to note down what they have seen and categorize the information easily. Reporters can write the article while researching the facts. Wearables can also be used for inventory control and other processes that are done manually within shops and factories.

5.2 Distributed Computing

In the good old days, monolithic mainframe systems contained all of their own presentation, business, and data access logic. They could not share data with other systems, and so each had to store a private copy of its data. Because different systems needed access to the same data, organizations had to store redundant copies on multiple systems.

These monolithic applications were inefficient and costly, and they soon gave way to relational database technology and the client/server model. Made possible by a convergence of technologies, client/server computing promised to simplify the development and maintenance of complex applications by separating centralized, monolithic systems into components that could be more easily developed and maintained.

Applications were partitioned into client components, which implemented the application's presentation logic and contained much of the business logic, and server components, which contained business logic in the form of stored procedures. Data access logic was handled either by the client or the server, depending on the implementation strategy. In the end, many client/server solutions simply created two monolithic systems where there once had been one. Today, it remains difficult to build, maintain, and extend mission-critical client/server applications.

Throughout this period, development teams have had to create the same functionality over and over again. Reusing code was difficult. Usually it meant copying a segment of code, modifying it, and then deploying the modified copy. Over time, a proliferation of similar modules had to be updated and maintained separately. A change to one module had to be propagated to similar modules throughout the enterprise. Because this often proved unmanageable, functional inconsistencies crept into enterprise information systems.

Distributed object technology fundamentally changes all this. Coupled with a powerful communications infrastructure, distributed objects divide today's still monolithic client/server applications into self-managing components, or objects, that can interoperate across disparate networks and operating systems.

The component-based, distributed-object computing model enables IT organizations to build an infrastructure that adapts to ongoing change and responds to market opportunities. In the age of global competition and increasingly narrow market windows, companies that can initiate rapid change, not just respond to it, are better prepared to capitalize on opportunity and are more likely to succeed.

Distributed applications provide an opportunity to establish and maintain a competitive advantage by creating a flexible IT infrastructure. However, they also bring new requirements. To operate in today's heterogeneous computing environments, distributed business applications must work on a variety of hardware and software platforms. They must integrate old technology with new and make use of existing infrastructure. Furthermore, suitability for enterprise-class applications calls for capabilities beyond conventional web-based computing: scalability, high availability, ease of administration, high performance, and data integrity.

5.2.1 Distributed Object Model Overview

To create distributed applications, several distributed object models have been established. Most applications are based on distributed object models using various implementations of RMI, CORBA, and DCOM.

The ability to reuse code is a major benefit of the distributed object development. Component creation makes rapid application development a reality. It empowers programmers to quickly and efficiently develop highly functional applications from existing components. The reuse is also cost effective, because developers do not need to reinvent the wheel. Another important feature of components is that a tested component does not need to be retested in another environment. If it passed the test in one environment, it will most likely work in all other environments. There are always cases when things go wrong, but in most such cases the environment was not set up properly.

Isolated development and modification are needed to make the use of components secure. A complex distributed object system is broken down into several separate, self-contained modules that work independently of each other but have clearly defined interfaces to exchange information and services with other components. The module interoperation is handled by a common protocol. But since the functions and methods within a module are isolated, they can

---

Concepts of Distributed Computing

Moving from traditional programming paradigms to the distributed object application development has several advantages.

- **Code reuse** – By reusing code, developers can introduce true rapid application development paradigms.

- **Isolated development** – A change to one component does not affect other related components.

- **Code maintenance** – Distribution of code becomes easy.

- **Thin clients** – Processing power does not need to be available at the location of the user.

---

be developed without having to know what the other modules do or when they will be available. This feature enables large-scale projects with multiple teams to work synchronously on distinct modules of an application. Once a module is ready, it is put into the common architecture and accessed as if it was always part of the application.

The use of this modular approach makes the code extremely maintainable. When the functionality of an application is changed to fix known problems or meet new requirements, a complete application overhaul is not required. The module that needs modification is identified and changes are made solely to that particular module. This approach reduces the number of man-days for the change, and testing is heavily reduced. It also reduces the number of potential errors introduced to a system with each code modification and release.

Most distributed object applications are run on servers, so that the distribution of code to the client can be handled easily by putting the new components onto the server. Once the client connects, the new code will be downloaded immediately.

With larger parts of the application run on the server, clients accessing the service can be kept small and lightweight. The system resources of the client can remain free while the bulk of the application processing is performed on the high-end servers.

Distributing an object across a network of machines makes it easy to ramp up speed and availability of the whole service. It also makes memory and disk space on the client a non-issue, since these resources can be allocated on the network. When most of the application runs on the server, the clients only have to download small portions from the Internet. These could be distributed, for example, in form of applets, browser plug-ins, stand-alone applications, or ActiveX objects and would deal mainly with the visualization of the data.

5.2.2 One Computer

Okay, I think, so far nothing new. The technologies described so far have been proven to work and are widely used on the Internet. They have one major disadvantage. They require a homogeneous server network. If we look at the pervasive computing landscape, we see a heterogenous network that requires a different approach.

Another drawback of these traditional distributed component models is that a single instance of a component needs to run on a single platform. It is not possible to share a single task over several computers.

In the future, all networked resources, such as hardware, software, applications, and people, need to work together, no matter which platform, language, or location they use or share. Future strategies need to leverage the existing infrastructure to create a better, faster, and more reliable service for customers. In the future, it should no longer matter if someone uses UNIX or Windows, or a Mac, Pentium, Power PC, or PA-RISC processor, Java, Basic, or C++, or if a person lives in Brazil, Russia, or Japan. These new applications do not have to know where resources are located, their programming language, their operating system, or any other details.

Such an architecture connects networks, workstations, supercomputers, and other computer resources in a system that can encompass different organizations, architectures, operating systems, and physical locations. No central server oversees and controls each resource: instead, each resource is an independent element. The advantage is that nothing or nobody can pull the plug and hereby destroy the service. If a resource becomes unavailable, the service will use another resource providing the same service.

This approach has two effects. If such an architecture is implemented, any device can use the provided service and services can easily get additional resources to fulfil the request more quickly.

You don't need a huge, expensive computer to do the job; you can use a smaller computer but just take longer to do it, although data would pile up. But if you use lots of small computers, all working simultaneously on different parts of the service, you can do the job even faster than the fastest supercomputer today.

This technique allows you to execute complex problems very fast and run programs more efficiently without worrying about different languages, conflicting platforms, or hardware failure. The architecture will schedule and distribute your processes on available and appropriate hosts, and then return the results to create the illusion of working on a single, virtual machine.

More and more companies use new technologies to achieve these goals because they want to integrate more devices than ever before.

Another important area is processing power. Many devices today spend most of their time in idle mode, meaning that they are waiting for input from another system or a user. Many companies need to do complex calculations, and to execute the calculations, these companies need to buy a lot of expensive hardware. In the future, they can rent computing power from anyone who possesses a device with computing power.

To achieve this goal, companies need to divide these large projects into many smaller tasks that can be distributed to many individual devices running simultaneously on a network. Tasks are processed by individual devices and results are transmitted back to a coordination server for analysis. This process opens doors to new projects by providing access to previously unobtainable computational power to hasten a project's time to market or completion.

Several projects have already been started. Most of them are based on traditional technology, but as more and more projects move toward pervasive computing technology, the distribution and use of the processing power becomes easier. United Devices,[7] for example, is trying to find a cure for cancer. By downloading a small agent application, anyone can apply to become part of the project. The National Foundation for Cancer Research (NFCR) Centre for Drug Discovery in the Department of Chemistry at the University of Oxford, England, is using the architecture in the search for new drugs in the treatment of leukemia.

The heart of any United Devices solution is the so-called MetaProcessor platform, which provides a scalable, secure distributed computing platform that allows customers to access more computing power at lower overall project costs. The MetaProcessor can be purchased as a software package or leased as a service. It works by tapping into the idle computing resources of thousands of individual devices connected to a network, which can be either a corporate intranet or the general public on the Internet.

Another very famous implementation of the same idea is SETI@home.[8] The traditional SETI programs build large computers that analyze data from the telescope in real-time. None of these computers look very deeply at the data for weak signals, nor do they look for a large class of signal types. The reason is that they are limited by the amount of computer power available for data analysis. To tease out the weakest signals, a great amount of computer power is necessary. It would take a monstrous supercomputer to get the job done.

UC Berkeley decided to tap into new, low-cost devices. Most desktop computers today idle and waste electricity by displaying screen savers. Here is where SETI@home come into the picture. The SETI@home project hopes to convince people all around the world to lend their computers when they are

---

[7]http://www.uniteddevices.com/
[8]http://www.seti-inst.edu/

not using them. This will help UC Berkeley to "search out new life and new civilizations." All the user has to do is to download a screen saver that analyzes data if the user is not using the computer. Every client gets a chunk of data from SETI@home, analyzes the data, and reports back the results.

In the next two years the entire sky as seen from the telescope in Arecibo, Puerto Rico, will be scanned three times. By the time SETI@home has looked at the sky three times, there will be new telescopes, new experiments, and new approaches to SETI, and perhaps extraterrestrial life will be discovered. If you want to find out more about the project, read the "Declaration of Principles Concerning Activities Following the Detection of Extraterrestrial Intelligence."[9]

The most difficult category of distributed applications in the future is coupled applications, in which several initially distinct programs are glued together. For example, much current research in climatology focuses on coupling independent atmosphere, ocean, sea ice, and land models into a complete climate system. Such coupled studies require coordinating the exchange of information between the models and synchronizing the models. Because each component model is itself complex and requires significant computing resources, it is advantageous to be able to run the climate system model on different machines.

Only a few solutions are on the market. One of the companies providing such an architecture is provided by Applied Metacomputing.[10] Their software, called Legion, can facilitate such work by making it easier to run the component models in different computing environments.

5.2.3 The Grid

The World Wide Web, invented in the early '90s by Tim Berners-Lee and scientists at the European Organization for Nuclear Research (CERN),[11] is acknowledged and accepted worldwide. The WWW initiated the e-business revolution as data from the CERN testing environment was distributed to scientists everywhere. Even as the WWW was changing the world, the scientists at CERN were already working on the next generation: the Grid. The Grid will correctly answer complex questions from anyone in the world.

The major problem with the WWW is that it cannot create answers to unknown questions. The Web can only provide answers to questions that have been published on it. The Grid will create highly customized answers on demand without having to store the answer statically on the Internet.

The Grid will be a "dependable, consistent, pervasive access to resource." The Grid technology makes it easy to use diverse, geographically distributed, locally managed and controlled computing facilities, as if they formed a coherent local cluster.

---

[9]http://www.seti-inst.edu/post-detection.html

[10]http://www.appliedmeta.com/

[11]http://www.cern.ch/

For example, you submit your work and the Grid finds convenient places for it to be run. It organizes efficient access to data by caching, migrating, and replicating data over the network as such. The Grid deals with authentication to the different sites that you will be using, making it easy to treat an "answer" as a logical resource on the Net. It also provides interfaces to local site resource allocation mechanisms and policies to make integration as easy as possible. The Grid runs the jobs on your behalf, monitors progress, and recovers from problems. It tells you when your work is complete, and if there is scope for parallelism, it can decompose your work into convenient execution units based on the available resources and the data distribution.

The specialists at CERN are already using parts of the Grid to support distributed computing for special applications. Today, these distributed computing applications are developed by companies that provide closed solutions for their own applications. The idea of the Grid is to provide an open source framework for all applications.

The most important application the Grid will support is the new particle accelerator that is being built at CERN. It will go online in five years, but the amount of data that it will produce cannot be handled by the Web in a useful way. The old system provided two or three incidents per second; the new one will provide several billion incidents per seconds. CERN and 500 connected institutes in the world want to use the data from the particle accelerator, but the information needs to be sorted and segmented by different criteria and calculated in different constellations. The computers on the network can then download the data, and the associated applications can then address a particular need or answer a question.

The new Grid will consist of a piece of middleware that would be open source just like Linux. This openness allows the industry to add ideas to the scientist's network. The development of the Grid will involve at least 100 people for the next three to four years. CERN is willing to pay more than 200 million euros for the first version of the Grid. CERN is looking for partners, and the European Union has already provided more than 10 million euros. Several companies have also provided money, and four national research institutes and the European Space Agency in Italy (ESRIN) are working on the Grid. In addition, more than 15 associated partners, mainly scientific institutions, are willing to cooperate on the development.

Those that are part of the Grid right from the beginning will have some advantages. They will be able to develop applications that will run on the Grid. Consumer applications are expected to appear in 10 years, but the Grid is expected to attract many scientific applications in the next few years. Any science that works with a lot of data, such as genetics, molecular biology, or computer medicine, will perceive the Grid as a revolution. Without having to wade through the data, scientists can receive answers to specific questions, like the ratio between sold cigarettes and cancer in a certain area. The Grid will gather information from all known resources and build the answer on-the-fly.

The Grid Concept

The Grid tries to evade problems that have arisen on the Internet and solve complex knowledge and resource sharing problems.

- **Pervasiveness** – Unlimited, ubiquitous distributed computing

- **Accessibility** – Transparent access to multipetabyte distributed databases

- **Connectivity** – Ease of to plug in

- **Simplicity** – Complexity hidden in the infrastructure

- **Analogy** – Analogy with the electrical power grid

The Grid has no limits in the possibilities it offers to consumers. If, for example, you want to buy a house, you can enter its coordinates and immediately see on-screen all information about the house. You can get the history of the house, view it through a satellite passing overhead, learn how often the sun shines on the area, and determine the likelihood of tornados or blizzards in the region. The Grid can answer such questions without anyone having to collect and collate the data. It is just a matter of time until such things become possible. Check out CERN's web page for the Grid to keep up with the progress and to learn how you could contribute to the project.

Part II

Future Strategies

Chapter 6

Wedding Anniversary

You are sitting in the office, just about to go home. You check your diary to be sure you haven't forgotten anything important and you discover that today is your wedding anniversary. You remember how everything went wrong last year when the shops were all closed after you left work and you couldn't find any gifts for your wife. You are nervous now, but you use your WAP mobile phone to locate an open flower shop and an open jewelry store; you choose the flowers and a diamond ring while walking out of the office. Then you select a good restaurant in the area and book a nice table from your mobile phone. The car GPS is already programmed for the route home via the flower shop and the jewelry store, so you pick up the flowers and the ring and arrive home at the usual time, only to notice that your wife has allegedly forgotten the anniversary this year. She loves the flowers and the ring, though. You take her to the restaurant and you both enjoy the anniversary.

6.1 The Solution Today

In today's Internet world, it would be possible to do all those things through a set of services available online. Several web sites provide an online calendar, and companies that sell flowers and gifts over the Internet send out reminder e-mail. I, for example, receive every year at the beginning of February an e-mail from FTD[1] to remind me about Valentine's Day, because I once bought flowers on this day.

Netscape[2] and Microsoft[3] provide calendar functionality in their Internet suites. These calendars can also be downloaded to a portable device, such as

---

[1]http://www.ftd.com/
[2]http://www.netscape.com/
[3]http://www.microsoft.com/

the Palm[4] or the Jornada[5] handheld devices. Dates that have been entered are available anytime and anywhere.

The major problem is the synchronization of the data that you are storing in different locations. Some Internet sites may have valuable information about you. Your desktop, laptop, handheld, and mobile phone will contain similar information and more. This means that a lot of inconsistent data that is difficult to keep updated and in sync is floating around. Another problem is that the data is stored in many different formats, so copying the information is also not easy.

There are problems, but the data regarding anniversaries and birthdays can be managed in a central database on the Web. A search engine or a directory will help to find the flower shop and the jeweler on the Web. The major problem in this case is that search engines or directories cannot measure distances from the current location to the shop premises. If you were to look for a flower shop in New York City, you would enter New York City Flower Shop into the search engine and receive a long list of web sites containing the information. There is no way to sort this data in a meaningful way and there is no guarantee that all flower shops are found. The search engine finds only these that are mentioned on the Web. The flower shops do not need to have their own web sites; it is enough that they are mentioned on some site.

The next problem is that the addresses of the flower shops are not stored in the same format, so it is more difficult to compare different shops. Another problem is that some sites may contain information about opening times, other may not, some very detailed, some may mention only the days the shop is open.

Once the search engine returns the names and addresses, you can enter the office address and the addresses of the individual flower shops into a route planner. If you know the neighborhood, you can skip this step and select the nearest flower shop that is open.

Once you select the flower shop, you repeat the same procedure for the jeweler. To complicate the issue, you want the jeweler to be between your office and the flower shop, or between the flower shop and home, to make the process as efficient as possible.

Once you are in the car, you need to program the GPS system to direct you to the jewelry store and the flower shop. You could use the mobile phone to call the shops in advance to tell them you are coming. If the shops have shopping sites on the Internet, you could shop on the Internet from the office and just pick up the goods from the shops. This would save even more time.

The next step would be to order a table at a restaurant. Typically people have some preferred restaurants, so the selection is rather easy, but the phone number is not always known. That's true in your case, so you use a WAP-enabled phone to obtain the phone number and call the restaurant to make a

---

[4]http://www.palm.com/
[5]http://www.hp.com/go/jornada/

reservation. Of course, you can use the mobile phone to call a Yellow Pages service for the number.

Payment for all services is made separately. Calendaring services and search engines on the Internet are mostly free. These services are typically paid by the advertisements you see on the screen while using the service. The disadvantage of this type of free service is that QoS is not guaranteed. The service is supposed to be up and running 24 hours a day, but if not, there is not much you can do about it: you did not pay for anything, so you cannot make the service liable for poor practices.

This is a big problem for businesses. Many people that travel a lot use their Hotmail[6] or GMX[7] mailbox for business purposes. They either forward their regular mail to these addresses to read while traveling or write business-related e-mail from that free e-mail address. The aforementioned e-mail services regularly break down, losing all e-mails from time to time. Hotmail is also famous for security break-ins, so it is unsuitable for business-related e-mail. Many businesses explicitly forbid employees to use these free e-mail accounts or, better, provide them with a secure external web gateway to their regular e-mail and calendaring services. Free online services are a good thing, but keep in mind that there is no guarantee that the site is available when needed and no guarantee that the site will not be switched off forever in maybe five minutes time.

The other services used in this case need to be paid for. The services used on the mobile phone are either charged by time or by traffic, depending on what type of contract you have. Charged by time means that once you connect to the Internet, you pay for every minute online. This model is used for WAP services in Europe, for example. The traffic model is used today in Japan. It means that you are always connected to the Internet without having to pay for it; instead, you pay for every page you download. Depending on the agreement with the service provider, either you pay the same fee for every page from the same server or each page is individually priced, depending on the value it may give you.

The GPS location service in the car is free, once you have built in the system. The GPS information is provided by satellites that orbit the globe and provide the required positioning information. These satellites work in one-way mode only, so there is no way to charge for the service because there is no way to tell who is using the service how often and at which time.

The flower shop, the jeweler, and the restaurant will probably all take cash, checks, and credit cards, so you can pay them individually.

As you can see, this scenario is possible in today's world but requires many interactions with different systems, processes, and people.

---

[6]http://www.hotmail.com/
[7]http://www.gmx.net/

6.2   The Solution Tomorrow

The solution in tomorrow's world will definitely look different. In the last section we saw all the services, processes, and people involved in the task of providing a seamless wedding anniversary. To integrate these services into a single one today is difficult, since many pieces of information need to be collected, compared, and put into a structure. The same applies to services; they often require information from various sources to be helpful. They often require input from other services as well.

To make things easy in the future, the different services should be grouped and generalized to make this particular example valid for many users around the world, and thus the basis for revenue generation. The following three devices were used in our example: the laptop computer, the mobile phone, and the car GPS. These three devices required information from each other to work more efficiently. They need to have a common architecture for exchanging services and information.

The services that are required in this case are summarized as followed. First, you need a calendaring service that reminds you about upcoming anniversaries. This means that you need to input important dates, and the service should output alerts to remind you about the events. The input and output should work on all above-mentioned devices; you should be able to enter a date through the car's voice recognition device and receive an alert on the mobile.

The next step in our scenario was to locate a flower shop and a jewelry store that were nearby and open. The first step could be to create several services, a florist and jeweler locator for every town; second, add a service that verifies that the shops are open; and third, locate the nearest ones. Technically, there is no difference between searching for a flower shop, a jewelry store, or a grocery. Therefore, it would be advisable to create a generic shop finder service that is open to any type of shop. To bring all shop-related information into a single format is not that difficult. It is quite easy to create an XML description that could contain all the required information. The XML description would contain the type of shop, the address, opening and closing hours and additional information that describes the shop less formally. Additionally, the description could contain a ranking by users to give the people an idea of how good the service is.

The bigger problem is the geographic location-matching system. Today, you enter addresses and find out exactly how far they are from a certain point. This is a processing-intensive task. To reduce the amount of resources used, the geographic location of a shop could be stored not only as an address, but also in a more computer-friendly format, such as the exact geographic location as found on a map. Shop owners typically do not know the latitude and longitude of the shop nor should they need to know to participate in the service. The geographic location finder should translate the street address into a geographic location once and save the information in the XML description.

Example 6.1 XML Description for Shop Location Service

```
<?xml version="1.0"?>
<shop>
<type>flower shop</type>
<name>rose empire</name>
<address>23, Hammersmith Lane</address>
<postcode>we18 b91d</postcode>
<city>London</city>
<geolocation>23.34n,12.34w</geolocation>
<openhours>mon:9-20,tue:8-18,wed:10-22,thu:11-21,
fri:9-22,sat:8-20,sun:0</openhours>
<info>Rose Empire specializes in roses that can be
delivered world-wide</info>
<ranking>7/10</ranking>
</shop>
```

This leads to the next question. Who is going to enter all the addresses of the shops? Ideally, merchants should own the data about their shop. This would mean that nobody would need to spend money collecting information or keeping it up-to-date. The only issue is that there should be only one XML description, to ensure that everyone needs to update only a single source. To make this work, the XML description file must be placed in public domain and be available for free. This process is the only way to ensure that a consistent set of data will be made available to all services.

All services should be able to extract the required information. One service connected to the data could be, for example, a data entry service that allows shops to enter their details. Another service could be the shop location service. The data could also be used in a different context, such as location-based advertising. For example, whenever a person walks down a street, a location-based ad service will check what types of shops are nearby and present advertising, rebates, coupons, or the like on the display of the person's mobile phone or car.

Once the shop has been located, the shopper would like to understand better exactly what the shop sells and what is on sale, for example. Therefore, all items that can be bought should be also available in an XML description file. A shopping service should be able to access this description file. This description file should contain the name of the product and a short description. There should also be an image, the price, stock levels, order times, item availablity, and many other things. The advantage of providing an XML description file over a stand-alone web site is that the shop owner does not need to design and operate a single web site that cannot be found in the wide space of the Internet. This means that shop owners that want their own web presence can use the same file description and add additional information to make the site unique. A shopping site for DVDs could contain additional information that is not part of the official XML description file, for example, a technology description, manuals, recommendations, and short previews of films. This would ensure that the web site is something special and a reason for customers to come back, but it allows also additional customers that are surfing the web to stop and shop.

Once the shoppers have selected a shop, they will look through the online catalogue, either through the shopping service site or through the shop site. The online catalogue can be used for browsing only, or if a shopping basket exists, it could be used for buying goods. In our scenario, you might want to buy the goods online and pick them up personally at the shop while driving home. As a requirement, every shop needs to provide stock levels as part of the XML description, otherwise customers must drive around to find whatever they are looking for.

Once you know the shop address, you can let the car's GPS system guide you to the shop. The shop location service must be able to transfer the necessary data to the car. This can be done through various technologies. The shop location service could send an e-mail to the car. The car would read the automated e-mail and pass the information on to the GPS system. Another possibility would be to use Bluetooth to transfer the data from the laptop computer to the mobile phone. You would take the mobile phone to the car and transfer the information from the mobile phone to the GPS system. Another way would be to store the information at a central location called "My Anniversary Service," which bundles all service related to the anniversary (see Figure 6.1) and stores all information that needs to be shared between the services.

Through special service and data access rights, every service can view, modify, or delete certain data in this central repository. The use of a central repository for data for this particular service ensures that only a single valid version of data is available. To ensure the validity of the data, service providers must build up special security services that reach beyond today's technologies and concepts. Services and people that want to access the data need to have a unique identifier and a temporary password that will allow them access to the data for a certain period of time. Only if privacy can be ensured will people be willing to use the service.

But back to our scenario. Once the GPS system is programmed, you will be able to find the shop easily. Since you have already selected a certain product, in this case a certain type of flower, you will be able to pick up the flowers immediately. Payment will be handled through a central service that will transfer the money from your bank account to that of the shop once you pick up

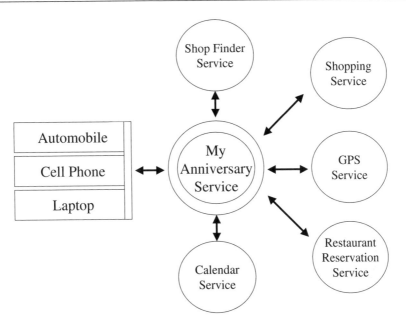

Figure 6.1. My Anniversary Service

the flowers. The service will pass on the money and retain a small fee for the transaction. This system works with the flower shop and with the jewelry and other shops. This decoupling of payment and the buying process is in the interest of all parties, as they are sure that a third party is handling all financial matters. This trusted third party should handle the payment process, and in case of problems should handle the flow of products and money in the opposite direction if you are not satisfied with the product, for example.

When picking up the goods, you will need to present special identification to assure the shop employee is picking up the right goods. The mobile phone could contain a personal identification module that, in conjunction with a bioscanner, makes sure that the mobile phone has not been stolen. A retina scanner, a finger-print scanner, or a voice recognition system could be used to verify identification.

Once you and your wife have celebrated at the restaurant, you should pay in the same way as at the shops, that is, without involving cash or credit cards.

6.3 Technology

To support the idea of an anniversary service, certain technologies need to be in place. In the last section we talked about the functional blocks that are required to support this particular service. In this section, we map the functional blocks to a technical infrastructure.

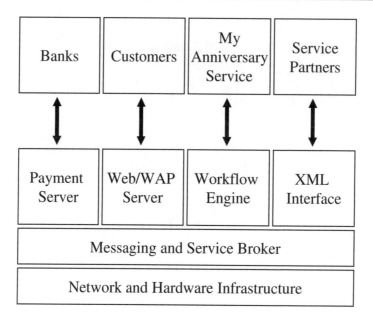

Figure 6.2. Central Anniversary Service

The central piece of the whole architecture is the anniversary service architecture. To manage the whole architecture (see Figure 6.2) the system needs to manage the flow of information and services. Therefore, the system requires a workflow component that checks that everything is going according to plan. This component checks whether a person received an anniversary alert and has chosen to look for a present online. If something does not work in the predefined way, the component will try to correct the workflow or, if this is not possible, send an alert to the involved parties.

The workflow will also create a protocol that will hold all information about the transactions and will deduct a percentage of all transactions that are made. A payment service will make sure that the payments are all made through this service and that the shops and restaurants are paid on time for their services and products.

In Figure 6.2 you can see the horizontal layer that consists of a standard hardware and network platform and, on top of this, a messaging and service broker that enables the creation of metaservices such as our anniversary service. The payment module ensures that all services can be paid for in a consistent way and that the money the consumers pay will be transferred in a timely manner from their bank accounts to the bank account of the company.

The web and WAP server ensure that all devices can communicate with the service, to allow customers to use the device to use the service. This server should not be restricted to the Web (HTML) and WAP (WML). By using XML to store information and services, the server could easily be extended to support, for example, imode, which uses cHTML or other output standards.

The employees of My Anniversary Service will need to control the whole environment and make sure that the business processes are properly implemented. Through the front end of the workflow engine, they control the status of existing orders and make changes to the workflow process, such as introducing new service partners, changing the order of the transaction, or removing information from the web site.

The service partners must define a standard XML interface that can handle all information and requests that they pass back and forth. If new information, services, or transactions need to be introduced, XML can easily be extended to accommodate them without harming the existing types of information, services, and transactions.

By specifying standard technologies, such as HTTP, HTML, WAP, and XML, the architecture makes sure that many devices and services can participate in the service without having to create special interfaces. This ensures that growth is not inhibited by technology that is either not accepted or not yet in place.

To make sure that My Anniversary Service works around the clock, the company must create SLAs with its partners. Every integration with a business partner needs to ensure that the partner service is always available when a particular customer is interested in this service. Several models are possible. Either the system of the business partner is guaranteed to be up and running 24 hours a day, or the most vital information about the service is transmitted to My Anniversary Service. The service must guarantee that people can get the most important information from the service whenever they want.

6.4 Business Case

As we have seen, it is technologically feasible to build up such a service. Before a service provider starts doing it, he must verify that the business case is watertight and unlikely to sink within the first year. Many companies have gone bankrupt because they tried something that could be done but was not necessarily profitable.

A business person must look at the target markets and evaluate how many customers could be interested in that particular service and how much they can charge for a transaction. The more people who will use the service, the lower the transaction fee can be. The provider must evaluate whether alternative income streams, such as banner advertising, are possible.

If we take a market, such as France, that is large enough to be attractive, we can expect about 10 to 15 million people online. Let's now assume that 50 percent are married, which would be about five to seven and a half million people. I must admit that I don't have the real figures, but they are not really important for now, since they will change anyway. What counts is the logic behind the calculations.

If we assume that these five million people are married, it means that there are 2.5 million anniversaries every year or an average of about 6,850 anniversaries per day. If we are the first service in that country, we can expect a market share of 5 to 15 percent, meaning that the service will receive between 340 and 1,027 anniversaries a day. If we were talking about low-cost transactions, we would not need to continue with the business plan. In this case, let's look further to determine if money can be made.

A typical transaction will consist of flowers and a restaurant visit; in some special cases, jewelry will play a role. If we expect flowers and the restaurant tab to be in the 30 to 50 dollars/euros range each, normal anniversary transactions range from 60 to 100 dollars/euros. Next, let us assume that about 20 percent of spouses spend 300 dollars/euros on jewelry. This would create an average sale of 124 dollars/euros per transaction. Fifteen percent of every transaction can be held back as commission for the online service if the appropriate contracts are made with the business partners. Our virtual company would earn 18.6 dollars/euros on each transaction. In the worst case, with 340 anniversaries, the company would make 6,324 dollars/euros a day (or 2.3 million a year). In our best case, with 1,027 anniversaries a day, the company would earn 19,102.2 dollars/euros a day (or 7 million a year).

Seven million dollars/euros sounds like a great sum, but to get 15 percent market share, a company must establish a brand name, and that requires a large sum to be invested in marketing. A good way to save a lot of money is to let the business partners do the marketing. This means that flower shops offer their virtual service using the company's domain, for example. The solution must be easy to use and should have a nice front end that makes people come back.

Another large sum needs to be invested in the system itself. The hardware and software need to be bought, and someone needs to implement the solution, including all the interfaces to other systems. The costs are difficult to calculate without a work breakdown structure and a project plan. These analyses can be done after a short evaluation phase where the processes and features are described in detail. Typically, software, hardware, and services cost between one and five million dollars/euros. Some companies charge more than 10 million, some even 50 million. In my opinion, these figures kill startups, and the result is not better than a 3 million dollars/euros project. A quality system integrator will not rip off a startup in phase one of the project but will try to establish a long-term relationship that will benefit both the startup and the system integrator.

In the first year, about two million dollars/euros will be spent on hardware, software, and services, and about the same amount needs to be spent on marketing and staffing the company. The company would need to collect at least five million dollars/euros from venture capitalists to be on the safe side. The implementation time should be calculated as at least half a year, meaning that no revenues will be earned during this time. Going online does not mean that a company will have a stable number of transactions immediately. It will take at least another half year to establish the brand and the site. As a result, the owner of the company should envision a period of two to three years of no profits.

As the service is virtual, it can easily be extended beyond the frontiers of France. The content could be translated into Spanish, for example, but probably no additional hardware or software is required. Some adaption of the implementation will be needed, but if accommodation for multiple languages, multiple countries, and multiple currencies has been planned for right from the beginning, only a little work needs to be done. Spain is about the same size as France, so a presence there means a doubling of revenue, without a doubling of costs, resulting in a larger profit.

If the management of the company can raise money from venture capitalists and can create an expectation in the market that profitability will take at least two to three years, there is a good chance the business will be successful.

6.5 Similar Cases

A company, to be even more profitable, should try to expand the business with similar business models. The basic business model here is to support people in their wedding anniversary preparations.

With only a few modifications, the wedding anniversary service could be extended to support a birthday service. Although a birthday is an event that happens only once a year, the target group becomes much bigger. The major modification would be the selection of business partners. Instead of having flower shops and jewelry stores, bookshops and gift shops become more important. An additional functionality could be introduced to alert all friends and family and allow them to get together virtually to buy a birthday present online. By pooling their money, they can afford a much bigger present.

Another extension of the business plan would include special days, such as Valentine's Day and Christmas. This would extend the business model from providing support for wedding anniversaries to becoming a full-service provider for special occasions.

Risks are associated with extending the business model. Entering a market where others may already have established a brand name could open the door to an invasion of a company's niche market by established competitors. Although the growing company will significantly increase its number of transactions, its system must be able to handle the increased traffic. Many more people will require a service representative in case of questions or trouble. If the business cannot provide additional resources, a decrease of quality will follow and customers will return to the tried-and-true brands.

Often it is better to stay in a niche market and build up a quality service than to go into the mass market where margins are much lower and many companies are vying for market share.

Chapter 7

The Thief

While you are window-shopping on a busy street while on holiday, a thief steals your wallet and mobile phone, leaving you without money, documents, and Internet connection. You envision life abroad without money or passport and fear you will soon be thrown into prison. But then you get a brilliant idea: you go to an Internet café, log on to the Internet, identify yourself through a retina scanner, and e-mail the police and the credit card company. A credit card tracker web page then displays a map of the city on which are superimposed the store locations where the credit card was used over the past hour. A second map pops up, showing police cars chasing from one such location to the next so the police can question witnesses about the thief's appearance; as the witnesses recall the face, an image of the thief slowly appears on the screen before you. The police capture the thief and return all your documents within minutes. You buy a new dress and continue with your holiday.

7.1 The Solution Today

In today's world, it is hard to image how such a scenario could work. Most probably, the procedure will be an incomplete patchwork of technologies and processes. Imagine being a Norwegian tourist on holiday in Japan. If your wallet, documents, and mobile phone get stolen in today's world, you have to find someone who speaks Norwegian or English if you don't speak Japanese. Otherwise, it will be difficult to find the nearest Internet café. On the other hand, an Internet café today won't really help since the police won't accept e-mail in most cases. You will have to go to a police station and explain your case.

This does not mean that the situation is hopeless. It is already possible to track credit cards. The credit card company records all transactions in the back-end system. The credit card company normally collects all transactions for a period of a month and sends them out to the owner. To track a thief, this process is not good enough. Two things could be done. One could call the credit card company and tell them to lock the credit card from further use. This ensures that the credit card is not misused, but it probably prevents the credit card company from tracking the movement of the thief. The thief will try once and will be refused, meaning that only one transaction will be recorded. If the shop owner has a good memory for faces, she could describe the thief, but it will not be enough to create a behavioral pattern.

The credit card company could offer another tack. Let the thief continue to buy goods and service up to a specified limit of 200 dollars/euros, for example, allowing more people to see the thief and see in which direction the thief moves or in which area of the city the thief can be found. Although there is a risk of losing the 200 dollars/euros, the credit card company could save a lot of money by getting the thief quickly.

At the same time, you could contact the local telecom company responsible for the roaming of the mobile phone. The local phone company can track the movement of the mobile phone if switched on. Currently, it provides only very rough tracking. Typically, a mobile phone can be tracked within a kilometer. But this only works if the mobile phone is not locked immediately. Usually one calls their own mobile phone provider to lock the phone to ensure that nobody can misuse it.

By tracking the thief through the credit card and the mobile phone, chances are much higher of finding the thief within the first day. This only works if both the credit card company and the mobile phone provider give the required information in a timely manner, if possible in real time. The police should be able to coordinate the information and create a composite drawing of the thief. This image should be initiated by you. If you cannot describe the thief, the shop owners that served the thief should be consulted.

Video cameras in public places could also help to find the thief. Comparing the sketch of the thief with the output of the video cameras could make it even easier to find the thief. The picture could be run through the electronic version of a mugbook. Although this seems like a viable way of making theft unprofitable, it is still unpracticable. The coordination of police, credit card companies, and mobile phone operators can only be done manually, which is fine if a theft occurs only every week or so, but in real life thefts happen much more often. If the frequency of this coordination process were increased, the police, credit card companies, and mobile phone operators would collapse.

And this is not a problem of Japan or Norwegians; it can happen to anyone anywhere in the world. In many countries there are barriers, such as culture, language, and technology, that will inhibit the process. A major issue is to prove that you are really the person you claim to be. Otherwise, anyone could lock your mobile phone and credit card. Therefore, you should ensure that only you can lock and unlock your phone and credit cards by a secret password that is known only to you and the company involved. As you can easily see, there is room for major improvement in the future.

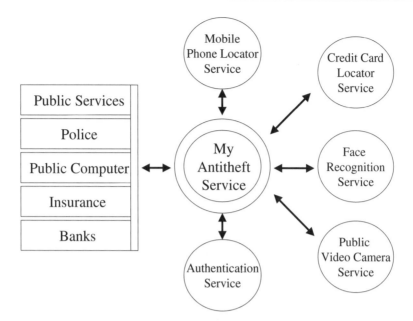

Figure 7.1. My Antitheft Service

7.2 The Solution Tomorrow

Several organizations will be more than interested in creating a more integrated approach in the future to reduce the number of crimes in the long run. If thieves can be easily identified through a new system and chances of catching them increase, the number of people trying to steal something will decrease. The police, insurance companies, and banks will be more than willing to invest in such a service if it can significantly reduce the number of thefts.

For this service to be easier to use and less error prone, it is enough just to connect a set of predefined services to each other to form a metaservice called "My Antitheft Service." Several organizations must also connect in an efficient way to ensure that appropriate measures can be taken to stop the criminal.

Let us look at Figure 7.1 to see how several organizations and devices need to connect to the service. First, public services must be involved. If a passport or a similar document is stolen, public or state services need to make sure that this particular passport is invalidated for the time it is in the hands of the thief. If someone tries to use the passport for identification at a bank or at border control, the staff at the bank and the border patrol would have been informed about the theft and would either cause the thief to be arrested or at least inform the police about the appearance of the document.

The police would need a full connection to the service to make sure that a composite image can be created and distributed to other organizations within the service. At the same time, the sketch will be distributed among the police to make sure that the thief does not slip through police controls. The police can also report updates on the case back to the service to make it available to the other parties involved.

The public computer will inform the service and start the investigations. From an Internet café you would log in to the web site of My Antitheft Service and report an incident. This report would be given in Norwegian. You should concentrate on the facts and should not care about translating the text, lest you make mistakes and give an inaccurate description. My Antitheft Service will provide a form with a lot of options to select from, to reduce the number of errors and time for completing the form. Some free text in the end will ensure that additional information about the case is not lost.

The input form will be based on the XML standard and will not only contain the fields you filled in, but also a description of the workflow and additional fields to fill in by the connected organizations. If this XML standard is certified by governmental bodies, the information contained within could be used for the lawsuit afterward.

Example 7.1 is an XML description for the credit card location. It is only an excerpt and contains only the basic information that will be needed: the name of the holder, the credit card number, the time of validity, and some information about the address. This basic information is not changed through transactions, so is valid for all transactions. Besides basic information, the XML description will store transaction-related information: the date, the address of the shop, and the amount of the transaction. The transaction-related information can help to trace the thief if it can be forwarded from the credit card company to the antitheft service, to determine the route the thief took.

The more transactions made after the theft, the easier it is to track the thief. A similar XML description needs to be implemented for the mobile phone provider. With little modification, the same XML description could be used for both credit cards and mobile phones. Instead of a credit card number, the phone number would be described, and instead of a shopping transaction, phone calls would be logged. By using the same XML description it would be easy to use a single location service to identify the spots where the thief has been in the past few hours. To receive transaction data in real time or near real time, the back-end systems must act in real time. This is not often the case today. In many cases, the back-end systems work in batch mode that typically stores incoming messages in a queue and processes them over night. Although this system works fine for most companies, it can be a major inhibitor in the online world. Banks, for example, often cannot process incoming orders immediately. Although instant processing is not really necessary in most cases, customers start to ask what the advantage is if an order is not processed immediately. In our case, real-time services and data are a must to ensure the availability and feasibility of the service.

Another important service is the facial recognition system that not only matches a face to a database but also generates a composite image based on

Example 7.1 XML Description

```
<?xml version="1.0"?>
<creditcard>
<type>credit card classic</type>
<number>3456 1239 1923 192</number>
<valid>02/02</valid>
<name>Clara Maarsson</name>
<address>Akerbrygge 145</address>
<postcode>1928</postcode>
<city>Oslo</city>
<country>Norway</country>
<shopping>
<date>17/Feb/2001</date>
<item>Trousers</item>
<shop>Jeans Corner</shop>
<address>Fisherman's Wharf</address>
<country>United States</country>
<amount>49,95 USD</amount>
</shopping>
</creditcard>
```

input from various sources, including the public video camera service. These closed-circuit television systems are widely used today to protect public places and shops and to prevent shoplifting. As the name says, these cameras operate in a closed circuit and are not available to the police, for example. In the future, it could be possible that the images from these systems will be made available to police computers for a particular purpose. The danger is that it can be misused to track innocent people, so all privacy issues must be resolved.

Privacy can only be ensured if strong authentication services will be implemented. Strong authentication means that it is difficult to falsify a person's identification. This ensures that only a few people will be able to see the information regarding the theft and those that have access will only see the information they require for their work. The police, for example, could import video material from public video cameras and compare it to the composite drawing only. Only if the facial recognition system finds a match will the police be alerted; if no match is found, the material will be removed from the police computer so that the police cannot use it for something else.

The insurance companies and banks should also be able to see the information that is relevant for them to do their job. This would require that every tag in the XML description contains a flag that describes who is allowed to see it and who isn't. The authentication service should provide several means for identification. For secure identification, the method should contain two components: one should be something a person has, and the other should be something a person knows. It could be, for example, a fingerprint and a password or the retina and the birth date. The information about a person must be stored in a central database so that it can be accessed from anywhere.

Ideally, the information should be stored at the passport office, which already saves a lot of information about citizens in an offline mode. To make the service useful, the passport office needs to provide a real-time online service to access the database. To be secure, the system should not give out the information to authentication services. It should be the other way round. Authentication services should send in the information they receive from a person, and the passport database should respond with "ok" or "failed." By providing two components that are not related to each other, authentication services can ensure that the result is correct.

Interfacing all services to a metaservice can help solve many cases of theft, making the world a bit securer. Although this service is a good idea, it won't change the world. Thieves will learn from the system and find a way to circumvent it. Therefore, I believe that curing the cause is a better way to solve the problem. Have a look at Chapter 10 for more on the social impact of technology.

7.3 Technology

The base technology for the information and service exchange will remain XML. It is the most flexible technology to date for formulating data structures and service information. No matter what type of information you want to share or which type of service you want to offer, you can create a structure in XML to define the information flow for all possible business cases. Knowing this, you won't be surprised to hear that all other scenarios described in the book use XML for the information exchange.

One of the biggest challenges of this scenario is to receive information in real time. Five minutes to find a flower shop may be a problem but it won't have an important impact on the business case. In our antitheft portal, minutes matter. The faster the portal collects and processes information, the greater the chances to find the thief and close the case.

To make real-time exchange of information a reality, the service must ensure that the environment is able to support it. This means that the antitheft portal needs to be highly available; this can be achieved through redundancy. Depending on the needs, every device can be cloned to make sure that one system fails, the other one can take over. Imagine a web server, an application server, and a database server—typical three-tier architecture that is used by most companies to run online business solutions. These servers, to be highly available, must be backed up by a second installation of the same components with redundant network connections and power supplies. This ensures that if a network problem occurs, the system can reroute the information via the alternative network connection until the network segment recovers. If one power supply fails, the other one can take over. An additional layer of security can be implemented by means of several connections to ISPs. If one ISP fails to connect, the system can be rerouted through the other ISP. To some, this may seem to be overkill, but for many companies such a setup is reality.

Another important issue is security. As the portal will have access to all sorts of private information, all information must be stored in a secure place to which only authorized people are allowed access. End-to-end security can only be achieved if security technology and procedures are implemented properly. The data and the portal itself must be protected by a firewall that allows access only to limited resources within the company. Limited access to the portal closes all back doors, but by itself is not secure. To ensure that only authorized persons are allowed to see content, the system must require a login and a password. More secure systems will require a bioscanner to ensure the identity of the person accessing the system. A login and password can be easily copied, a retina or fingerprint can't (this may change in the future, though). The firewall and the authentication procedure make sure that nobody can break in to the system. Finally, to secure the whole system, portals must secure the transfer of data between the portal and the different parties involved. Today's Secure Sockets Layer (SSL) encryption will suffice for most cases, but many companies are developing more secure systems, and new versions of SSL try to remove today's flaws in SSL implementations.

An intrusion detection system records all unusual events, such as port scanning or unauthorized access. In case of typical break-in patterns, the portal locks out that particular user or shuts down the service until a manual intervention is successful.

Figure 7.2 shows a technical architecture based on the described technologies. Although this redundant architecture doubles expenses in hardware and software, it will ensure that the business model works and that the system is available 24 hours a day. A system failure can result in an immense and immediate financial loss.

7.4 Business Case

Crime is a serious problem, and many parties are interested in having criminal cases resolved. The police, insurance companies, credit card companies, and mobile phone providers were already mentioned, and many other institutions could be involved to reduce the number of fraud resulting from theft.

Therefore, these companies will be more than willing to spend money on such a crime detection system. Theft and robbery happen all around the world

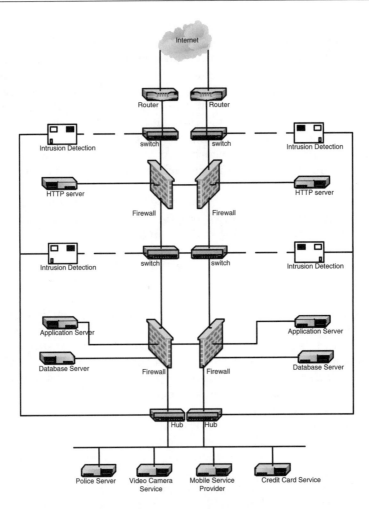

Figure 7.2. Sample Architecture for the Antitheft Portal

24 hours a day. Every few seconds a person is robbed or something is stolen. Only very few cases get solved, since the number of cases is too high for the police forces and the value of the stolen object is often too low for police to invest a lot of time and effort in its recovery. A cheap and efficient way to find criminals frees the police forces from paperwork so that they can work more efficiently on more complex cases.

A country like Germany has more than 10 million cases of theft a year. The value per theft is about 250 dollars/euros of direct costs: money, keys, and mobile phones, for example. In addition, another 250 dollars/euros are spent on blocking credit cards and mobile phones and on actual police investigations, which are often omitted from the calculation. Theft, therefore, creates a loss of 5 billion dollars/euros in Germany a year. Today, only 10 to 15 percent of the cases are resolved. This means that only 375 million dollars/euros of direct costs are recovered.

The idea behind the business case would be to increase the number of solved cases and reduce the indirect costs. Increasing the number of resolved cases by only 5 percent would save 125 million dollars/euros. Automating many of the manual processes involved after a theft, a business could reduce the cost per case by at least 20 percent, that is, to 200 dollars/euros. This reduction would drop the loss to 4 billion dollars/euros. Although still a gigantic sum, it reflects a step into the right direction.

The antitheft service can help the victim recover the stolen goods and can relieve the police of a lot of work. So, victims and police would be more than willing to invest in the service, for example, to give a percentage of the saved costs to the service. If customers were willing to spend 10 percent of the recovered items and the police also 10 percent of the saved cost, the antitheft service could generate 30 dollars/euros from each solved case (25 dollars/euros from the victim and 5 dollars/euros from the police). Considering that 5 percent of all cases can be solved, revenue of 15 million dollars/euros could be created per year for the antitheft service. A company should charge a minimum of 10 dollars/euros per transaction, whether or not the case can be solved, especially in the beginning when the number of solved cases is unknown. After some time, the company could reduce the base fee to make the service more attractive to customers, but only if a certain percentage of cases can be resolved successfully.

Additional money could be generated through a premium subscription service, which would store credit card and mobile phone numbers on the system. In case of theft, these people would call a number and enter their login and password to start the crime detection. Instead of calling a number, alternative channels, such as e-mail, the Web, or SMS start the process. The premium customers would get a higher priority on the system, and they would get status updates by phone or e-mail.

People would be happy to pay 5 dollars/euros a year for a good service. Through this subscription-based service, a certain base revenue can be guaranteed that makes life easier for the online service. It can be expected that 100,000 people will subscribe to the service in the first two years. Although peanuts compared to the 15 million dollars/euros revenue for each solved case, the fees offer a starting point for more diverse services in the future and ensures that people understand that extra service costs extra money. (This is a problem for many online startups; they offer something for free or at very low cost and then increase the price, losing most customers. Instead of increasing the price, startups should create value-added services that will lock in existing customers.)

As the service relies very much on other systems, it is important that SLAs be made with the information and service providers. Only this will ensure that the service will work in the predetermined way and will result in the predetermined revenue forecast.

This type of environment requires a larger investment than does the anniversary service from the last chapter. Scalability, stability, security, and real-time operation are features that are a must for this service, and they require redundancy in the hardware, network, and software components. In addition to the rather complex setup, a lot of integration needs to take place, so an investment of around 10 million dollars/euros will be needed for the first implementation. If the service works as designed, it won't be difficult to attract more customers. Therefore, it is not necessary to spend more on marketing and brand awareness than with the anniversary service. Staffing, marketing, and branding should not cost more than 2 million dollars/euros for the first year.

The service should first be introduced into one large country, such as France, Japan, or Germany, because it requires a large user base to be successful. On the other hand, the integrations that need to be made have to be repeated for every country, so a market analysis should evaluate the possibilities for every single market. Although there may be a need in every country, the solution relies heavily on other services that are not available in all countries. These services are only available in rich, technologically advanced countries.

7.5 Similar Cases

To attract more customers in the first place, the site could offer some tips on how to behave in case of robbery and theft and how to avoid being the victim of such an event. More information on crime prevention could be included, such as information on countries in which it is unsafe to travel or information about certain areas of a particular town. If this information is regularly updated, it will be valuable to every traveler. Offering travelers a subscription to the site will be valuable to both parties.

The business can also be extended to other forms of theft, for example, of cars or valuable jewelery. In this case, insurance companies are glad to invest a percentage to retrieve the stolen goods. For other forms of crime, such as kidnapping and murder, the business may provide some input, but these cases are often too complex and too individual to be solved in a standard way.

The antitheft portal could also try to sell related products, services, and information. The most obvious products are forms of travel insurance, which could be sold at a lower price in conjunction with a subscription to the portal and information about self-defense, with links to self-defense courses in the neighborhood. Many other things around security can be provided on the site.

The site has great potential because web sites today deal with this subject, and virtually none offer a service to the customer. The major issue will be to persuade the other partners that need to be involved to integrate their services and data into the portal. If they can be convinced, it is easy to convince venture capitalists and increase public interest in the web site. Again, the figures mentioned here are based on some assumptions. If you decide to create this or a similar service, please check the assumptions and make sure that the conditions are the same. This chapter does not replace a business consultant, but it should give you some ideas about what you need to look for.

Chapter 8

Party People

A family is going on holiday, except for the eldest son. As soon as the rest of the family leaves, the son initiates plans for a party at home. On the Internet, he sets up a party page that his friends can access over the Web or by mobile phone and logs in to the "after-party" service, using the credentials of his father's bank. Teens driving along the street are notified on their mobile phone to join the party. The house fills with teens, who inadvertently break glasses, one of the TV sets, and other devices. Meanwhile, the family has decided to return home because of bad weather. As more things break at the party, the after-party service monitors the damage remotely: each item that breaks has a built-in chip that notifies the after-party service to order a replacement immediately. When the family's car crosses the city limits, the after-party service declares a red alert and loads a team of cleaners into vans, which races to the house. The team cleans the house and leaves shortly before the family arrives. When the family walks in, the teens are sitting on the sofa, watching a talk show on an unbroken TV. The next day, the father checks his bank account balance from the Internet and sees a large sum debited from the bank account to the after-party service. He shouts for the son.

8.1 The Solution Today

In today's world it will be difficult to implement such a complex service, since many parts of the solution either do not exist at all or do not exist in the form required. The biggest challenge will be the assets in the house; they are too diverse at the moment to be treated by a single system. Although many of the devices used in a household have chips built in, they lack an Internet connection or at least a local connection to exchange information. No system knows about the existence of the others and there is no central point that knows about all items in the house, be they furniture, consumer electronics, or other objects.

To realize such an after-party service, it would be necessary to create an online service where homeowners can register all the items they have within the house. There are several problems with this approach. First, there is no standard way to describe the objects. The service either builds a catalog of all products that have been built and sold over the last hundred years or lets the homeowners describe their goods themselves. With the catalog, the providers could be sure that every item is precisely described, but the catalog would be too big to handle by the homeowners. Every category would contain thousands of different items, and often the owner does not know which one best describes an item.

The option of free text does not really help either, because it can't guarantee that an item can be found in a store. Probably the best way would be to create generic categories, such as table, define some attributes, such as size, make, and color, and add a free text field where additional information can be entered to make sure that the item is described as well as possible. This approach still means a lot of work without immediate reward.

To work, the system could focus only on consumer electronics and household devices. This means that the television set, the DVD player, the stereo, and the refrigerator would be registered at the service. These devices are easy to register because they have unique names and numbers and are all standardized. Having their model names and numbers will ensure that a certain product is correctly described and will provide the age and approximate cost for the object. This information makes it easier to find a replacement.

The number of objects to be entered into the system will be probably around 10, meaning that the effort is manageable and will ensure that many people will participate.

Once people have registered and the party can start, party-givers will want to announce the party on a web site. In addition, the information should be pushed to news services and party web sites so that the information can be found immediately. This means that a party portal needs to be built to provide information about ongoing parties for all cities and regions in a particular country. Registered party-goers could be informed by e-mail or SMS if the profile fits their requirements.

The setup of the information should be easy if the party person is preregistered. During the registration some details about the types of parties could be entered: what type of music is played, what type of people typically attend, and what criteria exist for acceptance to a party.

Once the party is under way, there is no way today to check what is broken and what is not. To make the system work, the party people would need to enter what has been broken into the system to allow for replacement. Another problem is tracking the parents in their car. It would be possible to track the mobile phone of the parents, but without their consent, doing so would be illegal in most countries around the world. Without the parent-tracking system in place, the whole solution will be difficult to implement, but there are ways around it, of course. The party portal could provide web cams on major roads into town, scanning for certain number plates. This simplified form of car tracking could work in many cases.

With geocoding software, the distance of the car from the house can be measured. If the car is moving toward the house, an SMS could be sent out to the party people, informing them about the return of the parents and how long it may take until they are back. The party people could enter the objects that were broken into the system and hope that replacements would arrive before the parents.

Although very complex today, the basic idea can be implemented with today's technologies, but I doubt that there is a business plan to support the effort or implement the technology with reasonable costs. Too many unknowns are in the project to make it reality.

8.2   The Solution Tomorrow

In tomorrow's world, things are changing, as we have learned in the previous chapters. More things will have built-in chips that will enable communication with other devices nearby and with the Internet in general. The above-mentioned consumer electronics and household devices will most likely have hardware and software to support this built-in functionality, meaning that these devices can be automatically categorized. Many other objects will also have built-in chips, so why shouldn't a cupboard or a couch have one to identify itself or to communicate with the rest of the furniture? The technology for this is becoming cheaper every day and would enable people to register at least all new objects in the house. Over time, fewer objects would have to be manually keyed in to the system.

Figure 8.1 shows which services and devices need to be connected to the after-party service. A home object surveillance service will be needed to check the status of every object in the particular house. A party announcement service will make sure that all relevant information is collected and forwarded to online party portals and registered customers. A party-people locator service will make sure that all registered customers that are near the event will be informed about it if their profile fits. The authentication service will make sure that only the right people have access to the party database. This would enable party organizers to invite friends only, for example. Last, a parent-alert service that makes sure that parents are still away needs to be implemented.

A person who wants to participate in the party service would collect information about all objects in a local database and export it after registration to the online service. This would mean a huge reduction in effort and lower the entry barrier significantly, but the party service portal must ensure that the information is securely stored and only authorized systems and people are allowed to see it. Otherwise, thieves could use the system to spot lucrative houses for break-ins, for example, or unwelcome guests could crash the party.

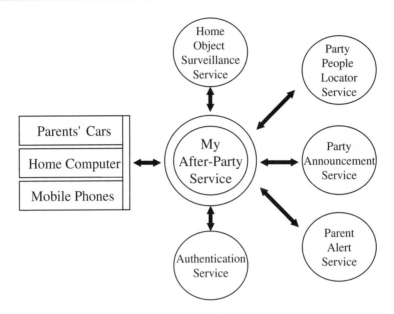

Figure 8.1. My After-Party Service

After the party-giver is registered, he can announce a party by several methods. In the future, he will have several methods by which to input the necessary data. He can enter the data from a web site, through a mobile phone using WAP or imode, or through voice recognition systems, just to mention a few examples. SMS, WAP or i-mode, or traditional e-mail will inform registered party-goers. Specialized announcement portals will broadcast the event. Television and radio programs tailored to the needs of the party generation would be informed and provide the information to the target group. One-to-one marketing and community-building features invite only those people who fit with the rest of the party and ensure that others are not informed about the event.

Once the party has started, objects with built-in chips would monitor their own status and if possible the status of neighboring objects and report the status to the party portal. Broken objects would be reordered or scheduled for repair. To communicate the status of the objects, an XML description would be used. Example 8.1 provides an excerpt of the data structure. Either in regular intervals or in real time status changes are reported to the party service, which then tries to locate a shop that can immediately deliver the broken object. The after-party service could also add information into the XML description about the shipping status. Another XML description will be used to define the type of party and what types of guests are welcome. This information is filtered through the party-goer database at the after-party service, which will then send messages to all people that may be interested.

Example 8.1 XML Description for Objects in a House

To make sure that all objects in the house can be collected in a central database, an XML description would be used.

```
<?xml version="1.0"?>
<homeobjects>
<type>HP Omnibook 4150</type>
<options>ABD</number>
<bought>05/Feb/1999</bought>
<owner>Daniel Amor</owner>
<currentlocation>living room</currentlocation>
<status>ok</status>
</homeobjects>
<homeobjects>
<type>IKEA Billy</type>
<options>none</number>
<bought>12/Mar/1989</bought>
<owner>Daniel Amor</owner>
<currentlocation>bedroom</currentlocation>
<status>ok</broken>
</homeobjects>
```

The parent alert service could connect the car with the house and report the distance of the car to the house. If the car gets nearer than the specified distance or time, an alert would inform the after-party service and the party people so that everything can be back in place when the parents arrive at home. As you can see it will become much easier in the future to implement such a service, driving the costs down and the revenues up.

8.3   Technology

From a technological point of view, the solution will require a platform that converts messages to and from many different formats and devices. Again, the use of XML will ensure the exchange of information across different platforms and devices.

The central piece of the whole architecture is the after-party service architecture (see Figure 8.2). To manage the whole architecture, the system needs

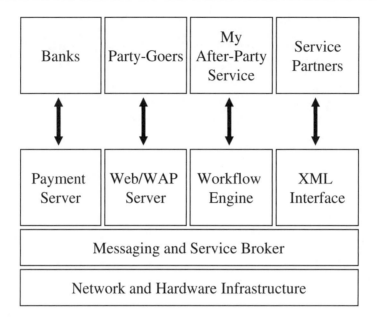

Figure 8.2. After-Party Architecture

a way to manage the flow of information and services. Therefore, the system requires a workflow component to check that everything is going according to plan. This component checks if a party needs to be announced and filters the party information through the party-people database. If something does not work in the predefined way, this workflow component will try to correct the workflow or, if correction is not possible, will alert the involved parties.

Every entry to the after-party service will be redirected to the other systems involved. A number of services are required to run the solution. They will be connected by an open standard XML interface, allowing maximum flexibility.

A WAP server will ensure that all party people will receive information about the party on their mobile phone. Others that are at home will receive e-mail with a URL containing detailed information about the party and, if available, a web-cam view of the actual party. It will show how many people are there and how lively the whole thing is. If the party host can set up an audio connection, potential party-goers can listen to the actual music at the party and maybe even receive a list of CDs that are in the house to see what type of music is available and what is missing.

A virtual jukebox could enable all party people to select their favorite song and download it to the home stereo system, where through a special licensing agreement, it will be played only once and deleted. That way either all party people participate in the music selection or a DJ selects the music, and no one needs to bring piles of vinyl records and CDs. Record label and online music shops would need to build up a new infrastructure to support this business model. Songs would be available in various formats for download, and payment would be based on different models for different occasions. A few cents would be paid for a single download that can only be heard once; around a dollar/euro if the host wants to keep the music. Although Napster[1] or Gnutella[2], for example, offer the download of music, there is still a big market for such a solution, since Napster does not guarantee quality or download times. Party people don't want to search for a piece of music, wait sometimes hours for the download, and then listen to a song of poor quality. They want it now and they want good quality.

The party people may have to pay a small fee for receiving the information. This cost could be automatically billed to the phone bill, or a direct link to the banking system could directly debit the fee from the party people's account.

Although security is always important, it is not on the same level as in the previous scenario, where we were treating very personal details. In this scenario, personal information, such as addresses and party times, is involved. Therefore, it is important to secure access to the information and make sure that the transmission is encrypted. The difference is that if information does slip out, it won't ruin the business, since security is not the major driver behind the business. A standard security infrastructure, which includes firewalls and a security concept, will suffice for this business case.

The service also does not need to provide a real-time infrastructure, since it does not matter if information is transmitted a few seconds or even minutes later. If people get a message about a party that starts at 10 p.m., the information may be of interest the whole day. More time critical is the parent surveillance system, but because a maximum of two adults per party needs to be checked, few resources are involved in that aspect.

Scalability is more of an issue because many people are involved in any transaction. It needs to be ensured that the technical infrastructure can be easily expanded by adding new hardware and networking components. Many solutions lack scalability, which is not an easy task if not done right in the first place. It is important to modularize the solution as much as possible because it is much easier to scale components than a monolithic solution. Often it is not necessary to duplicate the whole solution, but only to expand the bottleneck within the system. The use of components and modules makes it is much easier to identify these bottlenecks and remove them by adding additional hardware or by recoding them to be more efficient.

8.4 Business Case

Although the initial idea is quite good, I doubt it will be successful. As we have shown in the previous section, we are even able to build the solution,

---

[1]http://www.napster.com/

[2]http://www.gnutella.com/

but there is a major flaw in the business case. The whole idea works only if enough teenagers will be able to pay the bill for the after-party service. There is no doubt that the youth will accept the party announcement service immediately because it reduces the effort and time to tell everyone about a party. The parent-alert service will also be highly accepted, just as all other value-added services that surround the after-party service. The problem is that the preparty services are designed to be free and that the money will be earned with the after-service party.

Let's suppose that in a particular country there are at least 1 million parties every week. In 0.1 percent of the parties, the teenagers are rich enough to pay for their damage themselves. Let us assume that another 0.2 percent have access to their parents' credit cards and use them in emergencies. This is a total of 0.3 percent of all parties, that is, about 3,000 parties a week for which the service is of interest. This means that per year about 156,000 party-goers will use the after-party service.

If we consider that the service will have a transaction volume of about 200 dollars/euros per party and that about 5 percent of the transaction will be charged as a fee by the after-party service, the service will earn about 10 dollars/euros per transaction or about 3,000 dollars/euros a week or 1.56 million dollars/euros a year. This is not too bad, but the revenue probably is lower. The number of teenagers with access to the credit cards of their parents will reduce over time, as a result of the popularity of the service. The more people know about it, the more parents will make sure that their kids do not have any access to the money.

In most business cases, we see increased profit with increased popularity; with this business case, popularity could mean a reduction. Instead of having the parents pay for the party, teenagers could collect money from the friends that participate in the party and pay for the service themselves collectively. But this is also a number with many unknowns in it. Let us be optimistic and project revenues of 1.56 million dollars/euros a year. To build up the solution, a company must invest about 1.5 million to 2 million dollars/euros for the software, hardware, and network infrastructure. On top of that, the company needs to be built up and the service must be marketed. Owing to the nature of the project, marketing costs can be quite low because teenagers will spread the word very fast if the service works. So, let us expect another million dollars/euros for this part of the service. This would add up to at least 3 million dollars/euros. With an expected revenue of 1.56 million dollars/euros, it would take several years to make a profit.

As this case is the most optimistic one, it could well be that 1.56 million dollars/euros is far too high. I would not invest in this business. The technology will work, but the business case will most probably fail. In late 2000, when the fad for investing in startups began to wane, those startups with a good business case survived, albeit with lower share values. Those without a proper business case disappeared—and quite a few disappeared! A sound business is a must to ensure the longevity of a business. It does not suffice to have the technology in place and have the proof that the job can be done. Many people think that they need to continue once they have taken a project so far, but in my opinion it is better to stop a project that is set up for failure and concentrate on something else.

8.5   Similar Cases

Our rejection of the business case does not mean that we have to throw away the whole idea. We make it successful by modifying the business plan. We have identified single components of the solution as being very useful, and those components could become highly successful. The issue with the business case is the composition of the modules. To resolve this issue, we could split the business case into several business cases by adding new services, to ensure that the strengths and advantages of the components are reinforced.

The home object surveillance service is not only very interesting for party people, but also for the homeowners and maybe even more for insurance companies. If insurance companies had access to the objects in a house, they could calculate the value of the objects and offer more personalized insurance packages to their customers. In addition, they could track stolen goods very efficiently. For the first time, they would be able to track the location of the goods, check the status of them, and get them back more easily.

If a house burned down, an insurer could later tell which objects burned with the house and which were saved. This reduces the probability of fraud since the objects can be tracked very easily; their status will be transmitted to the insurance company. The scheme also reduces the time and effort spent by the homeowner in declaring what has been destroyed. The same concept might also be interesting to insurance companies in cases of theft.

The concept of a party service could also be expanded to be more successful. The first step would be to find a target group that is willing to spend money on services, for example, for wedding parties. An after-party wedding service would probably be profitable. The number of weddings is lower than teenager parties, but the amount spent per party is much higher. The next step would be to build a new business plan, verify the revenues, and estimate the costs. The numbers would probably be favorable, and we could start to think about the implementation issues.

One of the major obstacles for business cases is that startups write their own business plan, which is good, but someone else should also look it over, to make sure that it is not only a good idea, but also a viable business. To become successful, a company must be open to new ideas and be willing to modify the business plan if someone else has a better idea. The original scenario in this chapter tells us that it is not enough to have a good idea. A market, customer acceptance, and an architecture that supports the idea are as important as the idea itself. Complex technology can be handled by very few companies. Service ideas on top of an established technology can be created by a lot more companies. These companies should focus on translating technology into solutions for the customer.

Chapter 9

Toothaches

A small girl with a toothache tries to avoid going to the dentist by saying that everything is okay. She imagines how awful it would be at the dentist, with all those dreadful, noisy instruments. Finally, her mother, realizing that something is wrong with her daughter's teeth, replaces the normal toothbrush with a high-tech toothbrush, which lets the "Internet dental care service" check teeth while a person is brushing them. The service passes the daughter's dental information to a dentist locator, which finds the dentists in the girl's neighborhood and checks to see which one of them has an opening. The available dentist receives an image of the girl's teeth and a description of the problem. The dentist diagnoses the cause of the toothache and informs the mother by e-mail. The mother tells the daughter that she has made an appointment for her with the hairdresser. At the appointment time, the dentist and his office are transformed into a hairdresser and salon. The girl enters the room, sits down, and waits for the hairdresser to begin his work. In a second, the room is transformed back, and the dentist uses a high-tech laser to resolve the problem with the aching tooth before the girl even notices.

9.1 The Solution Today

Okay, so now we are getting a bit more into science fiction. But let us see how much we can do in today's world. The biggest challenge is to get all the required information together and pass it on to a dentist. Children who do not like to go to the dentist are not uncommon in today's world, and parents must check the teeth of their children regularly. Although it would be technically possible to build a toothbrush with a built-in camera, it would cost too much and would probably deliver poor results that would not help the dentist at all. So, a manual check by the parents cannot be replaced today with automatic procedures.

To help parents look for the right things, an education center for parents would be useful. This education center would explain everything about teeth, for example, to make it easier for parents to spot problems. This education center or portal could also contain a dentist locator that would list dentists in the neighborhood. The portal site could also manage appointments. The parents would enter the appointments manager of their preferred dentist and select a date and time for the appointment. As many dentists today won't have an online connection to the portal site, the site will need to send a request to the dentist for approval of the appointment. This could be done by e-mail, fax, or phone. The parents would receive an answer within minutes. For the parents, there is no added value in this service, since they could call their dentist directly. For the portal owner, it would offer an opportunity to present advertising to viewers and collect information that may be useful in the future.

The education part of the web site would allow the parents to specify the problem to let the dentist know what to look for first. The information will not replace the doctor's diagnosis, but it would allow the doctor to check for the painful things first. The educational portal also does not replace half-yearly visits to the dentist. If the symptoms are clear, the dentist could advise parents about possible remedies to reduce pain until the appointment.

The next building block in our solution was the camouflage of the dentist and his office. As described in our scenario, this was done with morphing technologies. But the intent can be realized anyway by creating a warm atmosphere with toys and colors that make the waiting room more pleasant for the children. In such an atmosphere, children will be less fearful and more willing to cooperate with the dentist.

As you can see, technology today can support current processes but cannot replace any of them. Technology enhances the processes very little so far: children must still brush their teeth daily, and parents must still check on their children and send them to the dentist when necessary. Many of the services that could be provided are inefficient. An online dentist locator and an online dentist appointment manager seem like good and simple-to-use technologies, but their use is limited. A dentist locator is only useful for people who have moved and don't know where a dentist is. People typically do not change their dentist with every appointment; they tend to stay with the same person. The appointment manager also does not relieve people from actively selecting the date and time of the appointment. It just replaces the phone call with a web interface. If the dentist has an integration with the portal site, it could reduce the number of phone calls, but the time saved is too little to compensate for the cost of integration.

Building up a dental care service portal today would be inefficient and probably unacceptable by the majority of people. Dental care is a problem that is the responsibility of all people, so there is a huge market, but the current technology won't attract many customers.

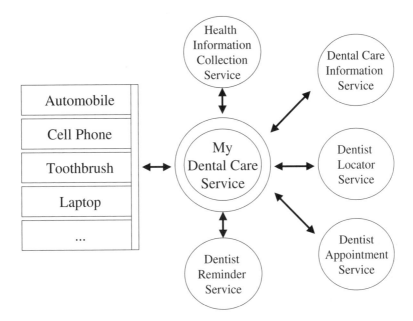

Figure 9.1. My Dental Care Service

9.2   The Solution Tomorrow

Tomorrow's solution will have one major advantage—it will offer the full integration required for efficient, effective use of the dental care service. Toothbrushes will have built-in sensors that look for problems. These toothbrushes will not only check for tooth decay, they will also measure the fluids in the mouth and check the number and type of bacteria. Other sensors will look for signs in the mouth that indicate the person's physical status; for example, sensors could measure body temperature or determine if a woman is ovulating. The toothbrush could detect bad breath and investigate its cause.

This multifunctional toothbrush would, of course, also check that all teeth were brushed properly and inform the user to spend more time on some teeth if necessary. Adding a connection to the network would not be difficult. The dental care service could upload collected information to a local information hub, generate statistics about the health status of a person, and provide tips to prevent future problems. When the user goes on holiday, the toothbrush would collect information during that time and update the system upon return.

Figure 9.1 illustrates which services and devices need to be connected to the dental care service to make it useful for the customers. The toothbrush will provide the information to a health information collection service. The health information collected by the toothbrush would be transmitted in SML format to be stored in a central database, as shown in Example 9.1. The collection service

Example 9.1 XML Description for Dental Care Data Collection

```
<?xml version="1.0"?>
<healthinformation>
<patient>Randalph Smith</patient>
<birthday>12/Apr/1967</birthday>
<sex>male</sex>
<dailyupdate>
<date>05/Feb/2007</date>
<time>07:02 GMT+1</time>
<temperature>36,5 degrees celsius</temperature>
<statusteeth>ok</statusteeth>
</dailyupdate>
<dailyupdate>
<date>05/Feb/2007</date>
<time>22:17 GMT+1</time>
<temperature>36,3 degrees celsius</temperature>
<statusteeth>ok</statusteeth>
</dailyupdate>
</healthinformation>
```

in turn will contact the dental care information service to check if problems occur and if they do, will learn what needs to be done. The dentist locator will provide information about the location and opening times of the dentist. The dentist appointment service would provide a real-time integration with the dentist's appointment system, and the dentist reminder service will make sure that people do not forget about their appointments.

The tight integration will make sure that the patients do not have to worry about details. They will have regular appointments, such as every six months which will be coordinated automatically between the personal calendar and the appointment manager of the dentist. The dentist locator will ensure that no matter where you are, you will find your way to the dentist. It could also be useful for travelers who have problems while away from home; the dentist locator will guide them to the nearest dentist. Through the dental care portal solution, the person's regular dentist will be informed about the problems abroad so that the patient can be checked upon return to ensure that the same level of quality was used for the dental care.

To be accessible to any dentist, the information needs to be stored in a central location, such as the dental care service itself or the health insurance company that insures a particular patient. The data should be stored in an application-independent format so that dentists with different applications can access the same data without trouble.

To make the exchange of data as seamless as possible, XML would be used. There is not much new to say about XML, since we have already seen three scenarios where it has been used. But there is one thing that should be noticed. Some of the data in the sample XML description (see Example 9.1) contains a unit descriptor, such as "degrees celsius" or "GMT+1." These unit descriptors make the measures independent of the measuring standards used. A patient living in the United States will most probably use Fahrenheit instead of Celsius and PST (Pacific Standard Time) instead of GMT+1 or CET (Central European Time). These pieces of information enable comparison of daily health status reports. The dental care portal could create statistics of the most common problems a certain group of people has and provide them as a guideline for reducing the most prevalent problems.

The dentist appointment service should make the regular half-yearly appointments and, in case of a problem, coordinate additional appointments with certain dependencies. It should check against the dates and appointments in the personal calendar of the patient. Depending on the urgency of the situation, the personal calendar should try to rearrange existing appointments. Once all changes have been made, the patient should be informed about the changes to make sure that everything goes the way the patient wants it to go.

To make sure that the patient is punctual, the dentist reminder service will remind the patient about the appointment regardless of where the patient is. If the patient is at home, a reminder will be displayed on the television screen or communicated over the radio. When at work, the patient will receive information by e-mail. When on the road, the patient will be called on the mobile phone. Depending on the distance and direction of the patient, the system will provide information at the right time. If the system detects that the patient is on the way to the dentist, it will not issue a reminder, but try to help the patient find the way. If the patient was a thousand miles away from the dentist the day before, an extra reminder will be provided. The reminder service will be strongly personalized to make sure that it does not interrupt the patients in their daily lives.

9.3   Technology

From a technological point of view, the different services in the future scenario can be designed. Several companies producing medical devices are working on intelligent toothbrushes. It will take some time before we see the version described earlier, but first steps will be made soon. Some of the features can also be implemented outside the toothbrush to make the first phase easier. Measuring the temperature will be included in a later phase (such measurement can

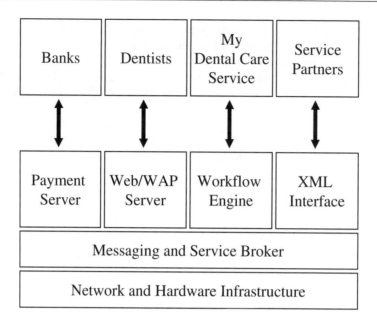

Figure 9.2. Dental Care Architecture

be done easily in the ear today). Measuring the breath will be probably easy to integrate. Other features will evolve and be incorporated over time. Each feature described is already available; the issue is to integrate all of them and to digitize the output. Putting in a transmitter to send the data to a health database is no longer an issue.

Once the health-related information has been inserted into the database, most of the other tasks can be easily automated. By putting the whole dental care service onto a single platform, the communication between the single entities and services is easy to create. To make sure that everything in the process works flawlessly, a workflow engine will check the status of each task and send out messages to the owner of the tasks in case of problems. The services surrounding the dental care portal are standard technology and do not require anything special. They could be built today but are useless because of the missing input. Integration will be the key issue to success. And that is the reason why such a dental care portal is not available today.

In some countries, dentists are already connected to a health network to automate payments with the health insurances. These private networks today are not connected to the Internet but work over private leased lines. Connecting these networks to the Internet is technically easy, but difficult from a security and privacy point of view. Many people object to the idea of free-floating health information on the Internet. To avoid a second source of health information, the dental care service should create a secure connection to this health network. This will ensure that the connectivity is controlled by trustworthy partners and will reduce the possible number of security and privacy breaches.

Privacy and security are especially important in this business case because this private information should not be in the hands of others. Although we are talking about limited health-related information, it can be expected that more information will be made available in the future. The service may be expanded beyond its original scope and may contain a complete health database. The toothbrush could analyze the DNA code of the person and discover more about illnesses that may happen in the future. The dental care service needs to state explicitly which information is collected and how it is used; otherwise, it is highly unlikely that people will trust the service. To make privacy waterproof, the service should create a legal framework to ensure that privacy breaches can be brought to court.

Availability is not a big issue for this kind of service as long as each component of the system works. If the toothbrush cannot communicate with the health database in real time, it does not matter. Nor does it matter if communication is delayed for several minutes. The information can be transmitted in batch mode without having a big impact on the business case.

Scalability, though, will be an issue. To make this service successful, many people will have to use it and every single person will contribute new data every day. This leads to the next technical aspect: storage. The amount of information stored in the database will be huge. Not only textual information will be stored, but also x-rays from the dentist and images taken by the toothbrush-camera. The information must be stored at least five years, probably even longer.

The information does not need to be available online all the time. Only when a person goes to the dentist must the information be present. This makes storage cheaper, since it can be offline on DVD or CD-ROM. Whenever an appointment is coming up, a storage robot will select the right DVD and upload the information to the online service. Depending on the date of the appointment, the information will remain on the online server or will be removed.

9.4 Business Case

Looking at the business case, we can see a lot of potential in the health business. People grow older and their health becomes more valuable. To prevent tooth loss, people are willing to spend a lot of money, and this dental care service could be very interesting to many people. If we look at a market like the United States, we are talking about more than 260 million people potentially interested in the service. The dental care service tries to reduce the effort and increase the positive results.

Several groups will be more than interested in pushing this service forward. Medical device manufacturers will be happy to introduce a new technology.

They will heavily promote the new technology because it will secure their profit for a few years. On the other side, dentists can lower their administrative overhead by automating the appointment process. By regularly checking the status of the teeth and making automatic appointments, they will substantially increase the number of patients. Today, patients are often not really willing to see the dentist. With the daily check of teeth and dental education, these people will see their dentist more often and reduce the number of difficult cases. The health insurance companies will love the idea since the cost of curing people is rising all the time. If people subscribe to a dental care portal and follow the guidelines provided by the system, insurance companies could lower the cost significantly and also lower costs to their clients. This would mean that if people had to undergo dental surgery, for example, they would pay much less because they regularly visited the dentist and took care of their teeth. The monthly insurance payment would also be lowered due to the cost savings.

These driving forces together with the desire of the people to remain healthy throughout their lives will drive the business scenario. If we imagine that only 1 percent of the population of the United States will subscribe to this service, about 2.6 million people would profit from the service. If every person paid a monthly fee of 5 dollars/euros, 13 million dollars/euros in cash would flow into the company, 156 million dollars/euros per year. This means that there is a huge money-making potential for the portal service. It would also be possible to charge the dentist a transaction fee, for example 1 percent of the cost of the visit. Over time, this amount would be reduced because of the good prevention technologies in place but would guarantee a good startup phase.

With increased popularity, it will be easy to reach 5 to 10 percent of the people in a country. With every additional customer, the cost is decreased, making the company even more profitable. Apart from the intelligent toothbrushes, the implementation will be easy to realize and relatively cheap. There will be some cost involved in setting up the company and getting the right knowledge on board to advise patients with dental problems. The software needs to be intelligent enough to track specific patterns of problems to make recognition easy. I assume that a first phase will cost about 3 million to 5 million dollars/euros in software, hardware, services, and organization. Little money will be required for marketing the services. Health insurance will include the service as part of their portfolio, and dentists will also be interested in promoting the service. The difficulty will be in getting all parties onto the same platform to make the exchange of information easy. In this very heterogenous environment, it will be necessary to support many devices and software platforms to make integration as seamless as possible for the dentists. They are not interested in setting up an IT department; they want to do their business, which is curing disease of the teeth, gums, and oral structures.

9.5 Similar Cases

Expanding the business case does not require a lot of imagination. Moving from a dental care service to a more generic health care service is easy. The most important part is to create a service that has no overhead for patients. They should be able to continue with their life and should only be disturbed if something is wrong. The intelligent toothbrush does not require people to change their habits. Assuming everybody in a house owns a toothbrush and uses it twice a day, the service will mean no change at all. Others who brush less frequently will still profit from the detection system but will also have more need for a dentist.

To expand the service, the owners need to think about invisible sensors in other areas of life to make the detection of problems as unobtrusive as possible. It would be possible to put a sensor in the toilet to check for problems there. Sensors could also be built into clothes, checking the temperature, blood pressure, and other signals sent from the body when problems arise. With a set of sensors controlling the health of a person throughout the day, the service provider can build up a complex database with a lot of knowledge about every single person. The service, to work properly, requires the intelligence of the person using the service. It does not help, for example, to eat only dietary products if you eat them in quantity. Common sense and good education are the basis for a healthy life, these health services only support these good habits.

The site has great potential; only small web sites today deal with this subject, and virtually none offer a service to the customer. The major issue will be to get the other partners that need to be involved to integrate their services and data into the portal. If they can be convinced, it is easy to recruit venture capitalists and to increase the public interest in the web site. Again, the figures mentioned here are based on some assumptions. If you want to create this or a similar service, please do check the assumptions and make sure that the conditions are the same. This chapter does not replace a business consultant, but it should give you some ideas about what to look for. Besides the technology and the business, please consider personnel, marketing, logistics, and other areas of expertise that need to be taken into account to make a business really successful.

Part III

Future Impact

Chapter 10

The Future of the Internet

10.1 Social Impact

Computers have revolutionized society over the last 50 years. Information technologies are taking on a large role in human social lives. Computers used to be tools that specialists employed to accomplish specific tasks. Today, individuals use computers to communicate with others and to work on a variety of tasks. Computing is no longer the domain of a few specialists. With the advent of pervasive computing, computers are leaving the largely sedentary and solitary desktop environment and are entering into human social lives in an unprecedented manner. Pervasive computing means a move from an interaction between an individual and a single device to an abundance of networked mobile and embedded computing devices that individuals and groups use across a variety of tasks and places. Pervasive computing becomes part of everyday life.

Pervasive computing will change the way we work and live. But it will be a transition rather than a revolution, from a technological point of view. Just as the telephone did not replace direct human communication and television did not replace the cinema, pervasive computing will not replace current computing technologies. Desktop computers will still be part of everyday life, but they won't be hot technology anymore, just a commodity for some of us. Big business will move on to new paradigms, technologies, and devices.

10.1.1 Effect on Daily Life

I think the most important question many people will ask is, "Do I really need this?" In many cases, I would respond, "No." But this question has always been valid for inventions. Do we really need to fly tourists to the South Pole? Do we need an elevator to get two floors up? Do we need to have the Internet? Life is definitely possible without these things, but one of the most important drivers in human nature is to invent things to make life more comfortable.

But many inventions have only been made because knowledge from past times has been lost. Look at air conditioning. Do we really need it? No. The reason for inventing air conditioning was the development of huge offices that were built very cheaply because the major driver was cost reduction. In Europe, air conditioning is still not very common. Especially around the Mediterranean Sea, people seldom use air conditioning, although it can be very hot in the summer. The reason is that builders still know how to build houses that keep people cool in summer and warm in winter without any technology at all. Builders know which stones to select and how to build the roof to protect from the heat in summer and preserve the warmth in winter. They also have a different rhythm for work. Although it seems strange to stop work from 1 to 4 o'clock in the afternoon (siesta time), it is a smart thing to do. After 4 o'clock when the sun is lower in the sky, the temperature is more agreeable and it is easier to work again.

The eight-hour shift was established to save costs, but as a result, many things were needed to make work comfortable again. There are many more examples of "new" inventions that were to make life "easier," but only because people had forgotten how to live comfortably with the conditions (weather, climate, etc.) that surrounded them. This technology-driven society believes that it is possible to solve all problems by inventing a new device, instead of determining whether a change in human behavior would solve the problem more elegantly. The drive to solve everything by technology has created a lot of problems, especially to the environment.

The power problems California experienced in the beginning of 2001 demonstrated that people become helpless if their electrical devices become inoperable. It could well be that California has not resolved the energy issue by the time you read this book. The reasons for the energy problem are complex, but some of the effects are quite clear. The power consumption per capita in the United States is high, the concept of power saving is not widespread, and the use of many electrical devices makes the problem worse every day. The price is now being paid in California, which only a few years ago was the motor of the technological future and now lacks the needed power to run its businesses.

Technology has changed society over centuries. Without technology we wouldn't be able to build up democracies and live the comfortable lives we are living today. Nevertheless, our lives would still be comfortable without the Internet and other high-tech gadgets. Look at Greece more than 2,000 years ago. The Greeks were able to build democracies. I often hear people say or write that the Internet will guarantee a democratic world. I don't believe so. The Internet is just a technology; by itself it is neither good or bad. But just like all technologies, the Internet can amplify any effort you put into something.

Consider a horse carriage and a steam engine. The steam engine increased the number of people a carriage could pull, which was good but also enabled more soldiers to be carried to war. The Internet is not very different from the steam engine. People expressed their thoughts and feelings without the Internet by talking to other people. Then someone invented a way that people could write down their thoughts and feelings. And basically, the Internet is just an extension of this line. Technologically, the Internet allows anyone to say anything or do business with someone. But other than in the United States where everything is possible, many other countries explicitly prohibit certain forms of speech. In some European countries it is forbidden to set up Nazi web sites, for example. Anything promoting Nazism and hate against foreigners is forbidden in Germany, and although Internet technology permits this, the society does not tolerate it. In other countries, the use of the Internet is restricted to certain web sites that promote only the propaganda of the ruling power. Before the invention of the Internet, these governments controlled the media; now they have added a new communication channel, the Internet.

In a democracy, the Internet will intensify the will for democracy; in a tyranny, it will intensify the will of the emperor. Of course, the Internet will enable tyrannized people to express their wills somehow, just as they did in former times with secret newspapers and radio stations, but it will also enable radical people in democracy to speak out. This is an important issue for society, because inventions and technology are always used for politics in the end. Only if people understand that technology by itself does not necessarily change anything will the society continue to exist. Society is harmed not by technology per se but by people who misuse technology. Therefore, one should not attack the technology but look at the people and their reasons to use a technology. Inventions cannot be undone, but the reasons for using them can be influenced.

The nuclear bomb is a good example. In the 1940s it seemed to be a necessity to build such a thing, and today every country with enough money can build its own nuclear weapons. Only if societies mutually agree that their use is not good are we safe. Therefore, society must come to believe that a nuclear war cannot resolve problems and that other means, such as political action and diplomatic communications, are more efficient in the long run.

The responsibility should always be with people and not with machines. Machines do not think, and they are not able to understand what is good or bad. They do whatever they are programmed for. Society should therefore always control technology, and not the other way around. And this is the problem today. Society in many countries is driven by technology.

10.1.2 Effects of Automation and Mobility

Technology presented in this book exhibits two trends: automation and mobility. These are not new trends, but pervasive computing is pushing them onto a new level. Automation of processes has already worked well in manufacturing; the Internet and especially pervasive computing can automate processes in every job. This relieves many people from repetitive tasks but also requires that the people working with the technologies have a better education to be able to use the technology. On the one hand automation is good because it enables people to concentrate on the creative aspects of a job and reduce the mind-numbing part. On the other hand, automation divides society because not everyone can afford the education that will enable them to work with automation technolo-

gies. Over time, the difference will narrow as knowledge becomes more pervasive and more people learn to participate, but in the beginning the digital
divide can create social problems, as we now see with the Internet. Pervasive
computing will advance those who already understand the technologies and
their possibilities; those who are still without proper education will lag even
farther behind. Again, technology magnifies an existing process.

To make sure that everyone can participate, the technology must be easy-
to-use. It needs to become invisible, as discussed in the first part of the book;
only then can it reach all groups within a society. Pervasive computing will
initially be a challenge to society, but the investment in education will make
it available to everyone. In some countries, writing and reading are skills not
possessed by all people. So that these people can participate without a formal
education, they need a shortcut—like voice control—to the technology. Pervasive computing could be a good incentive to more education and possibly also
a place to learn. Pervasive computing enables anyone to access services from
anywhere, so why not offer an online course people can do on their way to work?

Mobility will also change how society will behave. Many things that took
time and effort in the past will be done in the future on-the-fly. People will be
able to work from anywhere they want instead of going to an office everyday.
This will significantly change the way society works. With an 8-to-5 office regi-
men, society provided a frame around the workspace. With pervasiveness this
framework is gone. Leisure and work will not be easily separated anymore;
people will work on Sunday and relax on Monday. People will reject a society
that has strict rules on when to work and when to rest. Everyone will be able
to individualize their week. The advantage is that people will have the freedom to plan their week however they want, but the disadvantage is that social
contacts with friends and family become much harder to coordinate.

This may lead to a situation where nobody has time for anyone else because
work and leisure shifts are so different that they always collide. Because mobility will enable people to be wherever they want to be, it adds a timing problem
to the spatial problem; even if people have time to see each other, they may
not be very near each other. In the worst-case scenario, mobility could lead to
a society of individuals who no longer know anything about each other, which
would result in many unhappy individuals.

Although this technology may cause future problems, I don't see this destroying our culture. It will change culture and society, but human beings are
happier in company, so individual groups will create their own rules for when
to work and when to relax. Of course, a work group may not be the same group
as the leisure group, thus adding a layer of complexity. I am sure that some
new technology will resolve this problem, but I really hope that people will
reinvent the five-day working week with working hours from 8 a.m. to 5 p.m.,
to give society the framework that it needs to work properly. But we will see
what happens.

10.2   Political Impact

Technology has always had an impact on politics. Most inventions have been used for politics. Just like the nuclear bomb mentioned in the last section, many other technologies have been used to promote political ideas. Again, the technology by itself did not promote a "good" or "bad" political idea. Technology by itself is neutral.

A recent example of the political impact of technology is the 2000 presidential election held in the United States. Although the decision was finally made, the dismay and division caused by reaching the decision could have been avoided had the voting process not been subject to outmoded or misused technology. I don't think that I need to reiterate the whole story. The point was that technology for voting was set up in advance and approved by Florida legislators and the electorate. After unusually close results were posted, people distrusted the technology and denied its efficacy. In this case, again, technology was used to defend or oppose a political outcome. In reality, the outcome had more to do with the political climate than with the technology of voting machines.

Although many people believe that technology is perfect, it is important to know that most technologies have flaws and their results are not 100 percent correct. Applying technology to a complex task, such as vote registering and counting, is a good thing, because manual counting of the votes is error prone and therefore not really an alternative. A technology is only as good as the accompanying circumstances. In this case, the circumstances failed the technology.

Politics have never been so challenged as today. The technology is very fast, with the politics being left far behind. The basic problem is that developing a technology can take only weeks or months, but getting a consensus from the people of a country, formulating a political strategy, and implementing laws can often only start once the technology is known. In the business of genetics there is a lot of talk about what should be done to protect human rights and nature. But until someone invents something, its foundation is pure theory that many people do not fully understand. Only when technology is exemplified can society and politics create laws. Unfortunately, the time between the presentation of a development and the political action is often too long. Many countries still lack e-business-related laws and regulations, making it virtually impossible to be right on the Internet. If you take an Internet-related case to court, coincidence will decide who is right. Although the situation is improving, there are still many problems because not everyone understands the impact of the technology and of the court ruling.

10.2.1   Managing New Technology

Experts need to advise the governments on what to do with a new technology. Many governments already have some experts on board, but that is not enough. To be effective, the technology and its possibilities need to have their complexity translated into a simple language by experts. Only this enables politicians who may have studied law to grasp the possibilities and dangers of a new technology. At the same time, educators and the press need to adapt and inform the public about these possibilities and dangers in a neutral way. Neutrality is the biggest issue; most people who understand the technology will provide on opinion instead of an objective statement about its advantages and disadvantages.

Politicians therefore need to get a neutral overview before they start to agitate in one or the other direction. This would enable them to create a strategy on how to proactively create a framework for the new technology instead of having to react to the market, the press, and the potential voters. Most governments are in this reactive mode, making only tactical decisions that might promote their reelection goals. Knowing more about the Internet, e-business, genetics, pervasive computing, biotechnology, and other promising technologies would allow politicians to formulate strategies and reduce the number of errors in laws made today. It would also make the government responsible for the misuse of these technologies, and law enforcement agencies would need to ensure that no misuse will occur.

The technologies described in the book illustrate that the current pace of inventions will increase in the near future. Privacy, security, and many other issues arise from the use of these technologies without politics ruling on what is and is not allowed. So far, every new technology that was invented created a new hole in legislation. Connecting inventors all over the world will increase the introduction of new inventions. The only way politicians and law enforcement agencies can deal with the new technology is to become part of the inventor network so they can see what is going on and which inventions are about to emerge. In the past, it took quite a while to prepare a product for mass production. This time to market is also being reduced with new inventions by reducing the time to decide to market them.

10.2.2   Managing Global Technology

Governments and politics have always been bound to geographical limits. The limits defined the areas of influence a government had. Laws are enforced within these limits, and taxes are paid by the people living within these limits. The taxes pay for the infrastructure and the security, for example, of the inhabitants of a country that is defined by its borders.

The globalization of the economy has also created a situation where companies reside in a certain country but pay taxes in another. The Internet and e-business have a large impact on politics, much more than ever before. The Internet increases this dilemma for national governments because they are bound to the national borders, whereas e-companies work in a cyberworld without boundaries. Governments will still need to ensure public safety, for example, but their influence on the economy will vanish.

The European Union is one example of a transnational government that sets rules on a transnational level. While taxes still differ among the members of the EU, the laws are merging. At the same time as we see the creation of a transnational government, the influence of national governments is largely reduced and the influence of regions has increased. The European Union has become less a union of national states and more a union of regions, whereby the local identity becomes more important than the national identity. The economies of these regions compete against each other, since each region can be seen as a single economy competing against other economies under the same law and taxation system.

Politics will have to focus on regional and transnational issues in order to survive. The existing national states will not have a very bright future if they do not adapt to the changing environment, because the Internet and new paradigms in the economy are fast moving toward a borderless economy.

10.3 Privacy Impact

With these pervasive computing technologies, it is not only possible to enhance the service idea, but also to create George Orwell's Big Brother. The government could track every movement of every citizen if it wanted to. Today, this scrutiny is not acceptable, but that may change in the future. Thirty years ago nobody would have accepted the way privacy is handled today, and personal information is now often treated as a currency. It could well be that our children will grow up knowing that there is not much privacy left and in return for service will give up even more of it. Society and the government have to agree what is acceptable and what is not, and this perception will change over time. The more experience one has with technology, the easier it is to create the appropriate framework around it.

10.3.1 Effects from Marketing

As every device is collecting data on your spending and usage, one-to-one marketing can become even more effective. The more information about you that becomes available to merchants, the easier they can make appropriate offers to you. This has the disadvantage that you may eventually lose control over your privacy if you give out all this type of information to every merchant that passes by on the Internet.

The Big Brother from Orwell's *1984* could easily become reality now, but most probably not like he envisioned it. In my humble opinion, it will not be the government stealing your privacy, it will be the advertising and marketing agencies, who are interested in your profile in order to persuade you to buy even more things you do not need. This tendency can be seen already on many web sites.

To prevent such a situation, a new form of trust needs to be built up. The service hubs that have been mentioned throughout will trade human interaction for intelligent agents sitting in the media center and controlling the flow of services and information into the house. These agents will be the only ones to see your detailed profile.

The energy broker, for example, won't send your profile to every power supplier in the world to get the best prices, but to retain privacy, will ask the power suppliers to provide the broker with a detailed price list with up-to-date information. The broker can then compare the needs of the customer with the price lists of the suppliers and choose from every supplier the appropriate pieces for a solution that fits the needs of the client.

Most probably there will be a constant connection between power suppliers and energy brokers, so energy brokers can get the lowest prices for the washing machine, which is switched on once a week, and get instant power whenever the customer switches on an additional digital device. The communication between energy broker and power supplier needs to be encrypted to ensure that nobody intercepts the complete transaction. As energy brokers would most likely buy energy from several power suppliers at the same time, the suppliers won't be able to get the full picture of the customer, but someone who intercepted the communication with all power suppliers that might benefit from the information. Encryption technologies that are allowed at a high-level worldwide, without restrictions, would make break-ins impossible.

10.3.2 Effects on Security

Security also becomes very important. As the energy broker orders energy whenever it is required, nobody should be able to interfere with the energy broker or its connection to the power suppliers. The whole installation therefore needs to be highly redundant and highly available, meaning that the envisioned five nines of Hewlett-Packard (99.999 percent, which is equal to five minutes downtime a year), will need to be increased to at least six or seven nines. Only if this high level of availability can be guaranteed can it be used on a day-to-day basis. Hackers would otherwise find ways to black out whole towns with a few commands.

The next-generation firewall must allow secure access to your devices, for example, to switch your household devices on or off while you are on holiday, but prevent unauthorized access to them. New forms of authentication will therefore be required to make impersonation impossible.

Digital and biometrical authentication and authorization methods will be combined to form a new biodigital form of access to your home, car, and anything else that needs a way to restrict public access.

10.4 Financial Impact

Technology in general had a large impact on the economy in general and on the companies using it in particular. Technology has been used in the past to reduce costs, optimize processes, and create products and services. In many cases this worked out and it will also work out with Internet technology. History shows us two periods in which companies can generate a lot of money today.

The first phase can be described as the "hype" phase in which very few people know anything about the technology. Many people pretend to know something about it because selling knowledge about technology (in the form of consultancy) is very profitable, and most clients cannot distinguish good consultants from bad consultants. Because of the nature of the business and the market at this stage, there are more bad consultants than good ones. The result is that many businesses will fail because they listened to bad consultants, and the whole market could collapse. Even those with a good business plan will lose a bit, but once the market has understood what the problem is, it will take off to become a new prosperous market around a new technology. Continuous growth can be expected from there onward. With e-business, we are just moving away from the collapse. A look at the past will reveal similar movements for almost any other new technology and new paradigm.

Pervasive computing is not yet part of the hype, meaning that it is in a phase of development and discovery where companies are not really able to make money. Companies are still investigating the available technologies and how they could be used. As more companies become involved, marketing plans will be developed and more users will learn about the technologies and their promises. The more people know, the bigger the hype gets. In this stage, all sort of things will be promised without a real foundation. Many things will be tested, many of them possible, but only a few will be successful in the market. Many hopes will be raised and money will be invested; much of it will be lost during the hype phase.

The hype phase and the following depression are very important for maturing the market. The hype phase is important because inventors can try out whatever they want. Money is available because many people believe in the future of the market and there are basically no restrictions. Everything an inventor and developer dreams up can be implemented. During the following recession phase, investors lose confidence. The analysts and businesses can see a future for the technology but are unable to define the right vision to go forward. During the depression phase, strategies and visions are developed from a business point of view and are matched with the visions and strategies that have been developed during the hype phase by technology companies. These combined visions and strategies will define the way forward to a prosperous market, as they have in the past (see Figure 10.1).

For the investors, several strategies can be successful. Invest short term into new technologies and startups in the hype phase and get out before the recession. This rule of thumb guarantees a lot of money in a short time frame. The problem with this approach is that it is difficult to find out which company or technology will be on top of the hype. At this point, many different tech-

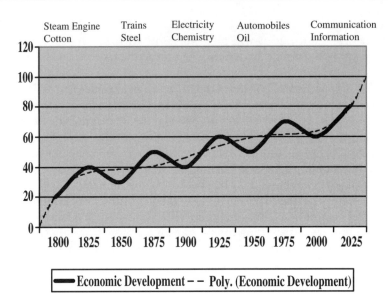

Figure 10.1. Economic Development Happens in Phases

nologies and startups compete, and it is unclear which of them will succeed. The result is a depression phase that sorts out the unsuccessful companies. Investors betting on the wrong horses will lose a lot of money.

The second strategy is a bit more conservative: wait until a clear focus for the market exists. This means to invest modestly in companies during the hype phase and wait until the market focus is clear on the technology and business sides.

Once the focus is clear, it is easier to invest in the right companies, but the stocks won't rise as fast as during the hype phase. But this strategy will most probably lead to a wealth generation that will last for a long time, as opposed to the hype investments that are high risk and short run. Figure 10.1 shows that this development is nothing new and happened basically with every major invention.

We will see in which way the information society moves on, but it will need to move into a knowledge society to survive. Except to the person who created it, information is context free and therefore useless. Knowledge puts information into context and makes it reusable.

10.5 Technological Impact

Technology in the past was often invented without a supporting network. This made it easier for the inventor to implement the idea, but often made it difficult to incorporate the invention into people's mind-sets. Many people cannot connect the idea of the invention with their lives. The universal network could make life easier for inventors. By adhering to the basic rules of the universal network, they would create inventions with a context, making it easier for people to come up with business ideas on how best to use the invention. Without this context, people need to be convinced about the usefulness of a product.

The disadvantage of this approach is that an invention will take longer to develop, because it needs to fit into an existing system. To make an invention fit into a system, in our case the universal network, the rules are predetermined and cannot be easily changed without destroying the known system. This leads to the second disadvantage: some inventions won't be made because people try to stick to the rules of the system. These rules may help to make it easier for the people to accept a new invention, but they may also be creating boundaries where there shouldn't be any.

Using the universal network as a foundation will have some benefits to developers and it will allow them to create a lot of new things over the next few years. But it is just a matter of time until the universal network will have more restrictions than benefits to the inventors and developers of the world. Once the restrictions take over, the next revolution will occur and something will replace the universal network. It won't be an extension of the existing network, but rather a completely new paradigm to make the use of knowledge much more efficient.

Different companies will try to create a universal network that will be based on proprietary technologies. This is a real danger and may mean a lot more restrictions than the real universal network would provide. We have seen in the past that proprietary technology controlled by a single company can restrict the development of a whole new generation of technology. All developments have been restricted to the platform, and extensions to the platform were only accepted by the public if performed by the owner of the technology. An open platform has trouble establishing itself because many parties are involved, but once the platform is ready, it will be much more powerful, scalable, and secure.

The universal network technology, to be as pervasive as possible, needs to rely on a technology-independent concept that is supported by the industry. It is not enough that two or three companies support it. Although the technologies used may be different, they need to adhere to the same concept. If such is the case, interconnectivity can allow the exchange of information and services.

There will be a battle about the technology and concepts over the next few years. I hope that this book helped to understand which technologies and concepts are available and how they can be used. It is impossible to predict which technology and visionary concept will win, but it is a good bet to expect the idea of pervasive computing and the universal network to be a success. With this book I hope to spread the word about the future as it is very likely to be shaped and to provide a basis for decision making. I also hope that the book helps to reduce the fear about new technologies and creates an awareness that something is happening and that there are risks that need to be managed.

Appendix A

Future Strategies for Customers

We have been talking about pervasive computing and the universal network from a company point of view, but every entrepreneur is also a customer who may want to participate in pervasive computing. Although the infrastructure is not in place yet, we can anticipate that the universal network will be a place for fraud as well. To protect themselves from fraud, customers should use the following checklist. By sticking to this list, consumers can deal in a secure way over the Internet today and in the future.

- **Compare prices online and offline**

  Pervasive computing will eventually enable all shops and service providers to share information with you, but it will take some years to enable all shops and service providers to have their prices online, even if they wish to remain offline. As long as not everything and everyone are connected, compare the online prices to the prices of offline goods to which you have access; call some of the shops in your area. Some may want to discuss prices in detail with you; others will just refuse to lower the price to that of the online retailer. In a few years time a single click will give you a complete overview on prices, but until then, remember to include offline prices in a comparison before deciding.

- **Check alternative sources**

  When looking for a certain item, for example, sport shoes, do not check only with sports hubs. Sport shoes could also be sold in online auctions or as special offers in shops that typically don't sell sporting goods. The disadvantage with auctions is that typically only one pair is available in one size. Another problem is that other people will also bid for the shoes, which may make them more expensive in the end. Once everything is connected, you will have a single interface to search through every resource on the Internet. Until then, try to find URLs of local shops and auction providers to make sure that you have checked every resource.

Items that are more difficult to find could be discovered in Internet newsgroups. The difference between pervasive computing hubs and Internet newsgroups is that the first are fully automatic and the second are fully manual. There are some advantages to the second approach. Pervasive computing technology focuses in the beginning on connecting as many devices as possible. To make the automation perfect, the input devices need to understand complex queries; this is the difficult part. People don't want to explain things in XML definitions. They want to use free text. Eventually an XML2FREETEXT (and vice versa) converter will be built, but until then you may have some difficulties describing exactly what you want.

One option is to wait for the conversion, the other is to use Internet newsgroups and online chats to express in your own words what you are looking for. The others involved in the newsgroup or the chat can respond to the request either with the appropriate answer or with additional questions to find out exactly what you meant. Through this interactivity, you clarify misunderstandings and you find the right seller and the right item.

When using newsgroups and chats, stick to those that deal with a certain item. This significantly increases your chances to find what you are looking for. Posting a request for sport shoes in an e-business newsgroup will anger the participants and result in e-mail floods.

Another good thing about newsgroups and chats is that one does not necessarily need to pay for a certain item. Bartering is a common practice. The exchange of goods can be handled informally because used items have individual value to people. If you are looking for sport shoes you may be willing to trade your old mobile phone for them. If you have something in exchange, mention it in your posting. Although this process is easy for humans to understand, it is complex to program formally because it relies heavily on informalities.

- **Check for hidden costs**

  Many digital offers in the future will seem to be cheap, but hidden costs may be involved. Before starting to use a service hub in the future, check if the use is free or if you have to pay a transaction fee. Typically, transaction fees are a low percentage of the price paid for an item or service. Read through the terms and conditions before starting to trade because other hidden costs, such as taxes and shipping costs, could be involved.

  Some service hubs will let you configure the pricing schema. Make sure that all hidden costs are shown; otherwise, you will compare apples to pears. Read through the FAQ pages to find out more about costs. If you cannot find any FAQs, don't use the service.

  In the B2B environment, shipping costs often do not play a role. A company that needs to buy 100,000 tons of steel will have a contractor for the shipping. They will concentrate on the price for the steel and calculate in a fixed price for costs.

Consider, too, the fees that need to be paid in cross-country transactions. Today, you have to pay a 20 percent customs fee if you buy a book from Amazon.com and send it to Europe. A good hub will automatically calculate the prices for customs. This is a huge task and it won't be done in the near future. So, check out whether these costs are calculated and if not, where you can get the information. Customs of 20 percent on top of the selling price may be acceptable for a book but not for 100,000 tons of steel.

- **Check the small print**

  Before using a service hub, read the terms and conditions stated in small print to find out how warranty and returns are handled. The easier the process, the better the organization of the hub. Read through the product descriptions. Often small variances or version changes may have a huge impact on the price. Do not rely on a single service hub, but try to consult a second one to make sure that you are being offered the best product at the best rate. In the ideal future, there will be only one hub for everything, but this is still some way off. Until then, different service hubs will have different offerings. Before buying a product, check with the manufacturer to make sure you get exactly what you were looking for.

  Always check with online reviews by actual users before buying a certain product. Many web services such as ciao.com[1] let users review their products. Read through the rants and raves and decide if the product is really what you wanted. With services, checking reviews is more difficult because services are more individual, but users of the service provider can describe the overall quality. Check also for fan or hate pages of the service hub.

- **Be patient**

  Once you have found the object you are looking for, consider the market situation and the importance of the item. If you don't need the item immediately, look at the market price and estimate its future price. Is it more likely to go down or up in the near future? If the trend is downward, being patient may mean you buy at a lower price.

  Once you have decided on a seller, try to get directly in touch with her and ask if the offering on the service hub was a standard offer and if discounts are possible. The perfect service hub would contain all preferences of the user and collect points and rewards for every transaction that could be

---

[1]http://www.ciao.com/

redeemed with sellers. Sellers would also be willing to give discounts to loyal customers. Until the architecture and infrastructure for such a perfect service hub are in place, some personal interaction may help to lower the price a bit.

- **Protect your data and yourself**

  To protect yourself and your personal data, don't automatically trust any service hub and seller on that portal site. Read through the terms and conditions and verify that the service hub is providing only the necessary information to its sellers. In most cases, it would be only the product-related information for the first round of offers. Check that the service hub will not give out your credit card details to anyone. The service hub should have the information and do a credit check, and the sellers should be able to trust the service hub to have checked your credit.

  Personal information should also not be transmitted to the sellers unless a transaction between buyer and seller needs to be conducted. The terms and conditions should explicitly state what type of information should be stored, how it is used, and who will be allowed to see it.

  Many web sites today in the United States have a privacy statement, but that does not mean that they are protecting your privacy. Read through the statements and you will discover that many will give your profile data to third parties. The privacy statement is not a sign of securing privacy; it is just a document describing the use of it. In Europe, few web sites have privacy statements. This does not mean that European web sites are less concerned about privacy. The difference is that in Europe laws explicitly forbid the trade of personal information, so a privacy statement is unnecessary.

  Also make sure that the information provided by you is transmitted in a secure way. Today, SSL encrypted web sites offer a good way to make sure that nobody can snatch the information in transit. In the future, 128-bit SSL encryption will not be enough—computers are becoming faster every day, making decryption faster every day. In the future, new algorithms will be used for SSL encryption to ensure data integrity and security at a higher level. We have to wait and hope that the United States will lift its ban on strong encryption. (128-bit encryption is the maximum that can be exported from the United States.) Although many standards are defined in the United States, security standards are not among them. Countries like Ireland, Israel, and Australia have become the centers of expertise in security and encryption standards because the technology is easily exported from these countries.

  Encryption is not good enough, though. You also need to verify that all personal data is secured by a login and password procedure to make sure that only authorized persons can access the information on the service hub. A password is only as good as you make it. If you choose as a password the name of the girlfriend or husband or any other word that is in a dictionary, your account will be easily hacked. A hacker will use a dictionary and try every word as the password and will eventually succeed. Smarter hackers will try to find out the names of the relatives and pets and try them first. To make sure that your account is not hacked, choose a password made of random letters and numbers. Do not pass on the password or write it down. The worst thing you can do is to write your password on a Post-it and stick the Post-it onto the display of your universal network device, such as LCD monitor, mobile phone, or refrigerator.

Credit card fraud is a big problem today and will become an even bigger problem in the future. The reasons are missing encryption standards, easy-to-guess passwords, or lax security policies. Therefore, check your credit card bills thoroughly. A good thief will grab all credit cards and deduct only small amounts to make sure that nobody notices. If you are afraid of using your normal credit card for Internet transactions, get a second one with a separate number. This approach makes it easier to track online payments. Today, the use of credit cards online is relatively secure. Because it is a transaction without a signature, you can easily get the money back from the credit card company since they cannot prove you conducted the transaction. In the near future, the introduction of digital signatures will make the return of credit card bills more difficult because a proof exists. The digital signatures, on the other hand, make it more difficult for hackers to steal information.

- **Use configurable online service hubs**

  For the service hub to be used as effectively as possible, it should be configurable and therefore personalizable. This will remove, for example, all offers you are not interested in. If, for example, you are not interested in water sports, you should not see anything related to them. The scheme should also work the other way around. If you are interested in climbing, the service hub should offer products and services for climbing, as well as links to information sites, newsletters, communities, chats, discussion groups, and the like.

  On the other hand, you have to be careful about the information you give the service hub. It allows the hub to create a rather accurate profile of you. Hub services could use this information to control your buying patterns, once they know what you have bought in the past. You will be surprised how predictable your behavior becomes with each return to the portal. The service portal will present you with items you may be interested in, but at the same time will try to steer you in buying certain services and products because the services know what is important to you and what should be neglected. Many people trust the portal because they believe it works in their interest.

- **Avoid service hubs that spam**

    To participate in a service hub, you register and provide some information about yourself. Again, read through the privacy statement to find out if the registration information will generate unwanted e-mail, so-called spam mail. To track the e-mail address back to the site you gave it to, use a free web mail address with autoforward to your normal e-mail address. That way, you can trace the source of the spam more easily.

    If the privacy statement explicitly states that it will send e-mail to all customers, don't use that service. If nothing is stated at all, check with country regulations and, if they don't forbid spamming, stay away from the site. Check with your friends about their experience with the service.

    As already mentioned, European regulations about privacy are quite strict, but there are always companies that ignore regulations and do what they think is best for business. If you are not sure about the commitment of the service provider, use a separate web mail address and a suffix to the postal address, for example. This makes it easier to trace the company that gave out the address without consent. Web forms are often processed automatically and nobody checks that the address is correct or whether anything has been added. You could add a letter to the house number or something similar. Normal mail would arrive anyway, but you would know where you left the information and who received it.

    Web mail providers can be easily found on the Web; almost all portal sites, search engines, and service providers offer this service for free. You could check, for example, GMX,[2] Lycos,[3] or Topmail.[4] If you are a very cautious user, create a separate e-mail address and an add-on for the postal address for every service hub and every seller. But after a while, you will need a database to manage all the different mail aliases.

    Before participating in a service hub, browse the site, watch other transactions, and check the quality of the goods, the bids, and the rules of the transactions. You should check that a transaction is always conducted according to the rules. Therefore, always check with sites like ciao.com[5] or online news providers such as News.com[6] or Wired.[7] These online news providers provide information about the success of the service hubs and eventual problems in the process. Hearing from other users is one thing, but having a reliable news source confirm the allegations of the user is always a good thing.

---

[2]http://www.gmx.net/
[3]http://www.lycos.com/
[4]http://www.topmail.de/
[5]http://www.ciao.com/
[6]http://www.news.com/
[7]http://www.wired.com/

- **Use an escrow service**

  If you are interested in using service hubs regularly, both as a buyer and maybe as a seller, you should consider using an escrow service. i-Escrow,[8] Trade-Direct,[9] or S-ITT[10] provide online escrow services. These service providers offer trusted third-party accounts which will hold the money until the physical transaction has taken place. The buyer puts the money into the trusted account, and the seller is notified and will send out the item. Once the buyer receives the item, the escrow service will be notified and the money is transferred to the seller. In Europe you pay 2 to 3 percent because everything is done through direct debit.

  In the United States often more than 5 percent is charged because the process is manual. Instead of using direct debit, many people use checks. The check must be sent to the escrow service, and the escrow service must send a check to the seller. Many escrow services also accept credit card payment to make things easier for the buyer and to add a layer of security through the credit check.

- **Subscribe to newsletters**

  Subscribe to personalized e-mail newsletters from your favorite service hub. They will inform you about special offers and discounts on your favorite products and services. You can be sure that many others will receive the same newsletter. There are two strategies to get a good bargain: either be the first or ignore the offers. Being first will ensure that you will receive what you wanted. Ignoring the offer and looking for other items that are not on sale will give you the opportunity to get into discussions with the seller. As the product is not especially promoted, it will be harder to sell and the seller might offer a discount anyway.

- **Create buying communities**

  To save money in online transactions, check whether your service hub will let you create virtual buying communities. The concept is simple: the more people who want to buy the same thing, the more pressure they can put onto the seller. This concept hasn't yet been successful, as you can see from companies like LetsBuyIt.com[11] that are struggling to survive. Community buying is a strong feature but can only be used on rare occasions. If your entire business model is built on buying communities, your business will not survive. The integrated approach of the service hub will make sure that buying communities become more attractive.

---

[8]http://www.i-escrow.com/
[9]http://www.trade-direct.com/
[10]http://www.sitt.de/
[11]http://www.letsbuyit.com/

- ## Check with regional service providers

  Regional service hubs may not always have the best price for a certain product or service, but their proximity may save you money in shipping and could in the end be the better option. It is also easier for returns, and acquaintance with the owner may make it easier to use the service.

  Entering the address into your profile may help you find sellers within walking distance, within a city, within 25 miles, or however far you are willing to travel. If sellers are in walking distance, you might arrange personal delivery or pickup. You could also pay in person.

Appendix B

Internet Addresses

This appendix contains a list of useful addresses concerning pervasive computing in general and mobile commerce and home automation systems in particular. I tried to keep this list as up-to-date as possible, but due to the nature of the Net, the information presented here could be outdated by the time of publication. Please consult the online directory on my web site for updates and new links.

Actiontec Online Tutorial The home networking info center of Actiontec Electronics provides information about technologies, standards, products, links, news, and where-to-buy of home networking. The web site includes a home networking tutorial: from "What is home networking" to "How to find a home networking solution".
http://www.yourhomenetworking.com/

ATVEF Advanced Television Enhancement Forum Home page of the cross-industry alliance of broadcasters, cable networks, TV-transports, PC and consumer electronics industry offers information (about ATVEF, directory, news/press and events), membership-related information, and a library (including specifications, white papers, supplemental information, and standards bodies).
http://www.atvef.com/

Official Bluetooth Web Site Applications examples for the Bluetooth wireless technology. Specifications available royalty-free. Qualification to use the Bluetooth interoperability symbol. News, products, technical information, the Bluetooth SIG. Plus the story of Harald Bluetooth (who was a fierce Viking king in 10th century Denmark).
http://www.bluetooth.com/

Broadcom ICs for Broadband Communications Broadcom Corporation designs, develops, and supplies integrated circuits for broadband communication markets, including the markets for home networking.
http://www.broadcom.com/

Bus Systeme German magazine for home automation technologies. It provides information about EIB (European Installation Bus). A special segment is dedicated to the "intelligent house" for end users. It also describes professional services company in this area.
http://www.bussystem.de/

CABA Continental Automated Buildings Assiciation Web site of the CABA, North America's source for information, education, and networking relating to home and building automation. The association's mission is to encourage the development, promotion and adoption of respective business opportunities in the industry.
http://www.caba.org/

Cahners In-Stat Group Market Research Cahners In-Stat Group "covers the full spectrum of digital communications research from technology to end-user." Includes studies on the development of networking, multimedia, wireless, computing and consumer electronics markets, and strategies.
http://www.instat.com/

Casadomo A Spanish portal for intelligent houses, includes an online magazine, links, and an online store.
http://www.casadomo.com/

CEATechHome Consumer Electronics Association (CEA) The Association of CEATechHome will show how to create an integrated home system using products that everybody may already own: heating, air conditioning, lighting, cable television, and other typical home systems. Integrated home systems link the independent systems and appliances so they can work together and be controlled from other sources.
http://www.techhome.org/

CEBus Industry Council CEBus Industry Council is a multi-industry organization of companies, incorporated as a nonprofit corporation, to develop and enlarge the market for products compliant with the CEBus standard and/or the Common Application Language (CAL) as implemented in the Home Plug and Play Specification. The site includes technical information about the CEBus standard EIA-600 (using the 120V, 60 cycle, electrical wiring of a home to transport data).
http://www.cebus.org/

CommVerge Magazine The web site of the monthly published magazine CommVerge, the "data stream for visionaries of the convergence area," provides information about convergence products and systems, including home networking technologies.
http://www.commvergemag.com/

Datatransfer Introduction A German introduction into the "wonderful world of networks." Includes detailed descriptions of modems, GSM, ISDN, and many other networking technologies.
`http://www.shamrock.de/dfu/`

DTV Information Source for Digital Broadcasting The site is structured to serve the needs of broadcast engineers, transmission network designers/installers, production engineers, videographers, sound engineers, film editors, and consultants who are involved in the production and broadcast of DTV, highlighting technologies s.a. format conversion, video editing, postproduction, signal processing, and products.
`http://www.digitalbroadcasting.com/`

DVB Digital Video Broadcasting The DVB project is a consortium of over 200 broadcasters, manufacturers, network operators, and regulatory bodies in more than 30 countries worldwide, committed to design of a global standard for the delivery of digital television.
`http://www.dvb.org/`

EasyLiving Laboratory Report on Microsoft's EasyLiving laboratory: "Houses will be build or refitted with all the light switches, thermostat controls, telephone jacks, alarm switches on the windows and doors...all tied together in a system monitored by cameras and sensors until the building becomes, in a sense, a living thing."
`http://www.research.microsoft.com/easyliving/`

eBiquity eBiquity.org is a slashdot-like portal for news, discussion, and community building for ubiquitous and pervasive computing. The site covers devices, communication technology and protocols, infrastructure, middleware, software architectures, mobility, applications, m-commerce, and theory.
`http://www.ebiquity.org/`

EIB European Installation Bus German web site with detailed information about the proposed European Installation Bus. Includes a very complete glossary.
`http://www.tirol.wifi.at/eib/eibAllgemein.htm`

EIB European Installation Bus German web site covering all about EIB, the international standard for intelligent houses. EIB is very flexible and can be extended later to create a link between the houses and the new service providers.
`http://www.eiba.de/home/explorer/eiba_main.htm`

EIBA European Installation Bus Association Web site published by the EIB Association. Offers information especially on international activities

and events around the European Installation Bus: in-home applications,
product guide, gateways, links to other sites, and downloads (info, software, etc.).
http://www.eiba.com/

EIB Forum German forum for EIB, includes a newsticker, a download area,
hints for marketing, a marketplace for buying and selling used EIB-de-
vices. The discussion groups allow the exchange of information within
the EIB community.
http://www.eib-forum.de/

EIB-Profis A German B2B Exchange for builder, architect, and planner. It
can search for EIB-certified electrotechnicians by postcode.
http://www.eib-profis.de/

EIB-News Online-Service This German EIB newsfeed provides experts and
interested people with information about the EIB industry.
http://www.eibnews.de/

elektroniknet Top News Dedicated German newsletter on electronic devices, including product news, industry news, market overviews, and specific expert subjects.
http://www.elektroniknet.de/

Elektro-Seiten German portal for electronics. Includes a search engine, a
product review section, and a forum where anyone can ask questions
about electronics. The answers are provided either online or at your local
electronics store.
http://www.elektroseiten.de/

Flash Commerce Newsletter Published as "Daily News and Discussion of
eCommerce and Small Business."
http://www.flashcommerce.com/

futurelife The Internet-enabled house in Hünenberg, Switzerland, demon-
strates state-of-the-art communication technology and modern furniture
design. The "future house" has been created to stimulate a discussion
about the future of life and society.
http://www.futurelife.ch/

HAA Home Automation Association The HAA web site provides its visi-
tors with a wealth of information about programs, products, services, and
initiatives—"all for the benefit of home automation professionals and enthusiasts."
http://www.hanaonline.org/

Haustechnik Verein A German nonprofit organization that offers electricians and plumbers that work in the area of housing technology to become active on the Internet. The organization provides free workshops, presentations, and seminars.
http://www.haustechnik.de/

HAVi Home Audio Video interoperability Home page of the HAVi organization, founded by eight consumer electronics companies (Grundig, Hitachi, Matsushita [Panasonic], Philips, Sharp, Sony, Thomson, and Toshiba).
http://www.havi.org/

The Home Automation Times A storehouse of up-to-date articles, links, FAQs, and so forth. Providing information, including case studies, for installers and consumers, and essentials and resources for builders, integrators, homeowners, and enthusiasts.
http://www.homeautomationtimes.com/

Home Networking: Is Your House Ready? "Just hook up a Microsoft Windows-based Personal Computer to a variety of low-cost sensors and controllers around your house, and all those dumb appliances will become part of your smart, future-ready house." Covers the kitchen, living room, baby's room, bedroom, bathroom, and garage.
http://www.microsoft.com/homenet/FutureHome.htm

Home Networking News HNN Newsletter HNN publishes special reports and excerpts of news stories about home networking. The complete articles are available for HNN-subscribers.
http://www.homenetnews.com/

Home Networking Solutions Information Site Connecting PCs together will open a new world of possibilities and save time and money. This web site will help you to understand the benefits of home networking and guide the choice of technology.
http://www.hnsolutions.co.uk/

HomePlug Powerline Alliance The HomePlug Powerline Alliance is a nonprofit corporation formed to provide a forum for the creation of open specifications for high-speed powerline networking products and services. Among the alliance members are AMD, Cisco, Compaq, Matsushita, and Panasonic.
http://www.homeplug.com/

Hometronic Applications, Overview, Technology Extensive German description of Hometronic systems developed by Honeywell that allow the

regulation and monitoring of heating, lights, and so forth, and an easy-to-understand description of the Hometronic System.
http://www.honeywell.de/

HWN Home Wireless Networks Offers its AirWay system for wireless telephone and data lines. The system has a maximum range of 1,500 feet; it operates in the 902–928 MHz range, and the throughput is 960 kbit/s.
http://www.homewireless.com/

IEEE 1394 The 1394 Trade Association Comprising more than 170 member companies, it was founded to "support the development of computer and consumer electronics systems that can be easily connected with each other via a single serial multimedia link." The IEEE 1394 high-speed multimedia connection standard is also known as Apple's FireWire or Sony's iLink.
http://www.1394ta.com/
http://www.askfor1394.com/

IGI Group Telecom Information Portal The   Information   Gatekeepers Group is a publisher, trade show organizer, consultant, and information service provider in the field of fiber optics, optical networks, WDM, ADSL, ATM, Internet, LANs, ISDN, wireless telecom, and the emerging telecom markets worldwide.
http://www.igigroup.com/

Infoline Elektrohandwerk German online service for electrotechnicians providing information about home networks. Product information, experiences, and user reports are available.
http://www.infoline-handwerk.de/

inHaus - NRW - Fraunhofer Institut IMS inHaus is a German demo house that provides many enhancements, such as automatic window opening and closing depending on the weather. All household devices can be controlled remotely. The devices also need less energy than normal ones. This project is coordinated by the Fraunhofer Institute IMS.
http://www.inhaus-nrw.de/

Intelligent House A German web site dedicated to builders. Includes information on the following topics: "life in an intelligent house," "how to make a house intelligent," and "which partner helps you to make your house intelligent."
http://www.das-intelligente-haus.de/

Jini Java Intelligent Network Infrastructure Web site of Sun Microsystems describing Jini connection technology "based on the simple concept that devices should simply connect and work together. No drivers to find,

no operating system issues, no wired cables and connectors."
`http://www.sun.com/jini/`

LCN Local Control Network The Local Control System by the Issendorff GmbH is an installation bus with extended functionality: it saves energy, controls the light, shades sunlight, opens and closes doors automatically, controls access, and activates alarms.
`http://www.issendorff.de/`

LON User Organization The user organization of the local operation network (LON) supports the LonWorks-Technology, bundles marketing activity, and is an information exchange. The web site informs readers about news, applications, and products in the area of home and building automation.
`http://www.lon.de/`

LonMark Interoperability Association The LonMark Interoperability Association promotes and recommends design guidelines for interoperable LonWorks (LON – Local Operation Network). The association offers latest news, information about upcoming events, and products/systems based on Lonworks.
`http://www.lonmark.org/`

LonWorks Networks for Connected Homes The web site of Echelon Corporation, developer of LonWorks networks, includes information about the company, products, solutions, partners, support, press releases, news, and events. LonWorks is a cross-industry standard for networking everyday devices in building and home automation and industrial, transportation, and public utility applications.
`http://www.lonworks.com/`

LonWorks Education and Consulting A partner of LonWorks in Germany that provides training and consulting for new LonWorks products.
`http://www.lon.de/`

Market Development Home network market to reach $5.7 billion. How the worldwide market for home network equipment and residential gateways is expected to grow. Many press releases about the growing market.
`http://www.hometoys.com/resources.htm`

MobileCommerce Forum for companies within the area of mobile commerce, phones, computing, and so forth.
`http://global.mobilecommerce.com/`

NextHouse Digital Home Network At the Consumer Electronics Show (CES 2000), Las Vegas, Nevada, Panasonic presented its digital home network solution "NextHouse." It demonstrated a new home gateway that

serves as a digital hub and router for the entire home network.
http://www.panasonic.com/ces2000/nexthouse.html

Nokia Finnish provider of mobile infrastructure and devices. The largest
manufacturer of mobile phones in the world.
http://www.nokia.com

PAN Powerline Area Network Media Fusion LLC (Dallas, Texas) developed
a powerline communications technology which solves problems such as
line noise, electrical load imbalances, and transformer interference that
hinder power-line communications.
http://www.mediafusionllc.net/northamerica/main/news/

PIMRC 2000 International IEEE Symposium on personal, indoor and mobile
radio communication, held 18.-21.9.2000, London, UK.
http://www.pimrc2000.com/

PLC PowerLine Communications FAQs about power-line technologies. It
answers questions such as "How to set up a PLC network and connect it
to the telephone system" and explains the test done by RWE in Essen,
Germany.
http://www.powerlinenet.de/

PolyTrax Powerline-Communication The hardware supplied by PolyTrax
allows fast and reliable transmission of data, audio, and video over existing power networks. Primary targets are home networks and industrial
automation.
http://www.polytrax.com/

PowerCom System Prepaid-Convenience Echelon announces that its Lon-
Works networks and PLT-22 power-line signaling technology are key components of Motorola's PowerCom system, which allows customers to buy
power on a (prepaid) as-needed basis.
http://www.echelon.com/company/press/powercom.htm

Powerline Data German document describing the history and applications of
data transmission through power nets. The concepts for high-, medium-,
and low-voltage networks are discussed, and an outlook into the future
development is provided.
http://speth08.wu-wien.ac.at/usr/h92/h9225559/mis/strom/98/art.htm

Project DNA A university project to extend existing Internet infrastructure
to behave like the DNA of the human body.
http://www.cs.umbc.edu/dna/

Set-top Home Networking This web site, a "new portal site for advanced digital set-top boxes," has been designed "to provide consumers and platform developers with a central hub for downloading TV applications, accessing the latest set-top news and participating in Web conferences."
`http://www.set-tops.com/`

ThinkMobile A very complete portal for the mobile community, dealing with many subjects connected to mobility and mobile computing.
`http://www.thinkmobile.com/`

UPnP Universal Plug and Play UPnP, developed by Microsoft, is an open standard technology for transparently connecting appliances, PCs, and services by extending plug and play to support networks and peer-to-peer discovery and configuration. The document includes an introduction to UPpnP, draft specifications and the UPnP vision.
`http://www.microsoft.com/homenet/upnp.htm`

VirtualVision VirtualVision is a manufacturer of head-mounted displays.
`http://www.virtualvision.com/`

VoiceRecognition 21st century eloquence, voice recognition.
`http://www.voicerecognition.com/`

Wearable Computing The introduction to Wearable Computing web page is a good place to look. It is updated more frequently than most other FAQs, and covers a wide range of topics.
`http://wearables.www.media.mit.edu/projects/wearables/`

Appendix C

Glossary

This appendix contains a list of all the buzzwords used throughout the book. You can use this glossary while reading the book or as a future reference.

3G The next (third) generation of wireless technology beyond personal communications services. The World Administrative Radio Conference assigned 230 megahertz of spectrum at 2 GHz for multimedia 3G networks. These networks must be able to transmit wireless data at 144 kilobits per second at mobile user speeds, 384 kbps at pedestrian user speeds, and 2 megabits per second in fixed locations. See also Universal Mobile Telecommunications System.

802.11 The Institute of Electrical and Electronics Engineers standard for wireless local area network interoperability.

Access Code Each baseband packet starts with an access code, which can be one of three types: CAC, DAC, and IAC. The CAC consists of a preamble, sync word, and trailer, and its total length is 72 bits. When used as a self-contained message without a packet header, the DAC and IAC do not include the trailer bits and are 68 bits long.

ACID Acronym and mnemonic device for learning and remembering the four primary attributes guarantee to any transaction by a transaction manager (which is also called a transaction monitor). These attributes are: atomicity, consistency, isolation, and durability.

ACL See Asynchronous Connectionless Link.

Active Box Loudspeaker box with built-in power amplifier or output amplifier (also for loudspeakers with separate amplifiers for high, middle, and bass frequencies).

Active Termination One or more voltage regulators for terminating voltage (ensures a uniform signal level over the entire bus).

ActiveX Controls A set of interfaces that access Windows resources: small additional modules, called controls, that can be embedded in a program. The module concept was standardized by Microsoft and dubbed ActiveX (for example, there is a calendar element that provides programs standard calendar functions, eliminating the need for programming them on your own).

ADC (Analog-to-digital conversion) An electronic process in which a continuously variable (analog) signal is changed, without altering its essential content, into a multilevel (digital) signal.

ADR See ASTRA Digital Radio.

ADSL See Asymmetric Digital Subscriber Line.

Advanced Mobile Phone Service An analog cellular phone service standard used in the United States and other countries. Compared to other standards, it is not very advanced.

Advanced SCSI Programming Interface Standard for developing SCSI drivers. The ASPI manager ensures that all devices connected to the SCSI controller function properly.

Advanced Television Enhancement Forum (ATVEF) Consortium of hardware manufacturers and program vendors interested in creating a single standard from various procedures of interconnecting TV and Internet. ATVEF is also aimed at the home-network market, particularly because the interfaces defined in the standards proposals call for controlling much more than TVs and computers.

Air Interface The standard operating system of a wireless network; technologies include AMPS, TDMA, CDMA, and GSM.

Aliasing Distortion of video images (or other analog information) of analog information is digitized or information is processed by digital means with an insufficiently small sampling rate. To reproduce the information properly, the sampling rate must be at least twice as large as the resolution of the original.

Alternate call A technique that allows the user to switch back and forth between two calls.

American Standard Code for Information Interchange Internationally used code for letters of the alphabet, digits, and special characters; a data format that allows text to be exchanged between computers having different operating systems. The original standard ASCII character set is based on a 7-bit code and has no special characters (ß, ö, ä, etc.) or formatting styles (bold, italics, etc.). The introduction of an 8-bit code expanded the ASCII character set to include a number of special characters and block graphics symbols.

AMPS See Advanced Mobile Phone Service.

Answer call A technique that allows the user to take a call.

Anti-aliasing Suppressing the effects of aliasing by filtering out rough, "step-like" edges or by smoothing the edges by mixing colors to form transitions (interpolation).

API See Application Programming Interface.

Application Programming Interface Software interface for user programs that allows programs to access the operating system or user interface resources.

Application Service Provider A service provider that makes applications available on a pay-per-use basis. ASPs manage and maintain the applications at their own data center and make the applications available via the Internet to subscribing business.

APS See Automatic Programming System.

Architecture Applied to data processing or information technology, general term for the structure of all parts of a computer system (hardware and software).

ASCII See American Standard Code for Information Interchange.

ASP See Application Service Provider.

ASPI See Advanced SCSI Programming Interface.

Assistant (also referred to as "Expert" or "Wizard"). A tool designed to help users create programs (e.g., databases).

ASTRA Digital Radio Transmission procedure for digital radio stations that have been broadcasting since 1995 via ASTRA satellites. It is based on the data compression procedure MUSICAM/MPEG-1. The data rate is 192 Kbit/s (including error correction 256 Kbit/s). In addition, 9.6 Kbit/s is used as overhead to transmit radio data signals (RDS), conditional access (access control for pay radio), and other signaling data.

Asymmetric Digital Subscriber Line A form of DSL, in which data flows downstream at a rate of >10 Mbit/s and upstream at >800 Kbit/s. Because of the different data rates involved, this form of data transmission is referred to as asymmetric.

Asynchronous Connectionless Link One of the two types of data links defined for the Bluetooth Systems, ACL is an asynchronous (packet-switched) connection between two devices created on the LMP level. This type of link is used primarily to transmit ACL packet data. The other data link type is SCO.

Asynchronous Transfer Mode A dedicated-connection switching technology that organizes digital data into 53-byte cell units and transmits them over a physical medium using digital signal technology.

AT Attachment ANSI version of the IDE interface.

ATA See AT Attachment.

ATAPI See AT-Bus Attachment Packet Interface.

AT-Bus Attachment Packet Interface Interface for AT-Bus hard disk and CD-ROM drives or CD recorders that "understand" the IDE controller.

ATM See Asynchronous Transfer Mode.

@ The commercial a—also referred to as the "at" sign. It has become a symbol recognized the world over as a separator in e-mail addresses.

ATVEF See Advanced Television Enhancement Forum.

Audiovision Combination of sounds and images.

Auto PC An in-vehicle combination AM/FM radio, Windows CE-based computer, compact disc and CD-ROM player, wireless phone, and navigational system. The units are about the size of a typical car stereo.

Automatic Programming System Automatically assigns all receivable television stations to the TV's preset positions when the TV is switched on for the first time.

Automatic Vehicle Location A system that combines a location-sensing device (such as a GPS receiver) with a wireless communications link to provide a home office or dispatcher with the location of a vehicle or mobile asset (such as a trailer or heavy machinery).

AVL See Automatic Vehicle Location.

Backbone High-speed cable—for example, within the Internet—that interconnects subnetworks. Online service providers or Internet providers are connected either directly or indirectly to a backbone.

Back-end The "side" of a client/server program that supplies data (typically a database server (front end)).

Bandwidth The maximum usable frequency range (measured in hertz) available for transmitting data: often—although not quite correctly—used as a synonym for the data transmission rate.

Bandwidth on Demand A component in the DECT-MMAP standard that provides the required channel capacity; dependent on the current service and data load.

Biometrics The science and technology of measuring and statistically analyzing biological data.

Bits per Inch Describes the data density on magnetic media in bits per inch.

Bits per Second A unit for measuring the data transmission rate, for example, the transmission path of a modem. The fastest modems operate today at 56,000 BPS. An ASCII letter consists of 8 bits; theoretically speaking, a 56-K modem can transfer 7,000 characters (nearly 2.5 pages of standard letter-size pages) per second.

BLER See Block Error Rate.

Block Error Rate Number of data blocks contained in one or more errors at the lowest level of error correction.

Bluetooth A consortium that introduced the open Bluetooth standard 1.0. (available as a PDF file from www.bluetooth.com) in 1999, led by the founding companies Ericsson, Nokia, Toshiba, IBM, and Intel. Bluetooth was developed especially for economical, short-range, wireless links between PDAs, laptops, cellular phones, and other (mobile) devices.

Bluetooth devices can detect each other automatically and set up a network connection. Using a modulation frequency of 2.4 GHz, they transfer data from one adapter to another, whereby the signals do not have a predefined direction and can, in principle, be received from any other device. Bluetooth functions with spread spectrum modulation, combined with frequency hopping (1600 frequency hops per second). There are 79 usable hopping frequencies available between 2.402 GHz and 2.480 GHz, spaced at 1 MHz. A unique ID plus data encryption ensures that only "authorized" devices will communicate with each other. The maximum data rate is 750 Kbit/s, and the range is limited to 10 meters. However, the standard also permits 100 meters with increased transmission power.

Bluetooth also enables devices to communicate with each other on the basis of Jini technology without being connected by cable. Many of the typical Bluetooth fields of application overlap with those of the IrDA standard for infrared data transmission. The first hardware and software products equipped with Bluetooth were introduced at the end of 1999. Experts predict that by the year 2005, nearly 700 million of these devices will be in use.

Bluetooth SIG Bluetooth Special Interest Group, with over 1,500 member companies and organizations.

Bookmark A technique that allows the user to find previously accessed pages on the Web by saving the relevant addresses (URLs). WWW addresses can be saved with any browser currently available.

BPI See Bits per Inch.

BPS See Bits per Second.

Broadband Describes a communications medium capable of transmitting a relatively large amount of data over a given period of time. A communications channel of high bandwidth.

Brokering The general act of mediating between buyers and sellers. In the universal network, brokering technologies such as E-Speak will enable universal service-to-service interaction, negotiation, bidding, and selection. See E-Speak.

Browser Software that provides a graphical user interface for navigating and searching or surfing the information pages of online services such as the World Wide Web. Browsers allow the user to access and display pages or documents that were written in Hypertext Markup Language (HTML). A browser also interprets mouse clicks on a link.

Building Automation Describes the sum of all automating measures in buildings (including rented housing and private homes). Building automation makes it possible to control and regulate technical systems to ensure efficiency, primary energy savings, productivity, and comfort.

Cache A small, intermediate memory area for exchanging or transferring data, for example, between the hard disk and central processing unit. A cache accelerates hard disk access.

Carrier A company that provides a communications service.

CASS See Conditional Access Subsystem.

CCIR See Comité Consultatif Internationale des Radiocommunications.

CCITT See Comité Consultatif Internationale de Telegraphie et Telephonie.

CD-DA See Compact Disc-Digital Audio.

CDMA See Code Division Multiple Access.

CDMA2000 A third-generation wireless technology proposal, which is based on the IS-95, or cdmaOne, standard, submitted to the International Telecommunication Union.

CDPD See Cellular Digital Packet Data.

CEBus See Consumer Electronics Bus.

Cellular Digital Packet Data A method of sending and receiving information via mobile devices. CDPD allows information to be sent in "packets" or blocks over the existing analog cellular network. It is best suited for short, periodic bursts of information. CDPD is a wireless transmission method that uses the analog cellular network, also known as Advanced Mobile Phone System (AMPS). CDPD allows information to be transmitted on idle cellular voice channels. Also referred to as "wireless IP."

Chai A product-family name for a set of HP products supporting intelligent interaction among embedded devices through the use of the Java programming language and today's web standards.

Chip Term for complex, integrated circuits that can contain several hundred thousand semiconductor circuits (transistor/diodes, etc.). By creating structures as small as one thousandth of a millimeter, manufacturer's can achieve higher levels of integration.

Clear call A protocal that allows the user to terminate a call.

Clear connection A protocol that allows the user to terminate an individual call. This service is required if the user wants to terminate a call to only one conference participant within a telephone conference.

Client/Server A method whereby databases in a network are administered from a central location by a server and client software installed on the user's computer retrieves required data from the server.

Code Division Multiple Access A spread spectrum, air-interface technology used in some digital cellular, personal communications services and other wireless networks.

Comité Consultatif Internationale des Radiocommunications An international advisory committee for radio and TV standards.

Comité Consultatif Internationale de Telegraphie et Telephonie An international advisory committee for international telecommunication protocol standards.

Common Interface An interface specified by DVB, for example, as PCMCIA interface in set-top boxes for connecting a conditional access module. This interface enables the user to add a decoder module to a generic set-top box with a common interface for receiving the services and programs offered by a pay-TV provider.

Common Object Request Broker Architecture See CORBA.

Compact Disc-Digital Audio Standard for audio CDs (defined in the Red Book drafted by Philips and Sony).

Computer Telephone Integration A term that describes the integration of telephones and computers. It enables solutions that go far beyond the limitations of a standard telephone. A classic example is the use of a telephone in combination with a PC database.

Conditional Access In the framework of the European project DVB, a European transmission standard, DVB/MPEG-2, was passed. Various systems (e.g., Irdeto, Beta, Conax, Cryptoworks, Seca, Syster Digital, Viaccess) are used in Europe for the additional encoding required by pay-TV channels.

Conditional Access Subsystem System of access authorization to (digital) TV and radio services that can only be descrambled, that is, viewed or heard, for certain user groups or if a service fee has been paid.

Conference Call An arrangement whereby users can converse with several parties on one line. The maximum number of conference members is limited by the PBX.

Constraints Logical rules stored in a database. These rules check certain conditions at the table level, for example, whether a particular range of values was violated for numerical fields.

Consultation Call An arrangement whereby a user can consult (call) a third party while the second party is still on the line.

Consumer Electronics Bus Communications standard for home networks; developed by the Electronics Industry Association (EIA) and the Consumer Electronics Manufacturer Association (CEMA).

Cookies Small files that are sent from a web site to the user's web browser and then stored on the user's hard disk. When the user returns to the web site, the web browser sends the information back to this site. Cookies allow the user, for example, to display individualized elements that appear as soon as the URL is selected.

CORBA Architecture and specification for creating, distributing, and managing distributed program objects in a network. It allows programs at different locations and developed by different vendors to communicate in a network through an "interface broker."

CRC See Cyclical Redundancy Check.

CTI See Computer Telephone Integration.

Cyberspace A term coined by William Gibson in his novel *Neuromancer*, published in 1984. Today, it describes digital communications and Internet data space.

Cyclical Redundancy Check Checksum for correcting errors that occur during data transmission.

DAB See Digital Audio Broadcasting.

Data Dictionary Area of memory in which all information on a database and the accompanying programs are stored and managed. This includes information on tables, triggers, constraints, relations, and indices.

Database A term with several meanings: refers to a DBMS (Database Management System) as well as a file that contains, for example, customer addresses or other data. A database can combine several tables into one file. Often, only one table is allowed per database file for PC databases. In this case, the user can still create a link to other tables from various files (referential integrity).

Data Throughput Transmission rate of the actual user data (excluding redundant data for error correction or data for delimiting individual data blocks, e.g., header). Specified in cps (characters per second).

Data Header Data structure at the beginning of a data packet header.

Data Packet A format for transmitting data within networks. These packets contain the header, the actual data (user data), and redundant data (CRC) for error correction on the receiving end.

Data Rate Also known as data transfer rate. Indicates the number of data units per specified time interval in bps (bits per second).

Data Record A logical entity that combines all the data for a specific table entry. Analogous to one file in a file-card box.

DCOM See Distributed Component Object Model.

Decryption The reconstruction of encrypted TV programs. Usually a chip or module in a television set or peripheral device (decoder/descrambler). See also Pay-TV.

DECT See Digital Enhanced Cordless Telecommunication.

DECT-MMAP DECT Multimedia Access Profile. A further development of the DECT standard as a "virtual cable" for mobile data devices; typically used for wireless Internet or intranet access within the transmission range of the base station with data rates of up to 2 Mbit/s. The most important DECT-MMAP features include service negotiation, dynamic resource management, and bandwidth on demand.

Deflect Call A way to forward an incoming call without the need to actually answer the call.

Descrambling See Decryption.

Digital Audio Broadcasting System for digital terrestrial transmission of radio and multimedia data services. The MUSICAM system is used for data compression—from 1.411 Mbit/s to 192 Kbit/s.

Digital Enhanced Cordless Telecommunication A technology (cordless telephone) that represents the most common application of DECT standards. Wireless, digital communication DECT-MMAP operating at ISDN speed (64 Kbit/s) or faster is growing in significance. The effective radiated power specified for DECT of 250 mW provides an effective range of up to 50m in buildings and 300m outdoors. The voice signal is 32 Kbit/s. Germany uses the 1.9 GHz band, whereas other frequencies between 1 and 10 GHz, commonly between 1.5 and 3.6 GHz, are also used. The access method used by DECT known as TDMA (Time Division Multiple Access, time multiplex) allows up to 100,000 simultaneous users in a single cell.

Digital Home See Intelligent Home.

Digital Satellite Equipment Control System for controlling satellite receiver equipment. Conventional satellite equipment uses a 14/18 volt switching voltage to switch between polarization levels (horizontal or vertical). An additional 22 kHz frequency on the input voltage line signals the direction of the satellite antenna to specific orbit positions. In contrast, DiSEqC uses a universal control concept, since the 22 kHz signal not only switches equipment on and off but also samples frequencies. This allows a number of commands (including polarization switching) to be transmitted within the DiSEqC system. DiSEqC level 2 also features bidirectional communication. Thus, the satellite receiver sends commands to the peripheral components capable of logging on to the receiver: Plug & Play in satellite receiver technology.

Digital Subscriber Line General description (also referred to as "xDSL") for high-speed, broadband data transmission over copper wires (i.e., "twisted pair" cables). See also ADSL, HDSL.

Digital Video Broadcasting Initially conceived as the European Launching Group (ELG) in 1991, the DVB project was founded in 1993. It comprises nearly 180 companies, institutions and organizations, equipment manufacturers, TV and radio stations, network providers, research institutions, and authorities from 23 countries. "The objective of the DVB, a project financed solely from membership dues without significant subsidies, is the shared and coordinated development of systems and standards in order to make digital television in Europe possible by means of satellite, cable, and terrestrial broadcasting (German Platform for HDTV and New Television Systems)." Although DVB was originally set up as a European project, a number of companies from Japan, South Korea, Canada, and the United States have since joined.

DVB can be used for more than digital TV and radio broadcasting. This technology can be applied as a generic "data highway" offering transfer rates of up to 36 Mbit/s. As a result, there have been proposals to rename the system Digital Versatile Broadcasting instead of Digital Video Broadcasting. DVB encompasses the following standards: (see) DVB-C, DVB-CI, DVB-CS, DVB-IPN, DVB-MC, DVB-MS, DVB-NIP, DVB-RCC, DVB-RTC, DVB-S, DVB-SI, DVB-Subtitling, DVB-T, DVB-TXT.

DiSEqC See Digital Satellite Equipment Control.

Distributed Component Object Model A set of Microsoft concepts and program interfaces in which client program objects can request services from server program objects on other computers in a network.

Domain An element in an Internet address. Domain names separated by dots are listed according to the protocol and service (e.g., http://www). An example is "ebusinessrevolution" (subdomain) and "com" (top-level domain). The top-level domain can contain a country code (fr for France) or an abbreviation indicating the type of server (for example, com for commercial companies, org for organizations, or edu for universities).

Domotik Widespread industry solution designed to connect Bosch products (security, telecommunications, household appliances, heating systems, etc.) by means of an integrated residential wiring system. All electrically controlled devices are networked by the European Installation Bus (EIB) and controlled by a multimedia PC. Domotik can also be operated with the HomeAssistant multimedia program used for entering the various functions. HomeAssistant runs on standard multimedia PCs. The user-friendly graphic interface is to a large extent self-explanatory.

Download To copy information (e.g., PDF files) or programs from a server (e.g., from the Internet) to the computer's hard disk or other data media. Common examples of downloaded data include drivers for hardware components or updates for software applications.

Downstream The data flow from the server to the client (client/server) or from the provider to the subscriber/customer. The opposite of upstream.

Dropout Error on the magnetic coating of a magnetic tape or on other magnetic media caused by dirt or surface damage. Depending on their size and severity, dropouts can cause read errors or data loss.

DSL See Digital Subscriber Line.

DVB See Digital Video Broadcasting.

DVB-C A standard compatible with DVB-S for distributing digital programs or services in a cable network. To convert the data transmitted from satellites to a channel-compatible 8 MHz bandwidth, QPSK must be transcoded into 64-QAM (Quadrature Amplitude Modulation with a bandwidth efficiency of [64 = 26] 6 bit/s/Hz).

DVB-CI DVB Common Interface; common interface for conditional access and other programs.

DVB-CS A DVB-C or DVB-S adapted standard for cable or satellite-supported reception of DVB signals via community antenna systems.

DVB Developments Further specifications and procedures that are in preparation or being developed for data radio via DVB, synchronization of single-frequency-networks, interfaces between the DVB world and ATM or SDH networks, Digital Satellite News Gathering (DSNG) based on DVB, bi-directional communication in GGA and terrestrial networks, networking DVB terminal equipment, and integration of HDTV and DVB.

DVB-IPN Gateways from DVB to the telecom world.

DVB-MC Specification for MVDS (Microwave Multipoint Distribution Systems) in the frequency range below 10 GHz. The procedure that is also used on the ground is based on the standards defined for digital channel transmissions (DVB-C) and thus uses similarly equipped receivers/decoders. (DVB-MS and DVB-MC are also referred to as "specifications for wireless broadband cabling").

DVB-MS (Digital Multipoint Video Distribution System/MVDS) The system uses microwaves for the terrestrial transmission of a larger number of TV channels directly to the audience. The microwaves are bundled and broadcast to receiver antennas that are positioned in the "visible area" of the transmitter antenna. Although they pertain to terrestrial broadcasting, the DVB-MS specifications are based on those for DVB-S. DVB-MS signals from standard DVB satellite receivers can be received by small rooftop antennas, but a corresponding MVDS frequency converter is used instead of the LNCs (low noise converter).

DVB-NIP Network-independent protocols for interactivity (protocols that permit communication in form of a data stream).

DVB-RCC Specification for interaction channels (forward and backward channels) in broadband cable networks.

DVB-RTC Specification for interaction channels (backward channels) via telephone and ISDN.

DVB-S System for satellite transmission with a 11/12 GHz bandwidth; it can be configured for various transponder bandwidths and transfer rates. The type of modulation is a four-phase shifting (QPSK, Quadrature Phase Shift Keying): at a constant amplitude, the modulated signal can assume one of four phase conditions, each of which can transmit 2 bits of information (given a bandwidth efficiency of 2 bit/s/Hz).

DVB-SI The Service Information System that transmits data within the transport data stream. It is used for the self-configuration of the DVB decoder (set-top box), for designing the user interface, and for identifying programs and services.

DVB-Subtitling Tools for subtitles and graphics display.

DVB-T Standard for terrestrial television; this transmission procedure uses a bandwidth efficiency comparable to DVB-C for 7-8 MHz terrestrial channels and is based on a COFDM system (Coded Orthogonal Frequency Division Multiplex). In this multicarrier procedure, the channel spectrum is divided into several thousand subcarriers, each of which is modulated with a part of the data stream.

DVB-TXT DVB specification for monitoring teletext (in special data packets).

Dynamic Resource Management Frequency-economic adaptation of the channel bandwidth to the current traffic load DECT-MMAP.

E911 Designation to be used when 911 service becomes E911; that is, when automatic number identification and automatic location information are provided to the 911 operator.

ECC See Error Correction Code.

ECMA See European Computer Manufacturers Association.

EDGE See Enhanced Data GSM Environment.

E-Die See Enhanced Integrated Drive Electronics.

EHS See European Home System.

EIB See European Installation Bus.

EIBA See European Installation Bus Association.

E-mail Electronic messages that can be quickly sent throughout the world through Internet or other networks. E-mail is one of the most frequently used applications in the Internet. In addition to text, multimedia data can be sent as an attachment.

Enhanced Data GSM Environment A faster version of the Global System for Mobile (GSM) wireless service. Delivers data at rates up to 384 Kbps and enables the delivery of multimedia and other broadband applications to mobile phone and computer users.

Enhanced Integrated Drive Electronics Advanced development of the IDE standard offering higher data transfer rates and support for newer drives.

EPOC Operating system designed for small, portable computer-telephones with wireless access to phone and other information services. EPOC is based on an earlier operating system from Psion, the first major manufacturer of personal digital assistants (PDAs).

Error Correction Code Redundant data that helps detect errors and eliminate them through recalculation. ECC On-the-fly: hardware error correction for hard disks that takes place while the data is being transferred.

E-service An electronic service, available from the Net, that completes tasks, solves problems, or conducts transactions. E-services can be used by people, businesses, and other e-services and can be accessed from a wide range of information appliances.

E-Speak The universal language of e-services. To accelerate the creation of an open e-services world, HP engineered E-Speak technology. The E-Speak platform provides a common services interface, making it easier and faster to create, deploy, manage, and connect e-services. Through the process of dynamic brokering, E-Speak lets an e-service discover other e-services anywhere on the Internet and link with them on-the-fly—even if they were built with different technology. See also brokering.

ESPRIT European Strategic Program for Research and Development of Information Technology.

Ethernet Technology for local networks based on the CSMA/CD protocol. In conjunction with IEEE 802.3, data rates of up to 10 Mbit/s can be achieved. The new IEEE standard 802.3ae slated for ratification by 2002 allows for data rates up to 10 Gbit/s.

European Computer Manufacturers Association Association of computer manufacturers with the goal of defining common standards.

European Home System A standard created under the auspices of the EU project ESPRIT (European Strategic Program for Research and Development of Information Technology). It uses electrical wiring as the installation bus and offers a data throughput of up to 2.4 Kbit/s. A separate two-wired cable can also be used instead of an electrical cable. This increases the potential data throughput to a maximum of 48 Kbit/s. EHS and EIB are to be united into a common standard.

European Installation Bus Association A widespread manufacturer association dedicated to establishing the EIB standard. Over 100 manufacturers and more than 8,000 licensers throughout Europe offer nearly 5,000 EIB components.

European Installation Bus Network technology for residential wiring. EIB is designed for two-wire cable only. EIB versions for electrical cables as well as wireless systems for radio and infrared—as a functional prototype—have recently become available. The Siemens Instabus complies with the guidelines of the EIB standard as does Domotik developed by Bosch. The version EIB.net can also use normal data networks in accordance with IEEE 802.2 with transfer rates of up to Ethernet 10 Mbit/s. The extension EIB.net "i" allows forwarding, for example, through the normal IP router and thus the EIB connection via the Internet. Maximum EIB data transfer rate is 9.6 Kbit/s.

European Telecommunication Satellite Organization A European agency founded in Paris in 1977 for managing satellite communication services.

Eutelsat See European Telecommunication Satellite Organization.

Extensible Markup Language A flexible way to create common information formats and to share both the format and the data on the Internet. Acronym is XML.

Extranet Segment of the intranet that can be accessed by authorized third parties (e.g., customers or suppliers). It uses Internet technology to establish communications between various company locations.

FAQ See Frequently Asked Questions.

Fast SCSI Transmission protocol compliant with SCSI-2 that allows data transmission of up to 10 MB/s on an 8-bit bus.

FAT See File Allocation Table.

Fibre Channel A technology for transmitting data between computer devices at a data rate of up to 1 Gbps (one billion bits per second). (A data rate of 4 Gbps is proposed.) Fibre Channel is especially suited for connecting computer servers to shared storage devices and for interconnecting storage controllers and drives.

Field The smallest unit in a record. Each field has a specific data type that contains, for example, text, dates, currencies, and so forth.

File Allocation Table The data table at the beginning of a partition used in operating systems such as MS-DOS and Windows 95/98. The data table stores information on where files are located on the disk.

Firehunter A comprehensive solution for measuring, monitoring, and reporting on Internet services.

Firewall A method to protect local networks from unauthorized access by intruders on the Internet.

FireWire See IEEE 1394.

Firmware Commands stored in a ROM chip for controlling the hard disk. This data can usually be updated (by a technique called flashing).

Frame A way to divide the browser window into several sections and independently configure and control their contents. Thus, a fixed menu can be shown in one frame while scrolling text, images, or animations are displayed in another.

Frame Relay Wideband, packet-based interface used to transmit bursts of data over a wide area network. Seldom used for voice.

Frequently Asked Questions Many home pages and nearly all Newsgroups offer FAQ lists to answer questions frequently asked by users. To save time, it is often sufficient to refer to the list of FAQs to determine whether specific questions have already been answered.

Front-end A part of a program that allows user uses to access the database (see counterpart back end).

Full-duplex Transmission protocol for the simultaneous transfer of data and signals in both directions.

General Packet Radio Service A packet-based wireless communication service that provides data rates from 56 up to 114 Kbps and continuous connection to the Internet for mobile phone and computer users.

Geographic Information System Enables users to envision the geographic aspects of a body of data. Basically, it lets users query or analyze a relational database and receive the results in the form of some kind of map.

GIF See Graphic Interchange Format.

GIS See Geographic Information System.

Global Positioning System A series of 24 geosynchronous satellites that continuously transmit their position. Used in personal tracking, navigation, and automatic vehicle location technologies.

Global System for Mobile Communication A digital mobile telephone system that is widely used in Europe and other parts of the world. GSM uses a variation of time division multiple access (TDMA) and is the most widely used of the three digital wireless telephone technologies (TDMA, GSM, and CDMA).

GPRS See General Packet Radio Service.

GPS See Global Positioning System.

Graphic Interchange Format Popular image format used on the Web for low-quality photos and drawings.

GSM See Global System for Mobile communication.

Handheld Device Markup Language Developed to allow Internet access from wireless devices such as handheld personal computers and smart phones. Derived from Hypertext Markup Language.

HAVi See Home Audio-Video Interoperability.

HDML See Handheld Device Markup Language.

HDSL See High data rate DSL.

HDTV See High Density Television.

Header The part of a packet that contains information about the type, meaning, or structure of the subsequent data packet. Since the header forms the beginning of a data packet, it can also be used to mark the end of the previous data structure.

High Data Rate DSL Transmission procedure capable of a transmission rate of 1,544 Kbit/s (T1) or with 2,048 Kbit/s (E1) with pulse-code modulation through dual copper wires.

High Density Television High-resolution television (i.e., doubled horizontal and vertical resolution).

Home Audio-Video Interoperability A consortium of manufacturers (Grundig, Hitachi, Matsushita (Panasonic), Philips, Sharp, Sony, Thomson, and Toshiba) for the development of a home network architecture for the (consumer) electronics and multimedia industries. Philips represents the eight companies as a primary contact for licensing issues. According to the HAVi version 1.0b standards (can be downloaded as a PDF file from www.havi.org), user programs can detect and control HAVi-compatible equipment from different manufacturers. These programs can also control individual components within various systems independently of their physical location. The HAVi standards refer to an IEEE 1394-supported, digital AV environment. The key specifications include components used for exchanging messages and events by IEEE 1394, the registration and detection of device capabilities through the network, and the management of digital AV streams and devices. Available features include a security system for virus protection, a component that supports functions such as preprogrammed (audio/video/data) recording, and standard programming interfaces for controlling equipment functions.

Home Automation See Building Automation.

Home page Starting page, that is, page 1 of a web site (WWW). It usually contains a table of contents and links to other areas or pages on the site.

Home Phoneline Networking Alliance Consortium promoting the use of telephone lines for data transfers of up to 10 megabits per second without restricting parallel telephone usage (members: AMD, Compaq, 3COM, IBM, Intel, and Lucent).

HomeWay Multimedia cabling system offered by Corning for apartments, houses, and home offices. The system requires only one cable and a universal wall receptacle for telephone, fax, PC, TV, home automation, and multimedia programs. The multimedia cabling system consists of a control center, a broadband cable, and a standard wall socket. All external wiring is connected to the control center. A broadband cable networks all rooms, and the wall socket provides connections for multimedia terminal devices. In terms of design, the sockets are tailored to the various switch programs. Their modular structure ensures that all services are available at any point in the residence. The inserts can be easily replaced if the socket is to be used in another way, for example, for a cable TV connection in another room. An integrated component of HomeWay is home automation based on the already available Instabus EIB (European Instabus). HomeWay also meets the specifications recommended by major providers including ASTRA, Deutsche Telekom, and property management companies.

HTML See Hypertext Markup Language.

HTTP See Hypertext Transfer Protocol.

Hyperband In the service channel network, the frequency used for distributing TV stations (300–470 MHz). It is the range of choice for digital transmissions according to DVB-C.

Hypertext Markup Language The language of the World Wide Web. HTML makes it possible for documents to appear virtually identical on all computer systems regardless of the software and hardware used. A voluntary consortium (W3) regularly proposes new standards to maintain this compatibility.

Hypertext Transfer Protocol The protocol regulates the transmission of hypertext files on the Internet. HTTP is the foundation for transmitting HTML pages on the Web.

IDE See Integrated Drive Electronics.

IEEE Institute of Electrical and Electronic Engineers.

IEEE 1394 The P-1394 bus technology, originally developed by Apple Computers, became the industry standard IEEE 1394/1995 in 1995; it is commonly known as FireWire. The IEEE 1394 technology describes a serial interface for computer and video devices for transmitting digital data up 400 Mbit/s. In 1997, Sony introduced its iLink logo for identifying standardized IEEE-1394 interfaces.

IES See Integrated Reception System.

Infranet Communication structure for networking equipment in the household or in other applications such as gas stations, restaurants, medicinal technology, or agriculture (a supplement to Internet and intranet).

Infrared Data Association An industry-sponsored organization set up in 1993 to create international standards for the hardware and software used in infrared communication links. In this special form of radio transmission, a focused ray of light in the infrared frequency spectrum, measured in terahertz, or trillions of hertz (cycles per second), is modulated with information and sent from a transmitter to a receiver over a relatively short distance.

Integrated Drive Electronics Hard disk with integrated drive electronics; referred to as an IDE disk drive.

Integrated Receiver/Decoder Receiver/decoder unit for digital data or TV services. IRD describes the device known internationally as set-top box digital decoder.

Integrated Reception System With the structure of the Integrated Reception System—promoted by the satellite operator ASTRA and, for example, implemented by WISI—existing distributor and communication structures (cable, terrestrial systems, telephone) can be supplemented through community satellite reception. The accompanying wall socket combines antennas and telephone connections.

Integrated Service Digital Network A digital network that integrates several different services.

Intelligent Home Control signals for building automation or transmitted multimedia signals. The forerunners of today's modern concepts: Professor Ken Sakamura's Tron house in Tokyo in the '80s and Chriet Titulaer's Huis van de Toekomst in Rosmalen (Holland).

Intelsat See International Telecommunications Satellite Organization.

Interleave/Interleaving 1. Multilevel, interleaved storage of user data for simplifying error correction. Interleaving is also used for digital television (DVB) as a means of splitting code. Bytes from a defined number of successive data packets are selected in memory in such a way that the successive bytes originate from various data packets. Through this interleaving, which is reversed in the receiver, transmission errors that have corrupted a longer section of the digital data stream, are parsed into single errors that are easier to correct. 2. Arranging the sectors in a similar way on a hard disk cylinder.

International Telecommunications Satellite Organization An organization of over 150 member countries promoting intercontinental telecommunications via satellite.

Internet Worldwide conglomeration of data networks. Initially intended for military use, the Internet was increasingly used for exchanging research data among universities and institutes. Today, online service providers and network providers have made the Internet available to everyone.

Internet Relay Chat A communication platform that allows users to synchronously communicate (chat) with other IRC users online via keyboard input.

Internet Server API Programming interface for Internet server programs that use the Microsoft Internet Information Server (MIIS) in conjunction with Windows NT.

Internet service provider A company that provides individuals and companies access to the Internet and other related services such as personal mail boxes. An ISP has the equipment and the telecommunication line access required to have points-of-presence on the Internet for the geographic area served.

Intranet Internal (corporate) network using Internet technology such as TCP/IP.

IP See Transmission Control Protocol/Internet Protocol.

IP address Location of a single computer in the Internet. The IP address consists of four numbers from 0 to 255, each separated by dots (example: 123.27.1.155). For ease of use, IP addresses are converted into alphanumeric names. IPv6 extends the range from four numbers to six numbers, thus making many more IP addresses available for appliances.

IPv6 The latest level of the Internet Protocol (IP), now included as part of IP support in many products including the major computer operating systems.

IRC See Internet Relay Chat.

IRC-Op IRC operators who administer the IRC servers on an international level. These operators have access to additional commands unavailable to normal users.

IRD See Integrated Receiver/Decoder.

IrDA See Infrared Data Association.

ISAPI See Internet Server API.

ISDN See Integrated Service Digital Network.

ISP See Internet service provider.

Java programming language Full network-capable, object-oriented and platform-independent programming language used to create web-independent programs (developed by Sun Microsystems).

Java intelligent network infrastructure Sun Microsystems introduced Jini technology in the summer of 1998. It is based on the Java and can programming language "spontaneously" connect network devices. In other words, devices that are dynamically connected to the network are immediately detected throughout the entire network. Jini regulates the communication between computers and other devices in the network and allows peripherals to be connected to the network without special configurations and used immediately. The self-identifying devices transmit their technical specifications and eliminate the need for "manual" driver selection. In contrast to Ethernet systems, Jini automatically allocates resources.

JavaScript Scripting language (not a programming language) developed by Netscape which expands the possibilities of HTML. JavaScript allows the user to integrate functions such as graphic effects, animated menus, ticker tapes, and so forth, in web pages.

JetSend A device-to-device communications protocol that allows devices to intelligently negotiate information exchange. The protocol allows two devices to connect, negotiate the best possible data type, provide device status, and exchange information, without user intervention.

Jini See Java intelligent network infrastructure.

Joint Photographic Experts Group One of the most popular graphic formats. The JPEG format frequently used in digital photography compresses large or color-intensive pictures to a fraction of their original size. This compression reduces storage requirements and file transfer time (i.e., on the Internet).

JPEG See Joint Photographic Experts Group.

Lag The delay caused by high traffic congestion or other overloading between IRC servers or Internet provider sites resulting in slow communications.

Last-Mile Technology Any telecommunications technology, such as wireless radio, that carries signals from the broad telecommunication infrastructure along the relatively short distance (hence, the "last mile") to and from the home or business.

LCN See Local Control Network.

Link A mechanism in the World Wide Web that allows the user to branch from one web page to another. Links are usually displayed as underlined text on HTML pages. Clicking these links makes it possible to "surf" the World Wide Web.

LMDS See Local Multipoint Distribution Service.

LNS See LonWorks Network Services.

Local Control Network An installation bus developed by Issendorff GmbH for residential and functional buildings. Conventional installation elements such as switches, pushbuttons, sensors, etc., are replaced or supplemented by "intelligent" modules. All modules in the building are connected to an additional wire in the installation cable (actually a 4-wire electrical cable that uses an added wire as a data channel). The data transfer rate is 9.6 Kbit/s.

Local Multipoint Distribution Service Located in the 28 GHz and 31 GHz bands, LMDS is a broadband radio service that provides two-way transmission of voice, high-speed data, and video (wireless cable TV).

LON See LonWorks.

LonWorks The field bus system originally developed by Echelon Corporation (Palo Alto, California) for production control. According to company information, it is the most widely used field bus system in the world for building automation (reference installations in Germany: Reichstag Building and Debis administration offices in Berlin). This technology was developed in 1988 and launched on the German market in 1991. In a LON (Local Operating Network), every bus participant, or "network node," has its own microprocessor or "neuron processor." The separate network nodes work independently and do not communicate with other nodes until it becomes necessary. A LON can be operated with two-wire cables, coaxial cable, electrical cables, or no wires (as a wireless system). Depending on the transmission path, the data rate is 10 Kbit/s (electrical cable) up to a theoretical maximum value of 1.2 Mbit/s (1,200,000 bits per second). According to press reports, integration into known data networks—for example, through cooperation with the Internet specialist Cisco—is the most widespread configuration. With LNS (LonWorks Network Services), LON systems can be integrated via gateways into Ethernet installations and the Internet.

LonWorks Network Services LNS allows the user to integrate LON systems into the Internet and Ethernet installations via gateways.

Look-up Service (Also known as "spontaneous networking" because each device is detected immediately as soon as it is connected to the network). A component of the Jini system architecture that registers every active Jini device in the network together with its technical characteristics in a table and makes the table available to authorized users (example: a handheld computer that has been registered in the look-up service detects available printers, free memory space on a hard disk in a desktop computer, or an Internet connection).

Magneto-resistive heads Write/read head in hard disks that can supply a stronger signal level when reading data from the disks because it has to go through a magneto-resistive element.

Make call A technique that enables the user to set up a call.

Make predictive call A technique that waits to connect a caller until the recepient answers. A user program transfers one or more call numbers to the PBX. The PBX sets up the connection automatically but does not place the call to the extension until the party called has lifted the receiver. This function is only useful if the extension is in an ACD group; otherwise, there is no guarantee that the call will be answered.

Masking pattern adapted universal subband integrated coding and multiplexing Complies with MPEG-1 Audio, Layer II. It reduces the data rate of audio signals from 1,411 Mbit/s (audio CD) to 192 Kbit/s.

MediaFusion A U.S. company in Dallas, Texas, that has announced a major breakthrough in transmitting data over electrical cables (www.mediafusionllc.net). The company received a patent for a system that can theoretically transfer 2.5 Gbit/s—more than fiber-optic cable—and bridge distances of over 3,000 kilometers without a repeater. The high-frequency carriers are microwaves from a maser (a "laser" for the microwave range) that are fed into the power supply. According to MediaFusion, the magnetic field surrounding the cable encapsulates the waves and transports them to the receiver.

Message Message or private messages refers to a message sent to one or more IRC participants. The message can only be read by the recipient and the sender.

MHP See Multimedia Home Platform.

Micropayments Payments in the penny range. Because of their "micro" value, the transaction costs must be considerably lower than, for example, credit card payments.

Microwaves Frequencies in the range above 3 GHz (Gigahertz = billion hertz). Microwaves can also be used to distribute digital TV services and are sometimes referred to as "wireless cable."

Monitor device A PBX is requested to forward all events at a particular extension (device) to a file server. A caller with the number 555-1234 is assigned to the extension.

Motion Picture Experts Group A workgroup—Working Group 11 (WG11), also known as the international MPEG laboratory—of the International Standards Organization (ISO) and the International Electrotechnical Commission (IEC). MPEG was founded in 1988 by over one hundred companies to negotiate proposals and define standards in specific expert groups (requirement or system groups).

MPEG See Motion Picture Experts Group.

MR Head See Magneto-resistive heads.

Multichannel Feed Data compression, encoding, and modulation processes are optimized for minimum bandwidths in Digital Video Broadcasting (DVB), resulting in a relatively large number of transmission channels. This is why a program can be transmitted over several channels from several cameras simultaneously. Viewers can view the event from a selected camera angle (and not necessarily from the perspective of the director). Typical applications include simultaneous broadcasts of Formula 1 racing events from inside different vehicles, from a helicopter, or from the pit lanes. Symbols displayed on the screen show the viewer which button to press and which perspective will be shown.

Multimedia Home Platform The MHP software package is the open, technical solution for all new multimedia programs and services within the framework of the DVB standard (digital television). MHP connects radios, the Internet, TVs, and computers. Essentially, a standard system for all services. With MHP, the DVB project has a uniform standard for the software interface (Application Programming Interface) of universally applicable DVB receivers. The standardized software interface (DVB-J) is based on the Java programming language, so all services and programs can be implemented in set-top boxes in the future. As an interface available to all program and service providers, MHP opens the door to manufacturing receivers that are compatible with all current and future standards. MHP will be implemented in DVB receivers and multimedia PCs.

MUSICAM See Masking pattern adapted universal subband integrated coding and multiplexing.

National Television System Committee U.S. TV signal with 60 Hz vertical frequency, a 4:3 screen format, and a resolution of 767×575 pixels.

Near Video on Demand A TV program broadcast in, for example, 20-minute intervals on additional channels. Audiences can then watch a program practically at any time starting within the 20-minute time frame.

Networked House See Intelligent Home. House or apartment with a cabled or wireless intelligent network.

Newsgroups The "blackboards" of the Internet. They include thousands of public information and discussion forums sorted according to topic. Participants can read and submit messages.

NICAM A transmission mode employed in various countries for two digital audio signals (stereo or bi-language) in the analog TV channel.

NTSC See National Television System Committee.

NvoD See Near Video on Demand.

Object-Oriented Programming A program philosophy made popular through Smalltalk, Object Pascal, and C++.

ODBC See Open Database Connectivity.

On-Screen Display A screen menu providing user instructions and simplifying operation.

OOP See Object-Oriented Programming.

Open Database Connectivity Interface defined by Microsoft for database systems. With an ODBC driver installed on a PC, the user can access other formats such as dBase, Paradox, or Access.

Operating System Software that controls and checks a computer's basic functions and logical devices. An operating system manages, for example, the resources and processes, input/output controls, file system, and the user interface.

OSD See On-Screen Display.

Packet The unit of data that is routed between an origin and a destination on the Internet or any other packet-switched network.

PALplus A system introduced in 1994 that is backward compatible with the PAL standard system for analog transmission of TV programs in the 16:9 widescreen format aspect ratio. Coordinated by Germany's ZDF network, PALplus was developed by a consortium of industrial companies, TV stations, and research institutes. On conventional screens (4:3 format), PALplus programs appear in the letterbox format with black strips along the upper and lower edges of the screen.

Partial Response Maximum Likelihood Digital procedure for interpreting the data stored as analog information on magnetic data media.

PASC See Precision Adaptive Subband Coding.

Pay-TV Subscription television. Audio and video signals can only be received (unscrambled) after a fee has been paid to the program provider.

PCMCIA See Personal Computer Memory Card Industry Association.

Personal Computer Memory Card Industry Association Originally designed as a memory expansion card for laptop computers, this interface is used today for miniature modems or for digital TV descrambling systems.

Picture In Picture An additional picture displayed within the TV picture. This system is used to simultaneously view a second TV channel or monitor the image from a remote camera.

PIP See Picture In Picture.

Plain Old Telephone Service Another name for traditional wired, land-based telephone service.

PLC See Powerline Communications Forum.

Plug-Ins Small, supplemental programs that can be downloaded free of charge from the Internet. Plug-ins add new functions to the web browser, making it possible, for example, to view new multimedia information on the Web.

Plug & Play Procedure for automatically configuring computer expansion devices or cards.

POTS See Plain Old Telephone Service.

PowerLine Systems that use the electrical network for data transfer. See also Powerline Communications Forum, MediaFusion.

Powerline Communications Forum A consortium founded in 1997 by members of the telecommunications industry and energy suppliers. This group tests applications and services supplied to homes via electrical cables to determine their feasibility and efficiency. See also PowerLine, MediaFusion.

Precision Adaptive Subband Coding Similar to MUSICAM. Coding and data compression process for audio signals. It offers a data rate of 384 Kbit/s and is used for DCC (Digital Compact Cassettes).

PRML See Partial Response Maximum Likelihood.

Protocol Rules that define how data is transmitted over "data highways," in online networks and between components within a computer.

Proxy Server Similar to cache memory. It increases "surfing speed" by caching pages previously visited on remote computers. If a web page is to be opened, the proxy server first checks whether the page is available on the hard disk. If so, the page is loaded from the proxy server. Proxy servers reduce the traffic on the data highway.

PSTN See Public Switched Telephone Network.

Public Switched Telephone Network The worldwide voice telephone system, also called the Bell System in the United States.

Pulse Width Modulation A standard means of encoding data read by a laser beam from optical media (CD, DVD).

PWM See Pulse Width Modulation.

QAM See Quadrature Amplitude Modulation.

QoS See Quality of Service.

QPSK See Quadrature Phase Shift Keying.

Quadrature Amplitude Modulation Digital modulation procedure. QAM is used, for example, for digital TV broadcasting via broadband cable.

Quadrature Phase Shift Keying Digital modulation procedure. QPSK is used, for example, for TV broadcasting via satellite.

Quality of Service The idea that transmission rates, error rates, and other characteristics can be measured, improved, and, to some extent, guaranteed in advance.

Referential integrity For databases, referential integrity in its simplest form means that, when a record is deleted from a main table, all related subordinate records in other tables will also be automatically deleted.

Relational database A database that does not have a predefined link structure. This allows the user to create new relationships between tables dynamically, that is, during the course of operation, for example, link customer names with invoices using the customer ID number.

Residential System Technology See Building Automation.

Residential Wiring Technology See Building Automation.

Resource Manager A component of the HAVi system capable of managing a number of operations. It resolves conflicts between devices, coordinates the programming of scheduled events (such as timer recordings on a digital recorder) and monitors the network to determine if reserved devices are still in place.

Retrieve call A mechanism that enables a caller, after parking and terminating his current call, to return to the first caller.

Runtime module A set of programs that allow the user to execute a database program without requiring the entire database development system needed to create the program.

Sampling Scanning analog signals in which samples of the current amplitude are taken at the sampling frequency and digitized. The quality of the digital signal depends on the sampling frequency (twice as high as the frequency of the digitized analog signal).

Scrambling Encryption of TV images to make them unrecognizable. In reference to pay-TV, programs that are scrambled can only be received by subscribers who have agreed to pay a fee for the program and have a descrambling unit (decoder) connected to their TVs.

SCSI See Small Computer System Interface.

Search Engine Databases containing information on documents available in the World Wide Web, that is, the "reference works" or "indexes" of the Internet. Search engines are created manually or automatically by computers.

Secure Electronic Transaction A method by which payments are encrypted and sent via a (trusted) third party—a bank, for example—checked, and customer identity verified.

Server Computer in a network that makes resources available to connected computers (clients), programs, storage space, printers, etc. (client/server, video server).

Service Negotiation A component in the DECT-MMAP standard for negotiating the minimum and maximum data rates for a particular service.

SES See Société Européenne des Satellites.

SET See Secure Electronic Transaction.

SGRAM See Synchronous Graphics RAM.

Shareware Programs that can be copied for testing purposes. Users who decide to use the program are required to register the software and pay a fee to the author. Shareware programs can often be used without restriction—based on the presumption that users are honest; sometimes, however, the programs are limited in function or expire after a certain period of time.

Short Message Service A feature of GSM phones that allows users to receive and sometimes transmit short text messages using their wireless phone.

Simple Object Access Protocol A way for a program running in one kind of operating system (such as Windows NT) to communicate with a program in the same or another kind of operating system (such as Linux) by using the World Wide Web's Hypertext Transfer Protocol (HTTP) and its Extensible Markup Language (XML) as the mechanisms for information exchange.

Simulcrypt An encoding method in which several CA systems (CASS) are transmitted simultaneously in a program packet. A decoder with one CA system suffices for reception. Example: a Seca or Viaccess decoder is required for the French ABsatPacket.

Small Computer System Interface Standardized interface for connecting peripheral devices to a PC.

Smart Home See Intelligent Home.

SMPTE See Society of Motion Picture and Television Engineers.

SMS See Short Message Service.

SOAP Simple Object Access Protocol.

Société Européenne des Satellites Company that operates ASTRA satellites.

Society of Motion Picture and Television Engineers An international organization that has developed a time code under the same name for controlling the synchronization of images and sounds.

SoD (Service on Demand). See also VoD.

SQL See Structured Query Language.

Structured Query Language A universal query language for databases; it is used primarily for databases in banks or in similar multiuser systems.

Symbian Joint venture between Ericsson Inc., Motorola Inc., Nokia Corp. and Psion to develop new operating systems based on Psion's EPOC32 platform for small mobile devices, including wireless phones or handheld personal computers.

Symbol A data block consisting of a defined number of bits (the most well known example of a symbol is a byte consisting of 8 bits).

Synchronous Graphics RAM High-speed video memory for video signals.

Table A format that combines identical records in columns (fields) and rows (records).

TAPI See Telephony Application Programming Interface.

TCP/IP See Transmission Control Protocol/Internet Protocol.

TCS-AT A set of AT-commands by which a mobile phone and modem can be controlled in the multiple usage models. In Bluetooth, AT-commands are based on ITU-T recommendation v.250 and ETS 300 916(GSM 07.07). In addition, the commands used for fax services are specified by the implementation. TCS-AT will also be used for dial-up networking and headset profiles.

TDMA See Time Division Multiple Access.

Telephony Application Programming Interface The Windows telephony interface developed by Microsoft, CTI.

Telematics The integration of wireless communications, vehicle monitoring systems, and location devices.

Time Division Multiple Access A technology used in digital cellular telephone communication to divide each cellular channel into three time slots to increase the amount of data that can be carried.

Transaction A procedure ensures that any modification to a database is carried out either completely, i.e., for all records, or not at all.

Transfer call A mechanism that allows the user to forward a call to another phone.

Transmission Control Protocol/Internet Protocol Technical basis for transmitting data on the Internet. This protocol divides the contents of a web page into small packets and sends them along different paths, if necessary, to the receiver where TCP/IP then reassembles the packets in their original order.

Transponder Satellite transmission technology. Combination of a receiver that receives signals from a terrestrial station (uplink) and a transmitter that beams down the signals as a satellite TV program to the earth (downlink). The term is a combination of transmitter and responder.

Ultra-SCSI Extension of Fast-SCSI that allows a data rate of up to 20 MB/s by doubling the clock frequency.

Ultra-Wide SCSI Extension of Wide-SCSI that allows a data rate of up to 40 MB/s by doubling the clock frequency.

UMTS See Universal Mobile Telecommunications System.

Universal LNB A receiver unit located in the focal point of a parabolic antenna (dish-shaped or satellite antenna). LNB (Low Noise Block Converter) is also used to describe an LNC (Low Noise Converter). In the

LNB, the signals received from a satellite are converted into a lower frequency range before they are forwarded by cable to the satellite receiver
in or next to the TV set. The term "Universal" indicates that the LNB can
be used for both analog TV (10.7–11.7 GHz) and digital TV (11.7–12.75
GHz) frequencies.

Universal Mobile Telecommunications System Europe's approach to standardization for third-generation cellular systems.

Universal Plug and Play Windows 9x and Windows 2000 offer "Plug & Play"
technology for automatically detecting all compatible devices within a PC.
UPnP is designed to expand this technology to include devices in an external network. Once devices are connected to a network supporting UPnP,
they automatically configure themselves, which eliminates the need for
setup and configuration. UPnP detects the devices along with the relevant product characteristics including communication protocols. For example, a camera can automatically detect a printer in the network, determine its ability to print in color, and print a photo.

Universal Resource Locator Address for Internet pages. A URL consists
of a server name, possibly a directory name or full path name, and the
document title (example: http://www.ebusinessrevolution.com/blgarski/).

Universal Serial Bus A technology developed by Intel. The Universal Serial
Bus based on a star topology can connect up to 127 devices on different levels to a PC and replaces earlier interface standards. Each device
forms the end or point of a star. Direct communication between connected
USB devices is not possible. Control is provided by a USB controller that
functions as a host. The complicated process of reserving address ranges
and interrupts has been eliminated. Only the USB controller requires
an interrupt from the BIOS. Thanks to the hot-plugging function, any
number of devices can be switched on, plugged into different sockets, or
removed while the PC is in operation. The USB host detects the change
and renumbers the device addresses. Windows 98 is the first operating
system to fully support the Universal Serial Bus.

In version 1.1, the USB operates at a maximum data rate of up to 12
Mbit/s. Version USB 2.0 will offer data rates that are 20 times faster,
that is, 240 Mbits/s and will be backward compatible. Devices are connected with a four-wire cable with standardized plugs that are polarized
to prevent them from being plugged in the wrong direction. The cable can
also supply current, if necessary, to connected peripheral devices. The devices are chained to the bus by passive hubs that can also be integrated
into separate USB devices such as keyboards or monitors. The maximum
cable length between hub and peripheral is five meters. Early in the year
2000, Intel introduced a USB system 2.0 that offers a maximum data rate

of 480 Mbit/s—40 times faster than version 1.1 (for more information, see www.usb.org).

Universal Wireless Communications Consortium An industry group supporting IS-136 time division multiple access and IS-41 wireless intelligent network technology.

UpnP See Universal Plug and Play.

Upstream The data flow from a client to a server or from a subscriber/customer to a provider; the opposite of downstream.

URL See Universal Resource Locator.

USB See Universal Serial Bus.

Video on Demand Procedure in which TV programs can be directly accessed by a subscriber through a back channel from a video server. The transmission, which requires special switching equipment with distributed structure and bidirectional channels from and to the subscriber, is enabled after payment has been made. Similar services are being discussed, such as Audio on Demand, Software on Demand and others.

Video Server Hard disk storage for video signals with computer-controlled file management. In contrast to magnetic tape cassettes, this type of storage offers fast random access to specific scenes or images. In conjunction with Video on Demand (VoD), proposed video servers will provide storage capacity for hundreds, or possibly thousands, of video clips and films. Instead of gigabytes, these storage capacities are being measured in terabytes (1 terabyte = 1024 gigabytes).

VoD Video on Demand.

Video Random Access Memory High-speed video memory.

Virtual Reality Modeling Language A programming language for displaying 3-D spaces on the Internet. VRML allows the user to design virtual landscapes or 3-D games. Current browsers are capable of displaying such data. Numerous browser plug-ins offer 3-D functions.

Voice Mail Similar to e-mail. Voice mail is a message sent or received within a network as audio data.

VoIP A term used in IP telephony for a set of facilities that manage the delivery of voice information, using the Internet Protocol (IP).

VoxML Voice Markup Language. A technology from Motorola for creating a voice dialog with a web site in which a user can call a web site by phone and interact with it through speech recognition and web site responses.

VRAM See Video Random Access Memory.

VRML See Virtual Reality Modeling Language.

WAP See Wireless Application Protocol.

W-CDMA See Wideband CDMA.

WebQoS See Web Quality of Service.

Web Quality of Service A product that ensures consistent quality of service on shared systems by preventing surges in online customer demand from overloading the server. It also allows service providers to safely host multiple sites on a single system by preventing busy sites from impacting each other's performance.

Wideband CDMA The third-generation standard offered to the International Telecommunication Union by GSM proponents.

Widescreen TV screen format with an aspect ratio of 16:9 (width/height). This format adapts to the perspective of human vision in which the horizontal range is wider than the vertical range. Widescreen images reduce eye strain, particularly for larger screen formats. From a technical standpoint, the 16:9 format can be implemented in conventional analog TVs (PALplus) as well as digital TVs (DVB).

Wide-SCSI Transmission protocol compliant with SCSI-2 that defines an extension of the bus width to 16 bits and thus requires special cables and plugs. Wide-SCSI is normally used with Fast-SCSI and is capable of data transmission of up to 20 MB/s.

Window-RAM Special type of VRAM with high bandwidth used by Matrox, Number Nine, and other video card manufacturers.

Wireless Using the radio-frequency spectrum for transmitting and receiving voice, data and video signals for communications.

Wireless Application Protocol A specification for a set of communication protocols to standardize the way that wireless devices, such as cellular telephones and radio transceivers, can be used for Internet access, including e-mail, the World Wide Web, newsgroups, and Internet Relay Chat (IRC).

Wireless IP The packet data protocol standard for sending wireless data over the Internet.

Wireless LAN Local area network using wireless transmissions, such as radio or infrared instead of phone lines or fiber optic cable to connect data devices.

Wireless Markup Language A language that allows the text portions of Web pages to be presented on cellular phones and personal digital assistants (PDAs) through wireless access. Formerly called HDML (Handheld Devices Markup Language).

WML See Wireless Markup Language.

WRAM See Window-RAM.

Xanadu Bill Gates' networked home. The house uses a variety of methods for electronic house control. According to press reports, the house has over 100 PCs connected to thousands of sensors and activators used to regulate lighting, air, and temperature. Chip cards identify the whereabouts of people in each room. Once a person has been identified, that person's music and video preferences can be preselected.

xDSL Designation for digital subscriber line technology that enables simultaneous two-way transmission of voice and high-speed data over ordinary copper phone lines.

XML See Extensible Markup Language.

Xpresso A processor designed for the Java engine by Zucotto Systems. It is used for broadband access to handheld devices via an integrated Bluetooth connection. The Xpresso core is formed by Sun architecture (KVM, Kernel Virtual Machine) around which the proprietary data slice (service layer in Consumer Electronics) was programmed.

Subject Index

.NET, 27, 151

Acer, 42
Adidas, 167
Advanced Mobile Phone Service, 43
AirPort, 112
Akai, 101
Allied Business Intelligence, 139
Amazon.com, 23, 119, 149
AMPS, 43
AOL, 92
Apple, 6, 41, 112
Application Service Provider, 18
Applied Metacomputing, 174
Ariba, 149
ASP, 18

Belluzo, Rick, 3
Berners-Lee, Tim, 174
Bertelsmann, 68
Big Brother, 231
BizTalk, 21
Bluetooth, 15, 137, 184, 259
Bluetooth, Harold, 137
Borg, 142
Brazil, 155
British Telecom, 66, 69
BT, 69

Canon, 140
Captura, 147
CC/PP, 57
CERN, 174

Chai, 131, 261
ChaiServer, 131, 132
ChaiVM, 131
Chase Manhattan Bank, 86
ciao.com, 239, 242
Cisco, 133, 137
Clancy, Tom, 9
Coign, 142
Context Awareness, 28
Continuum, 143
CORBA, 17, 137, 143, 145, 170, 262
Crusoe, 42
C#, 157

DCOM, 170
DCS1800, 43
DECT, 110
Delphi Group, 91
Deutsche Telekom, 50, 66, 69
DigiMarc, 39
Digital Bridges, 79
Digital Communication System, 43
DivX ;-), 69

E-blana, 77
E-Device, 106
E-Lancers, 160
E-services, 148
E-Speak, 17, 27, 140, 144
Echolon, 107
Electrolux, 105
Electronic Service Broker, 146
Embedded Devices, 131

Ericsson, 68, 69, 82, 87, 90
EuroTechnology, 60, 63

FCC, 77
Federal Communications Commission, 77
FireScreen, 146
Fremont, 144
FTD, 179
fusionOne, 25, 83, 123

Gameboy, 78
General Packet Radio Service, 53
GMX, 181, 242
Gnutella, 26, 209
GPRS, 53
Grid, 174
GSM, 43

HAA, 100
Helsinki Telephone, 147
Hewlett-Packard, 3, 9, 27, 41, 107, 120, 130, 131, 140, 144, 148, 158, 232
Home Automation Association, 100
HomeRF, 111
Hotmail, 181
Houseware Show, 106

i-Escrow, 243
IBM, 4, 9, 107, 120, 140
iBook, 41
ICA Ahold, 90
IEEE, 113
IEEE 802.11, 110
imode, 58
IMT-2000, 65
In-Fusio, 79
Inferno, 131, 133, 141
InfernoSpaces, 141
InfoBus, 143
InfoSplit, 39
Institute of Electrical and Electronics Engineers, 113
Intel, 41, 134

IntelliQuest, 86
International   Telecommunication Union, 67
Internet Sync, 123
IrDA, 15
ITU, 67

Java, 131, 133
JetSend, 140
Jini, 9, 27, 107, 120, 131, 135, 140, 144, 155
Job Description Format, 22
Jornada, 180

KPN, 66

LAN, see Local Area Network
Lavazza, 106
LetsBuyIt.com, 243
LG Electronics, 106
Limbo, 133
Linux, 133, 175
Local Area Network, 140
Loewe, 13
LonWorks, 107
Lucent, 112
Lucent Technologies, 9, 66, 107, 120, 131, 133, 158
Lycos, 242

McDonald's, 75
MediaTechBooks, xxii
Merloni Elettrodomestici, 104
MetaProcessor, 173
Microsoft, 9, 27, 107, 120, 130, 131, 134, 142, 151, 158, 179
Millennium, 142
Minolta, 140
MIT, 167
Motorola, 41, 87
MSN, 152
myAladdin.com, 77

Napster, 26, 68, 209
NeoPoint, 77

Netscape, 179
News.com, 242
NMT900, 43
Nokia, 13, 41, 68, 69, 78, 87, 88, 119
Nokian, 139
Nordic Mobile Telephone, 43
Norman, Donald, 6
NTT DoCoMo, 58, 67

Oasis, 21
Office of Naval Research, 164
Olympic Games, 38
Omnitel, 79
Open Service, 150
OpenSkies, 149
Oracle, 18
Orwell, George, 231

Palm, 180
Panasonic, 140
PCS1900, 43
Personal Communication System, 43
Personal James, 102
PersonalJava, 133
Pervasive Computing, 119
Philips, 101, 133
Pioneer, 101
PlayStation, 78
Power-line, 109

Qualcomm, 66
Quantum, 137

Rhodes, Bradley, 162
RMI, 170
RosettaNet, 21

S-ITT, 243
Samsonite, 167
Samsung, 68
Screenfridge, 105
SDMI, 39
Secure Digital Music Initiative, 39
Secure Electronic Transactions, 39
SET, 39

SETI, 173
SETI at home, 173
Short Message Service, 48
Siemens, 140, 167
Smart-SMS, xxii, 52
SMS, 48
Sonera, 75
Sony, 42, 68, 101
Sprint, 66
Star Trek, 136, 142, 143
Starlab, 167
StarOffice, 123
Starseed, 102
Strategis, 67, 92
Sun, 9, 18, 27, 107, 120, 131, 133,
        135, 140, 143, 144, 155, 158

T Spaces, 140
T-Online, 92
Tantau, 86
TDMA, 53
Tegic, 52
Telecom Italia, 66
Time Division Multiple Access, 53
Topmail.de, 242
Torwalds, Linus, 41
Trade-Direct, 243
Transcoder, 125
Transcoding, 125
Transmeta, 41
Turkcell, 96

UMEC, 134
UML, 126
Uniscape, 147
United Devices, 173
Universal Plug and Play, 131, 134
UPnP, *see* Universal Plug and Play

Verizon wireless, 66
VIAG Interkom, 28
Vodafone, 66, 69

W3C, 57
WAN, *see* Wide Area Network

WAP, 57
WaveLAN, 112
Webraska, 79
Weiser, Mark, 4
Wide Area Network, 136
Windows NT, 133
Windows .NET, 154
Wired, 242
Wireless Application Forum, 57
Wireless Location Industry Associ-
          ation, 77
Wireless Markup Language, 57
Wirelessgames, 79
WLIA, 77
WML, 57
World Wide Web Consortium, 57
WRC, 65

Xerox, 4, 140
XMI, 126

Yahoo!, 23
Yamakawa, 101

ZagMe, 77

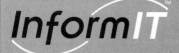

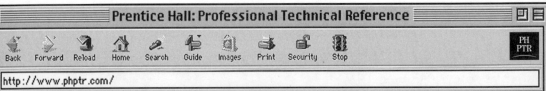